W9-BWH-894

ANDREA GROSSO CIPONTE

FREIHEIT!

THE WHITE ROSE GRAPHIC NOVEL

PLOUGH PUBLISHING HOUSE

Published by Plough Publishing House
Walden, New York
Robertsbridge, England
Elsmore, Australia
www.plough.com

Copyright © 2021 by Plough Publishing House
All rights reserved.

White Rose leaflets translated by Arthur R. Schultz, reprinted from *The White Rose: Munich, 1942–1943*, by Inge Scholl (Middletown, CT: Wesleyan University Press, 1970, 1983). Used with permission.

ISBN 978-0-87486-344-4
26 25 24 23 22 21   1 2 3 4 5 6

Library of Congress Cataloging-in-Publication Data

Names: Grosso Ciponte, Andrea, author, artist.
Title: Freiheit! : the White Rose graphic novel / Andrea Grosso Ciponte.
Description: Walden, New York : Plough Publishing House, 2020. | Audience:
    Ages 12-up | Audience: Grades 7 to 9. | Summary: Disillusioned by the
    propaganda of Nazi Germany, Sophie Scholl, a young German college
    student, her brother, and his fellow soldiers formed the White Rose, a
    group that wrote and distributed anonymous letters criticizing the Nazi
    regime and calling for action from their fellow German citizens.
Identifiers: LCCN 2020043257 (print) | LCCN 2020043258 (ebook) | ISBN
    9780874863444 (paperback) | ISBN 9780874863451 (ebook)
Subjects: LCSH: Graphic novels. | CYAC: Graphic novels. | White Rose
    (German resistance group)--Fiction. |
    Germany--History--1933-1945--Fiction. | Underground movements--Fiction.
    | Anti-Nazi movement--Fiction.
Classification: LCC PZ7.7.G79 Fr 2020 (print) | LCC PZ7.7.G79 (ebook) |
    DDC 741.5/973--dc23
LC record available at https://lccn.loc.gov/2020043257
LC ebook record available at https://lccn.loc.gov/2020043258

Printed in the United States of America

The Nazis have been in power for almost a decade.

The tide of World War II may be turning, but within Germany propaganda still trumpets a thousand-year reign. By now, the genocide of Jews and others in concentration camps is no secret.

Dissent has been crushed. Those whose consciences trouble them keep their thoughts to themselves. Anyone could be an informant, and any whiff of treason brings swift death.

A new generation of Germans has come of age, steeped in Nazi ideology through the Hitler Youth and League of German Girls. Millions enthusiastically march in lockstep and hail their leader unquestioningly.

Or will youth always hunger for freedom?

When they are not serving on the Eastern Front, Hans Scholl, Alexander Schmorell, Christoph Probst, and Willi Graf are medical students in Munich. Of these four friends, only Christoph is married, with two young sons. Hans's younger sister Sophie, twenty-one, is just beginning studies at the same school.

Behind closed doors, they ask themselves: Are we the only ones who find our government abhorrent? The lack of freedom suffocating? If only someone would find the courage to speak out, would not thousands of others rise up and put an end to the repression? If we don't take that first step, then who?

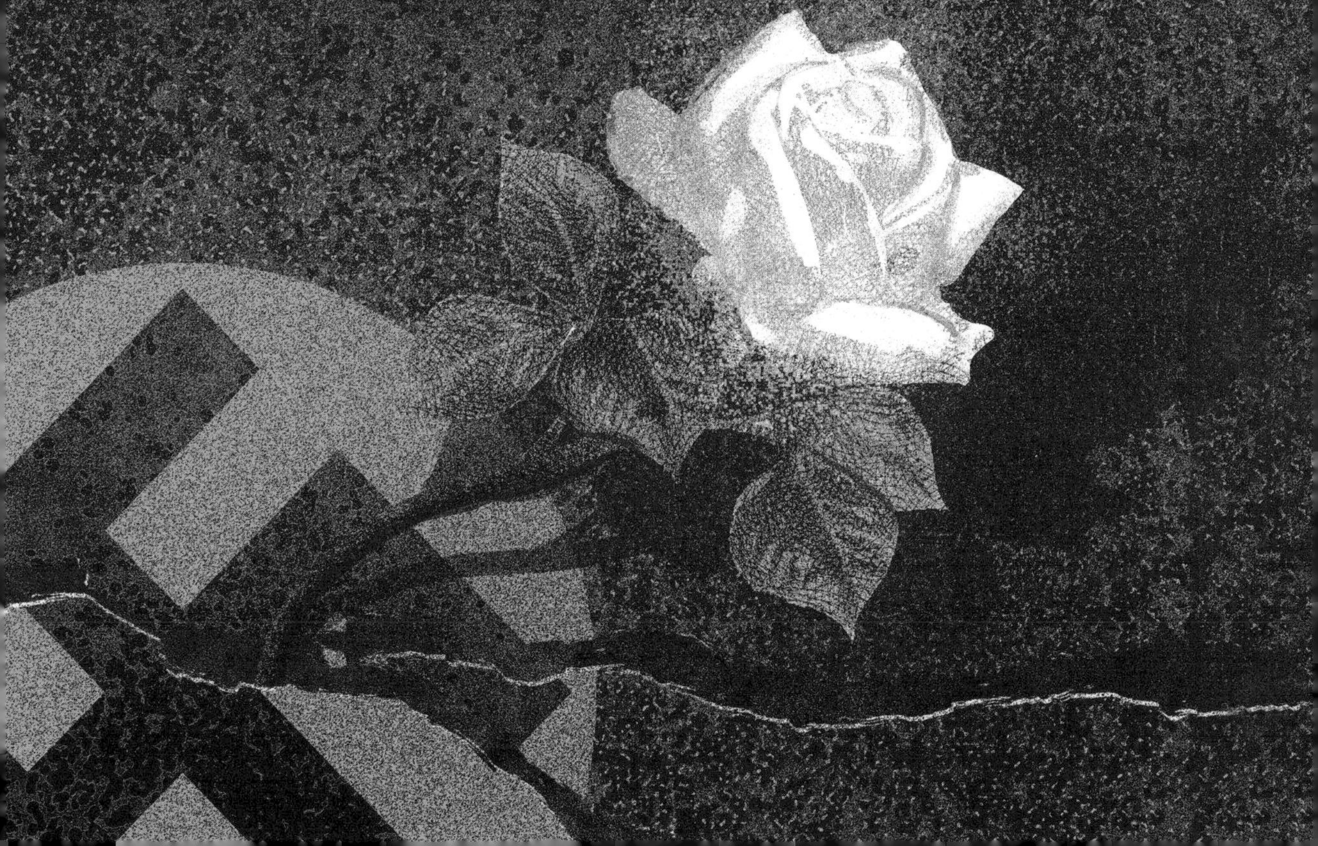

UNIVERSITY OF MUNICH, FEBRUARY 18, 1943

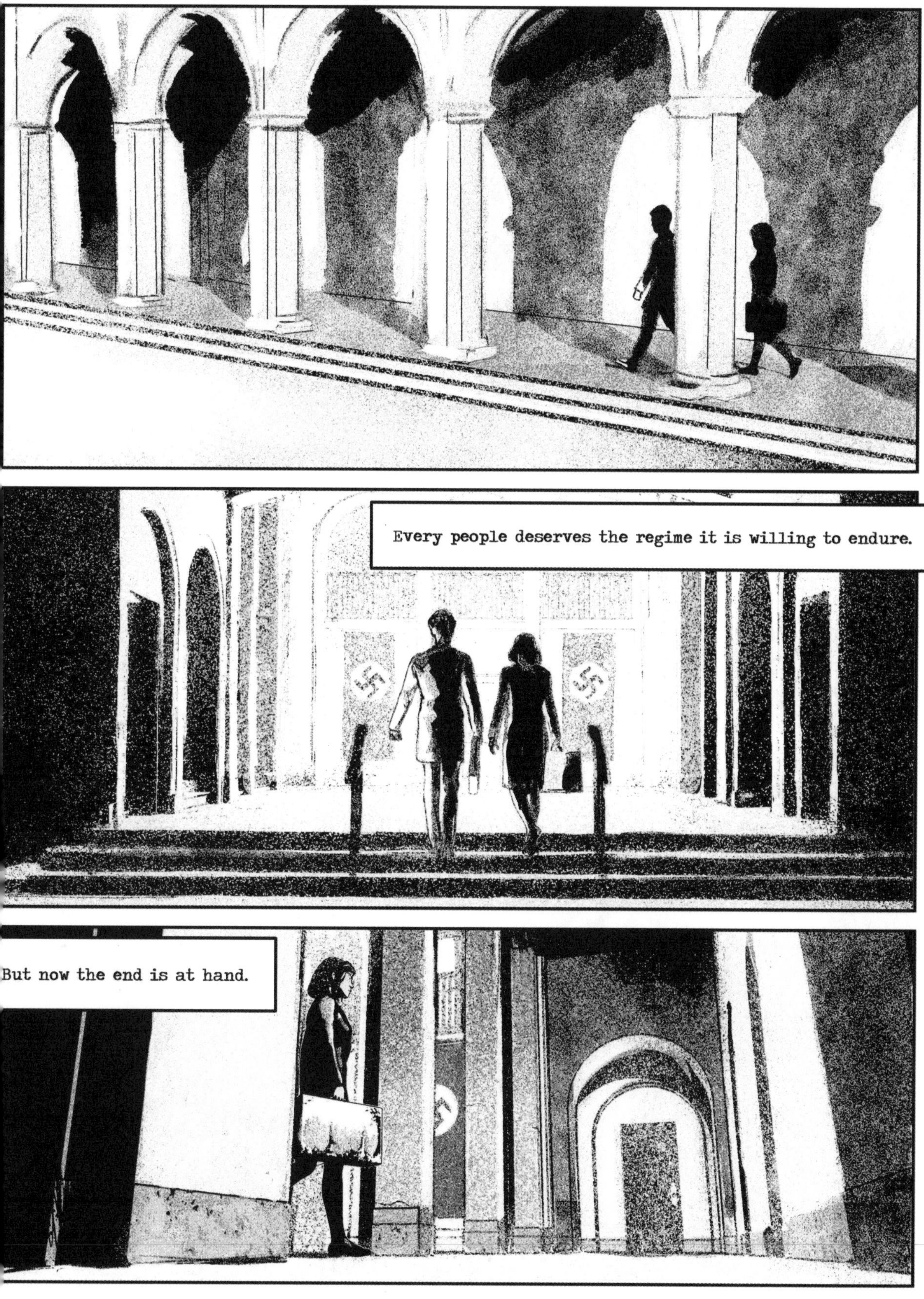
Every people deserves the regime it is willing to endure.
But now the end is at hand.

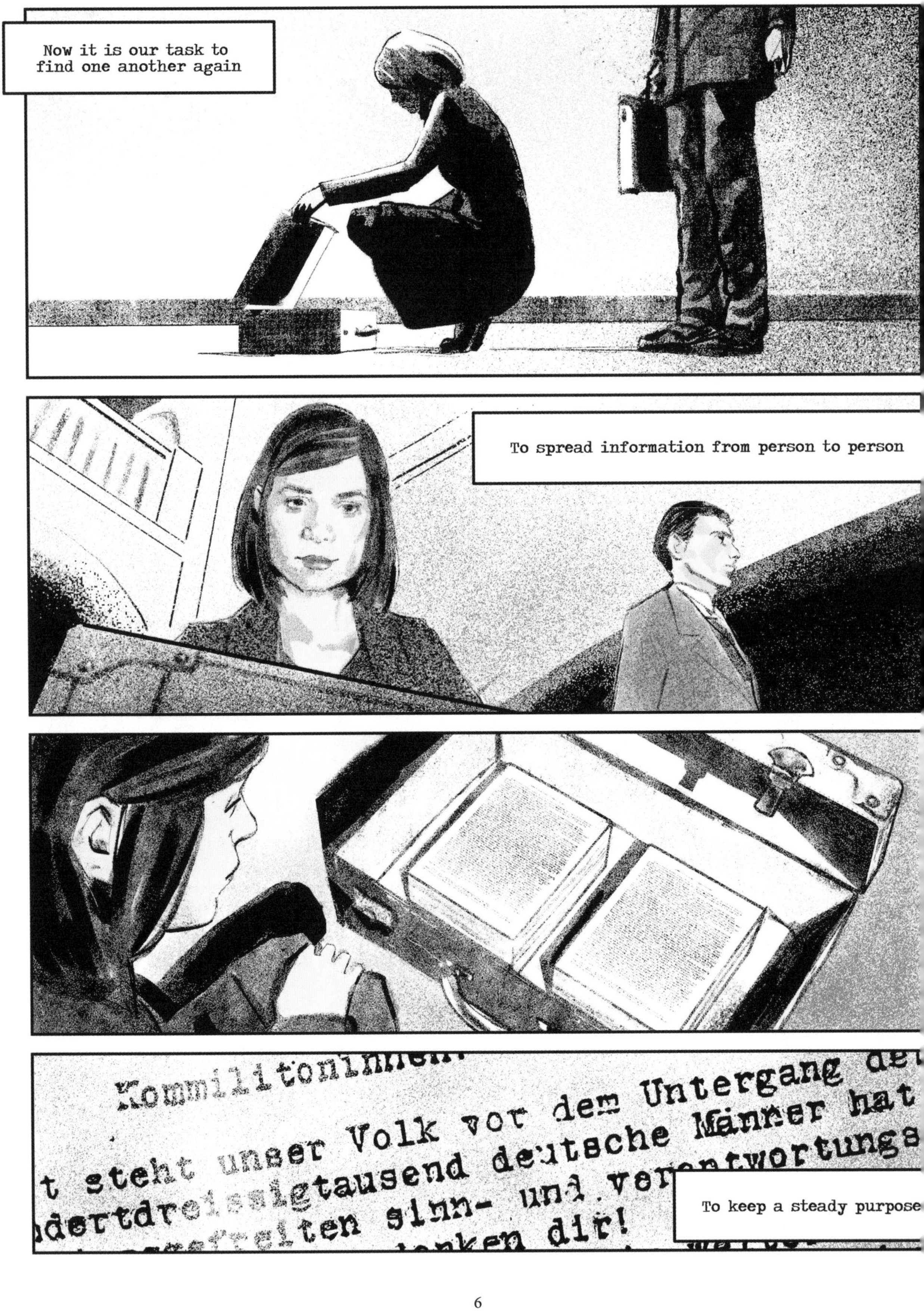
Now it is our task to find one another again
To spread information from person to person
To keep a steady purpose

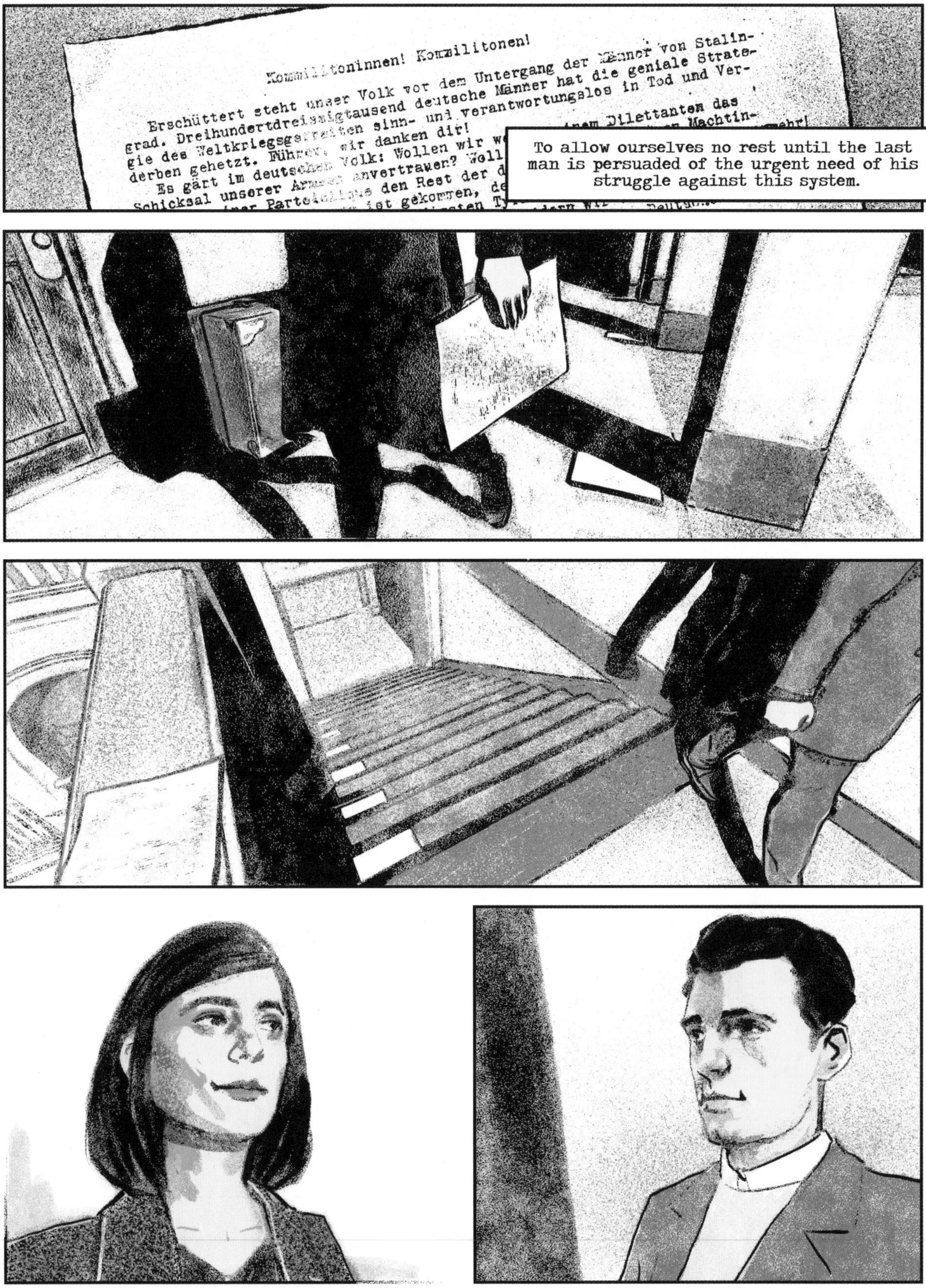
Kommilitonen!
grad. Dreihundertdreissigtausend deutsche Männer hat die geniale Strate-
derben gehetzt.
wir danken dir!
Es gärt im deutschen Volk: Wollen wir
To allow ourselves no rest until the last man is persuaded of the urgent need of his struggle against this system.

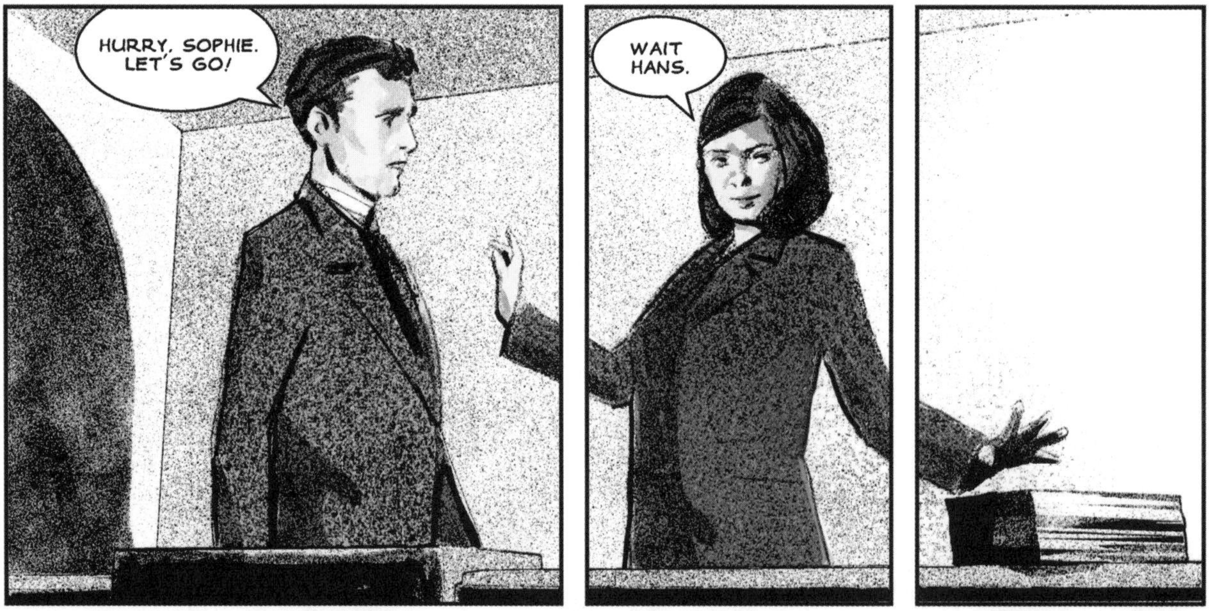
HURRY, SOPHIE.
LET'S GO!
WAIT
HANS.

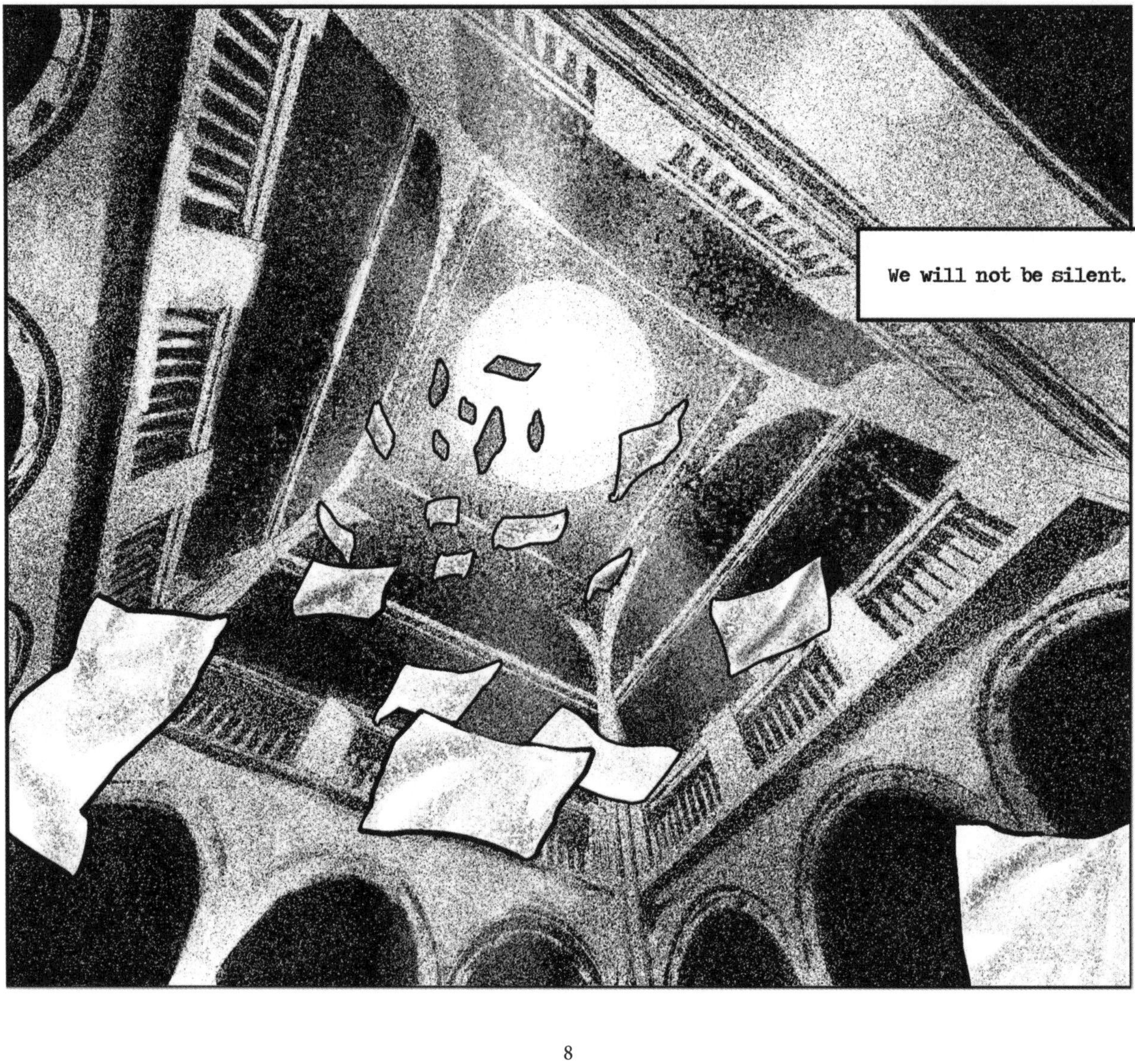
We will not be silent.

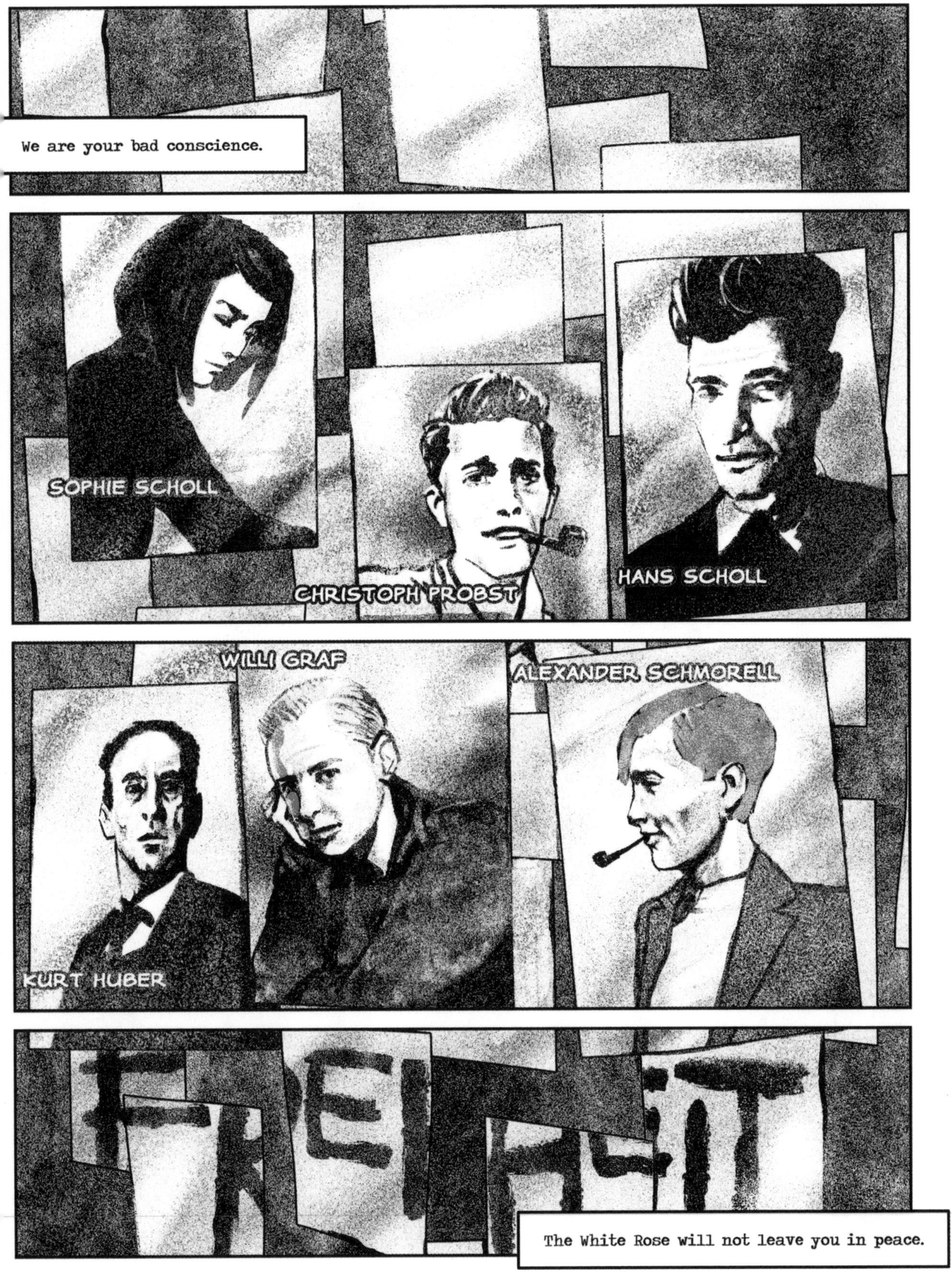
We are your bad conscience.
SOPHIE SCHOLL
CHRISTOPH PROBST
HANS SCHOLL
WILLI GRAF
ALEXANDER SCHMORELL
KURT HUBER
The White Rose will not leave you in peace.

NINE MONTHS EARLIER, MAY 1942, EN ROUTE TO MUNICH

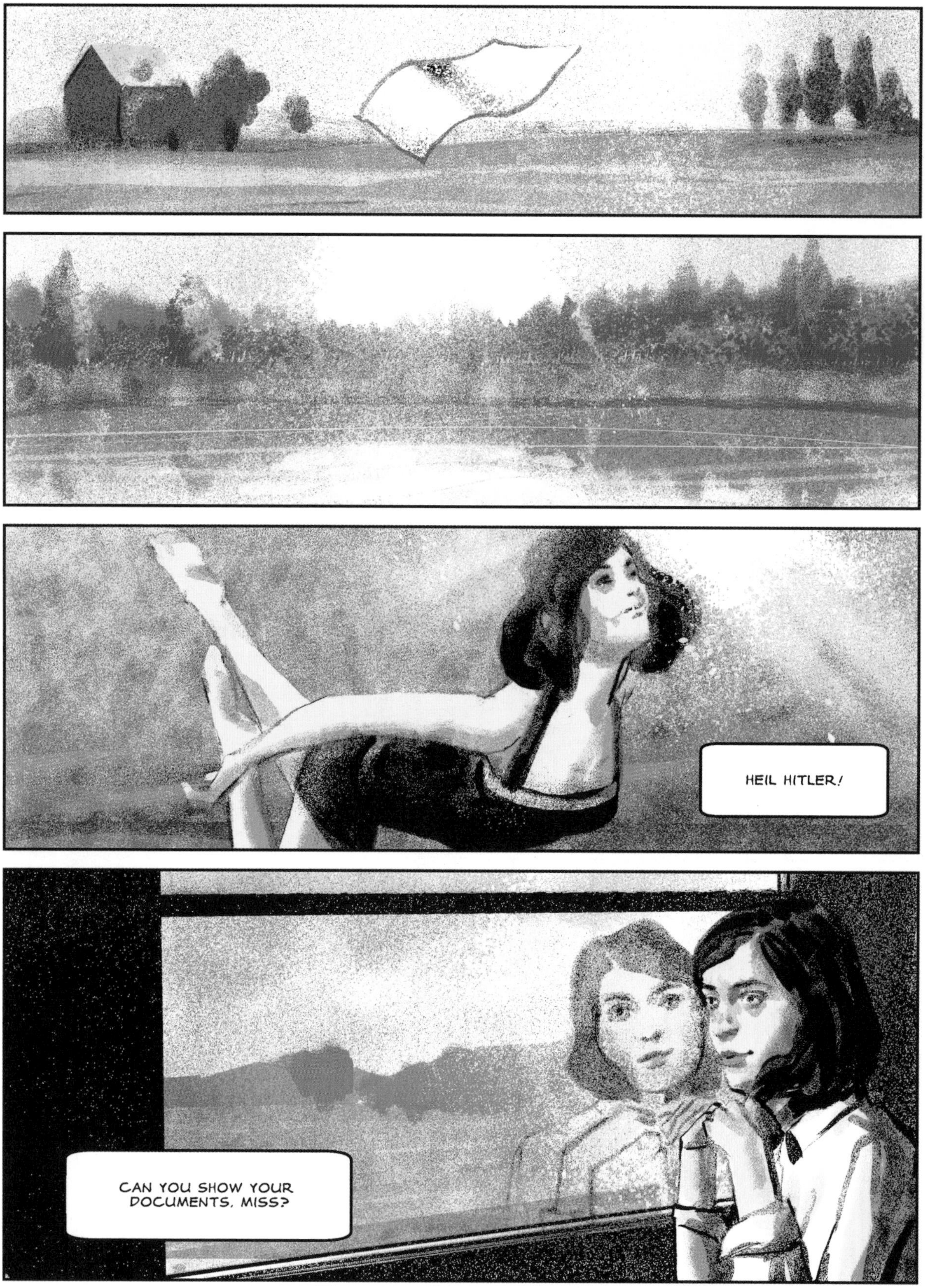
HEIL HITLER!
CAN YOU SHOW YOUR DOCUMENTS, MISS?

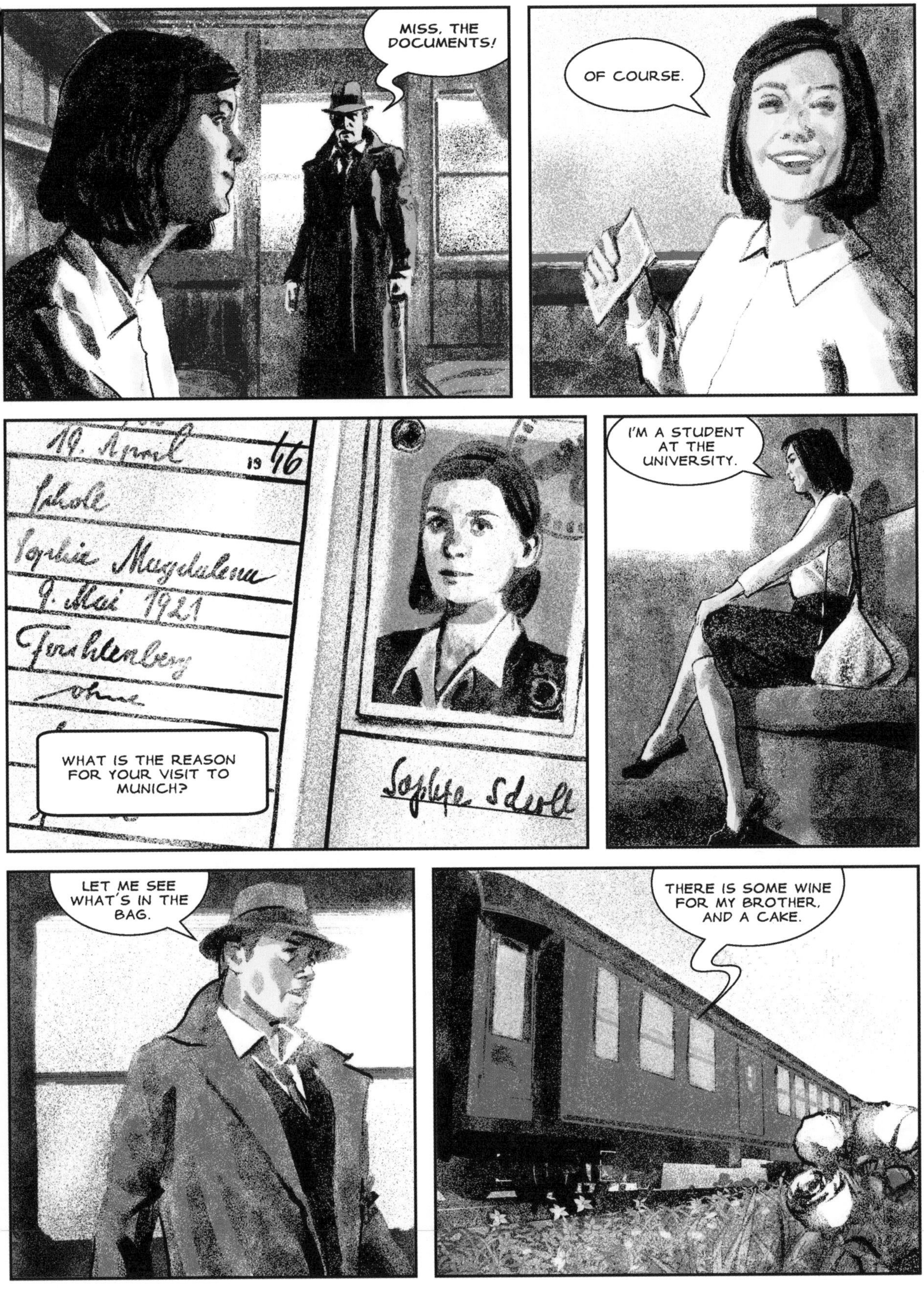
MISS, THE DOCUMENTS!
OF COURSE.
WHAT IS THE REASON FOR YOUR VISIT TO MUNICH?
I'M A STUDENT AT THE UNIVERSITY.
LET ME SEE WHAT'S IN THE BAG.
THERE IS SOME WINE FOR MY BROTHER, AND A CAKE.

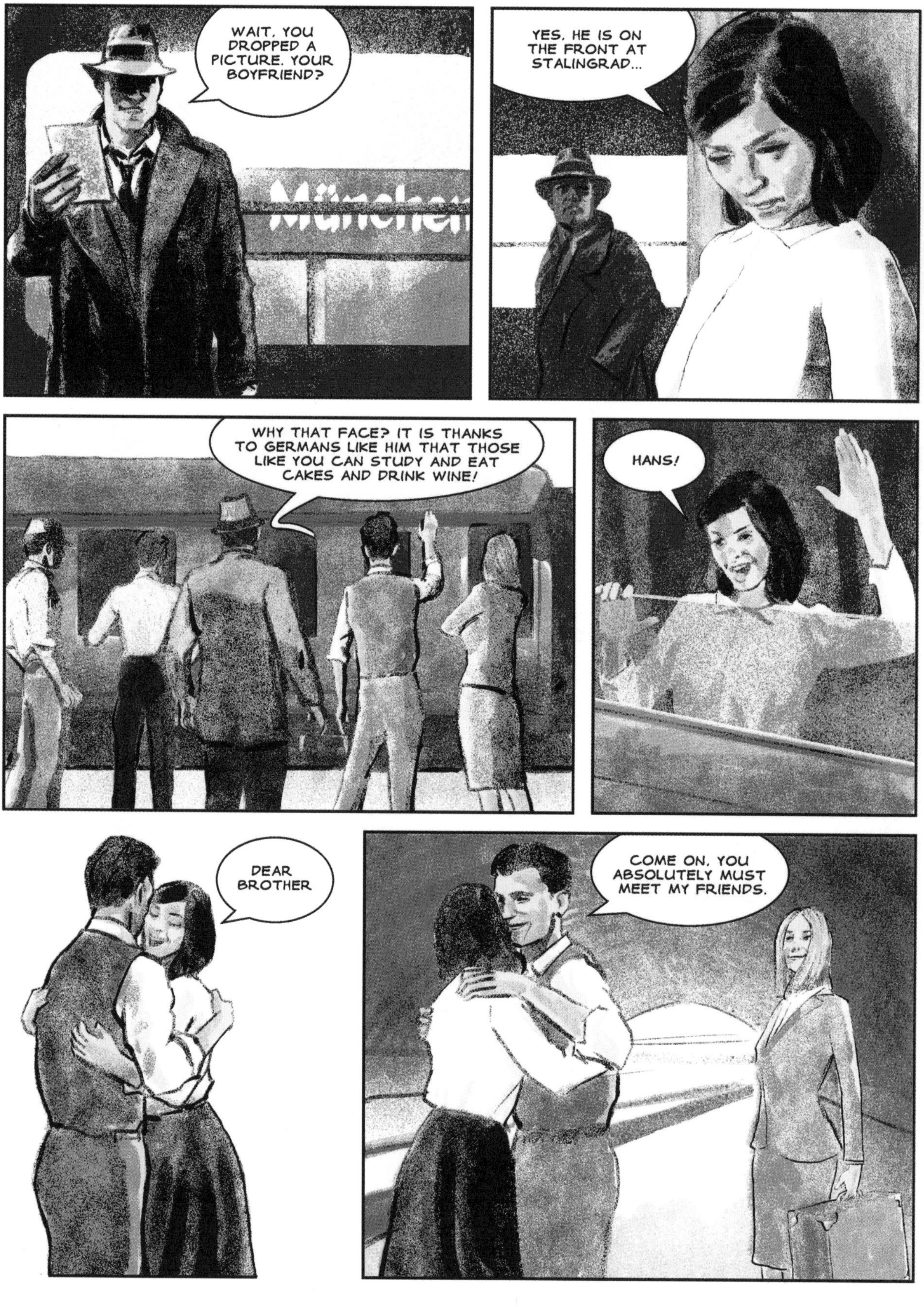
WAIT, YOU DROPPED A PICTURE. YOUR BOYFRIEND?
München
YES, HE IS ON THE FRONT AT STALINGRAD...
WHY THAT FACE? IT IS THANKS TO GERMANS LIKE HIM THAT THOSE LIKE YOU CAN STUDY AND EAT CAKES AND DRINK WINE!
HANS!
DEAR BROTHER
COME ON, YOU ABSOLUTELY MUST MEET MY FRIENDS.

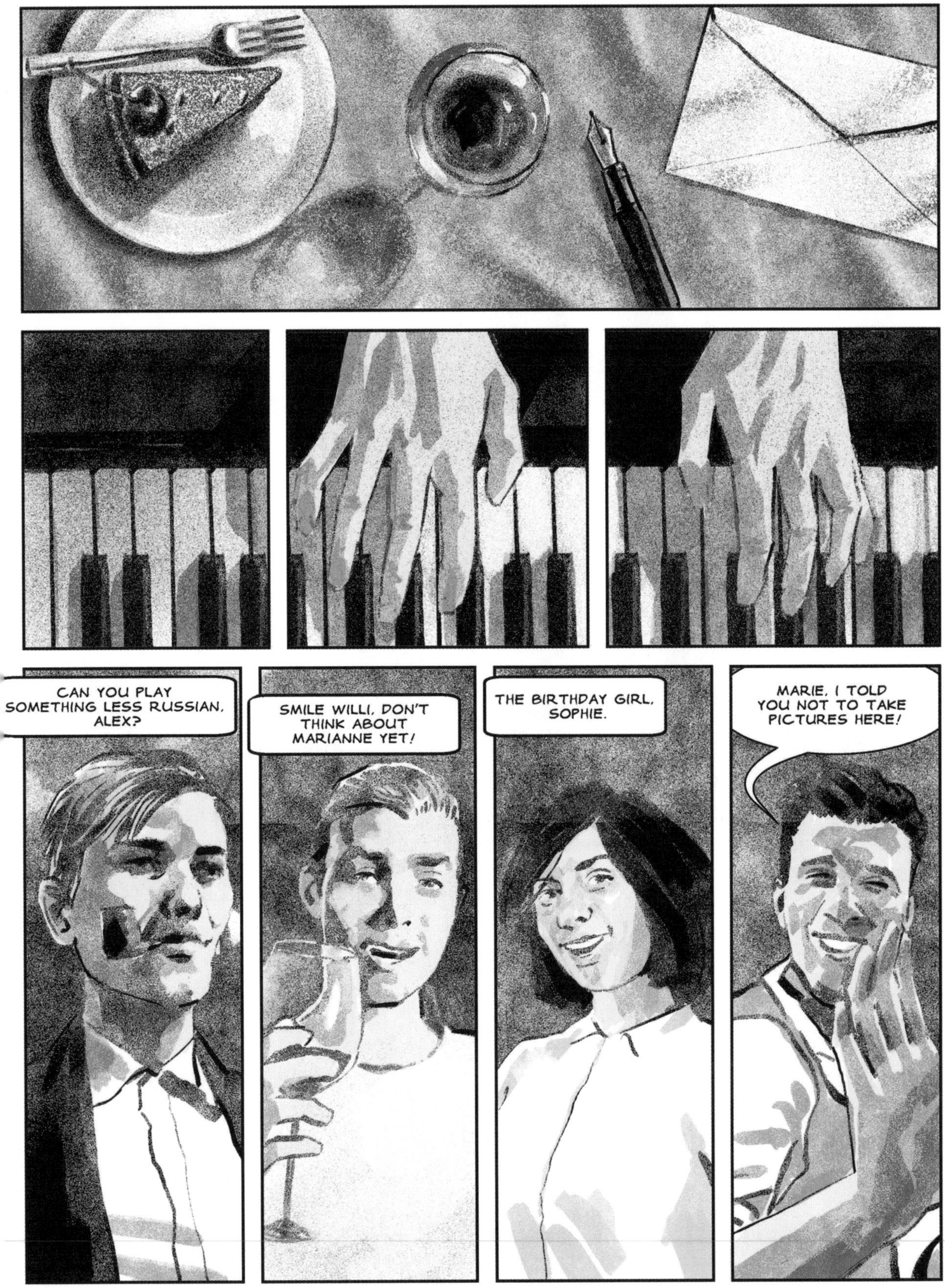
CAN YOU PLAY SOMETHING LESS RUSSIAN, ALEX?
SMILE WILLI, DON'T THINK ABOUT MARIANNE YET!
THE BIRTHDAY GIRL, SOPHIE.
MARIE, I TOLD YOU NOT TO TAKE PICTURES HERE!

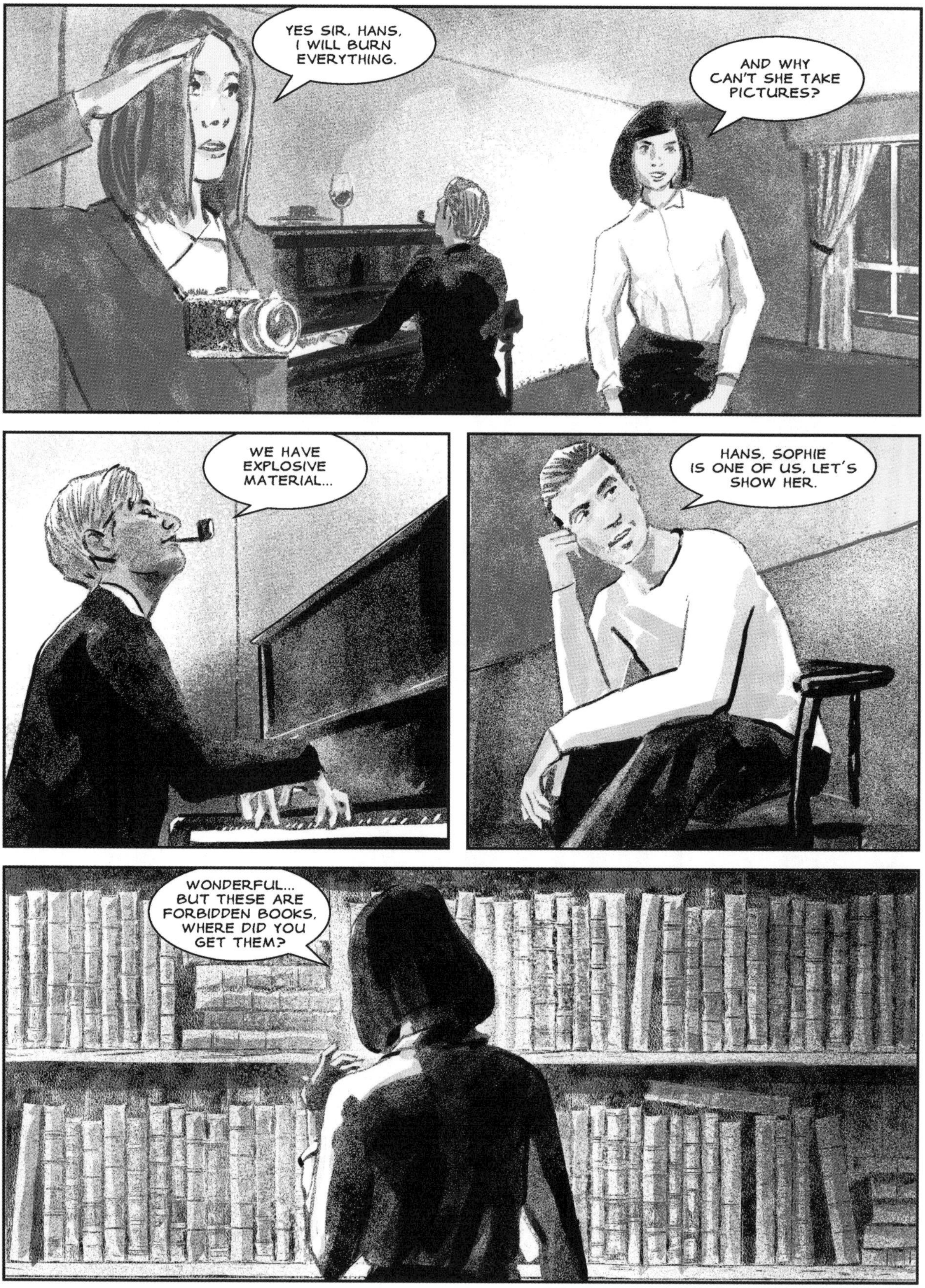
YES SIR, HANS, I WILL BURN EVERYTHING.
AND WHY CAN'T SHE TAKE PICTURES?
WE HAVE EXPLOSIVE MATERIAL...
HANS, SOPHIE IS ONE OF US, LET'S SHOW HER.
WONDERFUL... BUT THESE ARE FORBIDDEN BOOKS, WHERE DID YOU GET THEM?

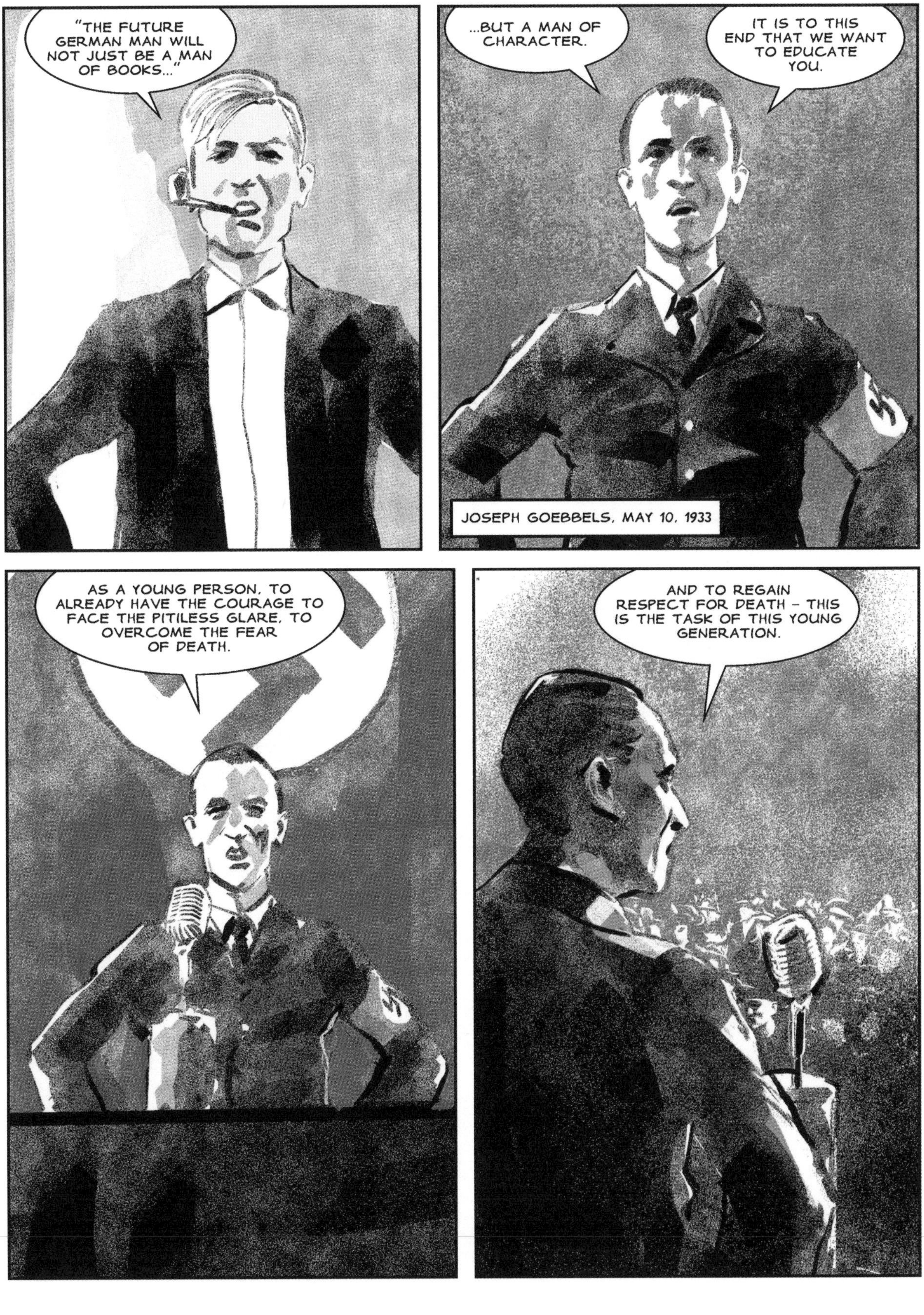
"THE FUTURE GERMAN MAN WILL NOT JUST BE A MAN OF BOOKS..."
...BUT A MAN OF CHARACTER.
IT IS TO THIS END THAT WE WANT TO EDUCATE YOU.
JOSEPH GOEBBELS, MAY 10, 1933
AS A YOUNG PERSON, TO ALREADY HAVE THE COURAGE TO FACE THE PITILESS GLARE, TO OVERCOME THE FEAR OF DEATH.
AND TO REGAIN RESPECT FOR DEATH – THIS IS THE TASK OF THIS YOUNG GENERATION.

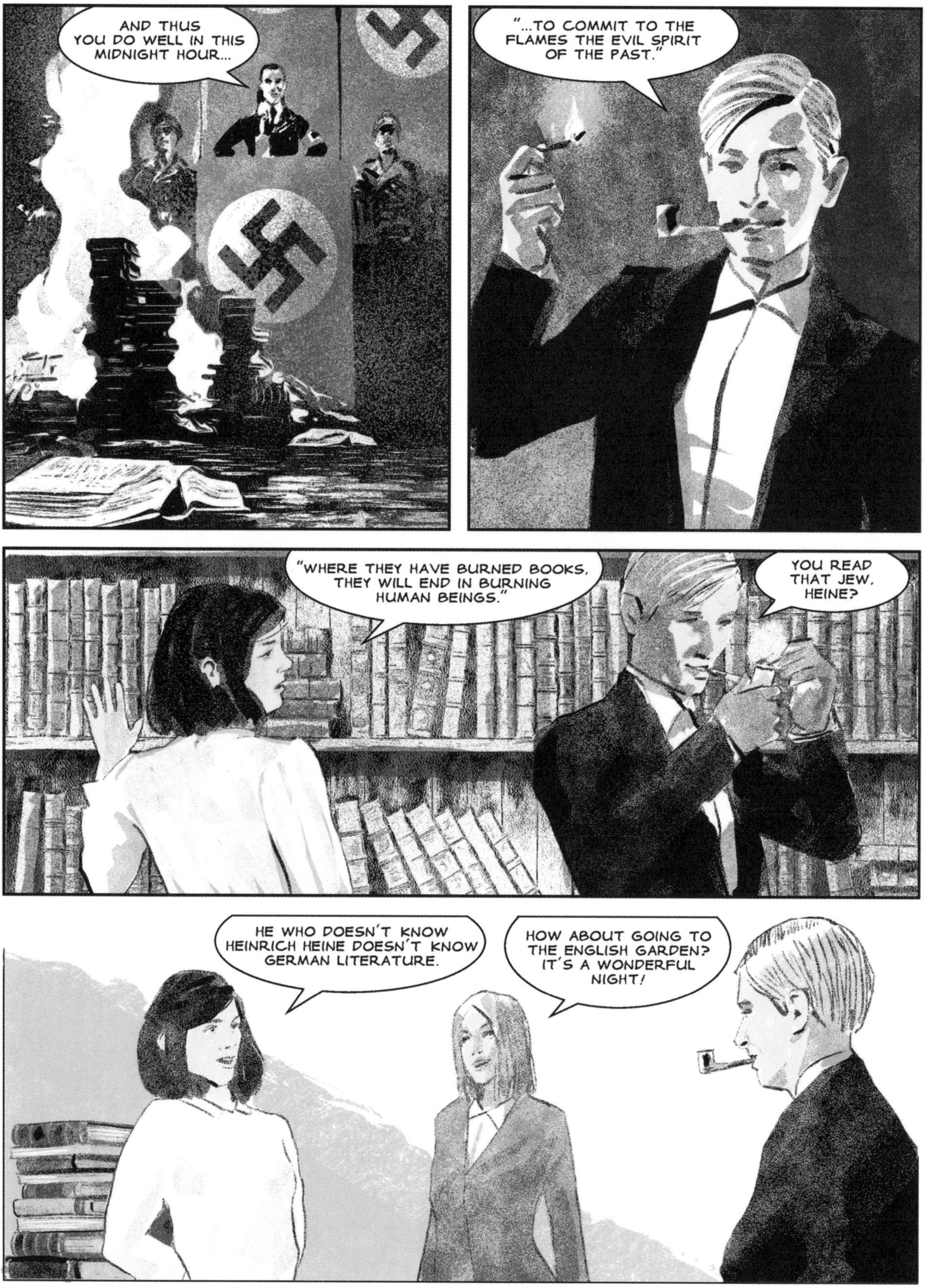
AND THUS YOU DO WELL IN THIS MIDNIGHT HOUR...
"...TO COMMIT TO THE FLAMES THE EVIL SPIRIT OF THE PAST."
"WHERE THEY HAVE BURNED BOOKS, THEY WILL END IN BURNING HUMAN BEINGS."
YOU READ THAT JEW, HEINE?
HE WHO DOESN'T KNOW HEINRICH HEINE DOESN'T KNOW GERMAN LITERATURE.
HOW ABOUT GOING TO THE ENGLISH GARDEN? IT'S A WONDERFUL NIGHT!

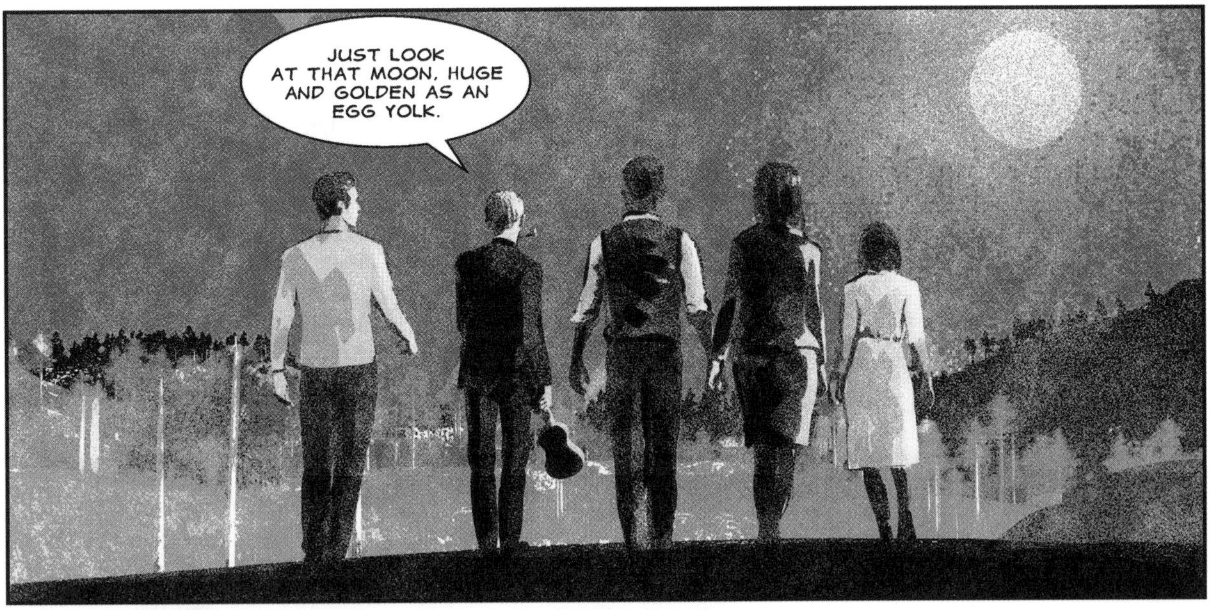
JUST LOOK AT THAT MOON, HUGE AND GOLDEN AS AN EGG YOLK.

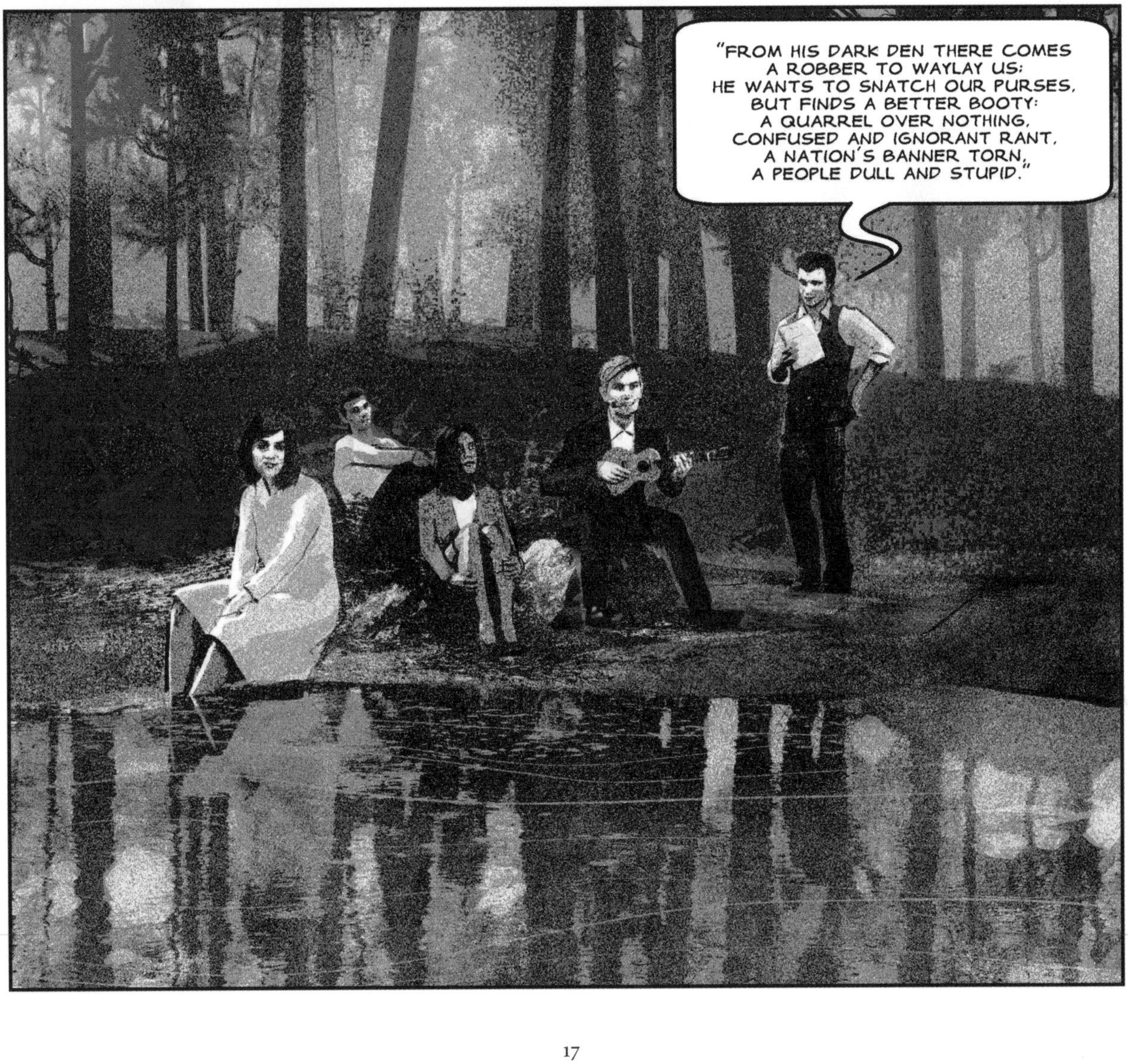
"FROM HIS DARK DEN THERE COMES
A ROBBER TO WAYLAY US;
HE WANTS TO SNATCH OUR PURSES,
BUT FINDS A BETTER BOOTY:
A QUARREL OVER NOTHING,
CONFUSED AND IGNORANT RANT,
A NATION'S BANNER TORN,
A PEOPLE DULL AND STUPID."

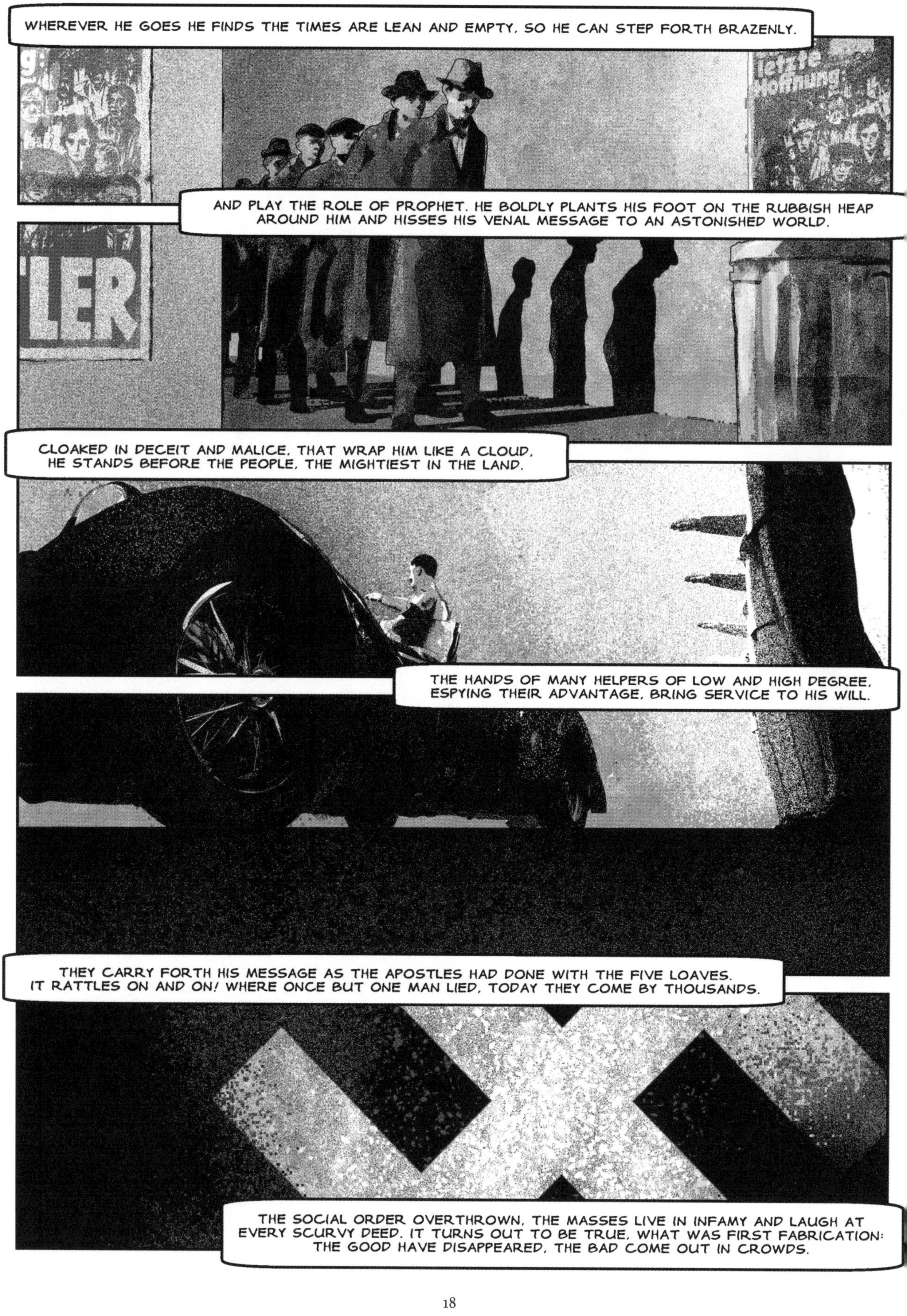
WHEREVER HE GOES HE FINDS THE TIMES ARE LEAN AND EMPTY, SO HE CAN STEP FORTH BRAZENLY.
letzte Hoffnung:
AND PLAY THE ROLE OF PROPHET. HE BOLDLY PLANTS HIS FOOT ON THE RUBBISH HEAP AROUND HIM AND HISSES HIS VENAL MESSAGE TO AN ASTONISHED WORLD.
CLOAKED IN DECEIT AND MALICE, THAT WRAP HIM LIKE A CLOUD, HE STANDS BEFORE THE PEOPLE, THE MIGHTIEST IN THE LAND.
THE HANDS OF MANY HELPERS OF LOW AND HIGH DEGREE, ESPYING THEIR ADVANTAGE, BRING SERVICE TO HIS WILL.
THEY CARRY FORTH HIS MESSAGE AS THE APOSTLES HAD DONE WITH THE FIVE LOAVES. IT RATTLES ON AND ON! WHERE ONCE BUT ONE MAN LIED, TODAY THEY COME BY THOUSANDS.
THE SOCIAL ORDER OVERTHROWN, THE MASSES LIVE IN INFAMY AND LAUGH AT EVERY SCURVY DEED. IT TURNS OUT TO BE TRUE, WHAT WAS FIRST FABRICATION: THE GOOD HAVE DISAPPEARED, THE BAD COME OUT IN CROWDS.

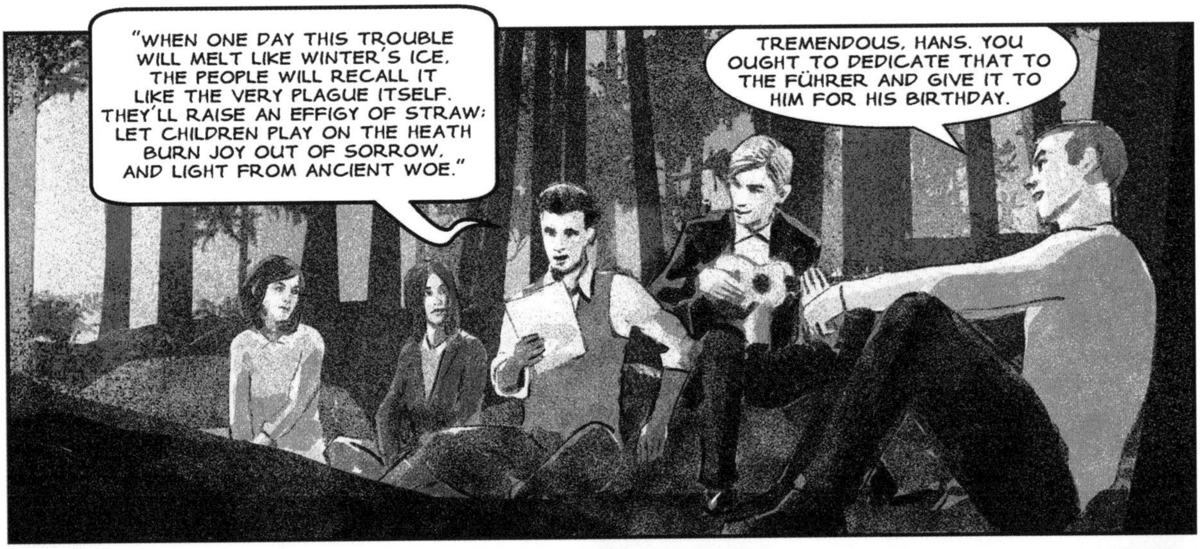
"WHEN ONE DAY THIS TROUBLE WILL MELT LIKE WINTER'S ICE, THE PEOPLE WILL RECALL IT LIKE THE VERY PLAGUE ITSELF. THEY'LL RAISE AN EFFIGY OF STRAW; LET CHILDREN PLAY ON THE HEATH BURN JOY OUT OF SORROW, AND LIGHT FROM ANCIENT WOE."
TREMENDOUS, HANS. YOU OUGHT TO DEDICATE THAT TO THE FÜHRER AND GIVE IT TO HIM FOR HIS BIRTHDAY.

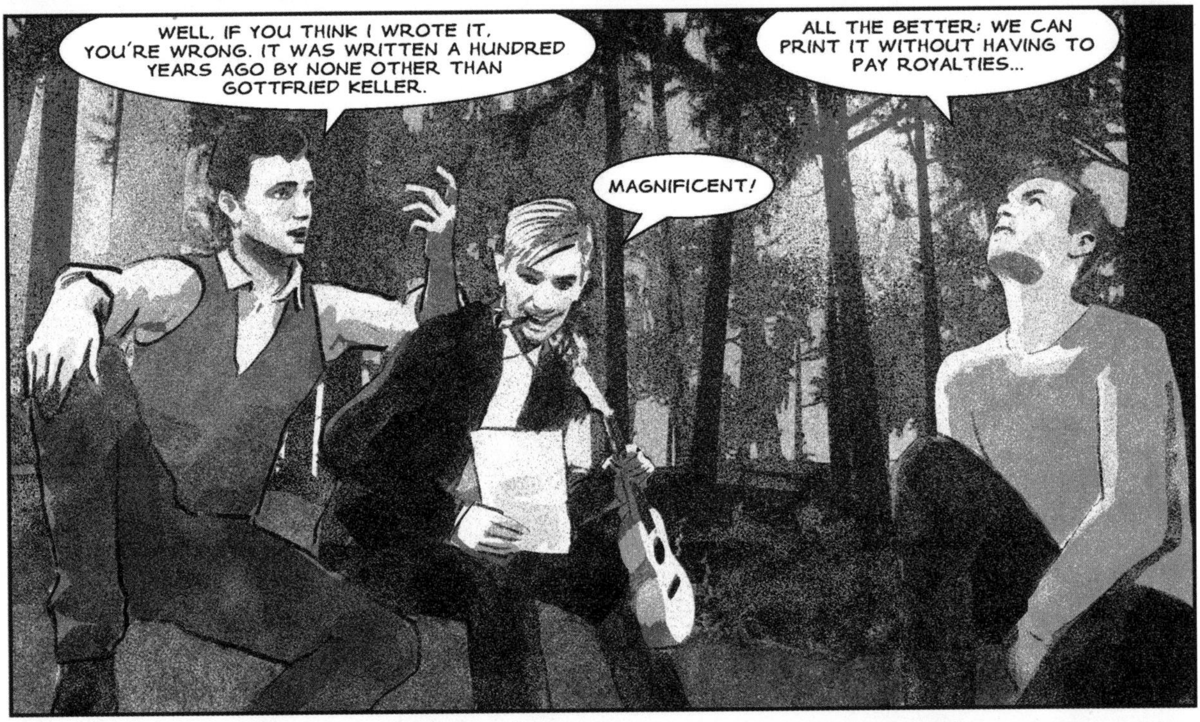
WELL, IF YOU THINK I WROTE IT, YOU'RE WRONG. IT WAS WRITTEN A HUNDRED YEARS AGO BY NONE OTHER THAN GOTTFRIED KELLER.
MAGNIFICENT!
ALL THE BETTER; WE CAN PRINT IT WITHOUT HAVING TO PAY ROYALTIES...

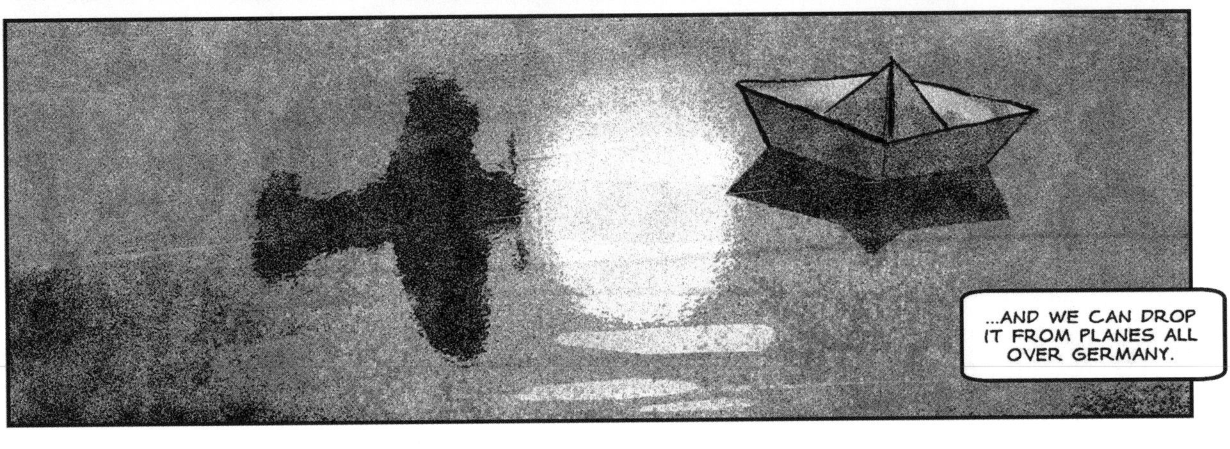
...AND WE CAN DROP IT FROM PLANES ALL OVER GERMANY.

UNIVERSITY OF MUNICH, JUNE 1942

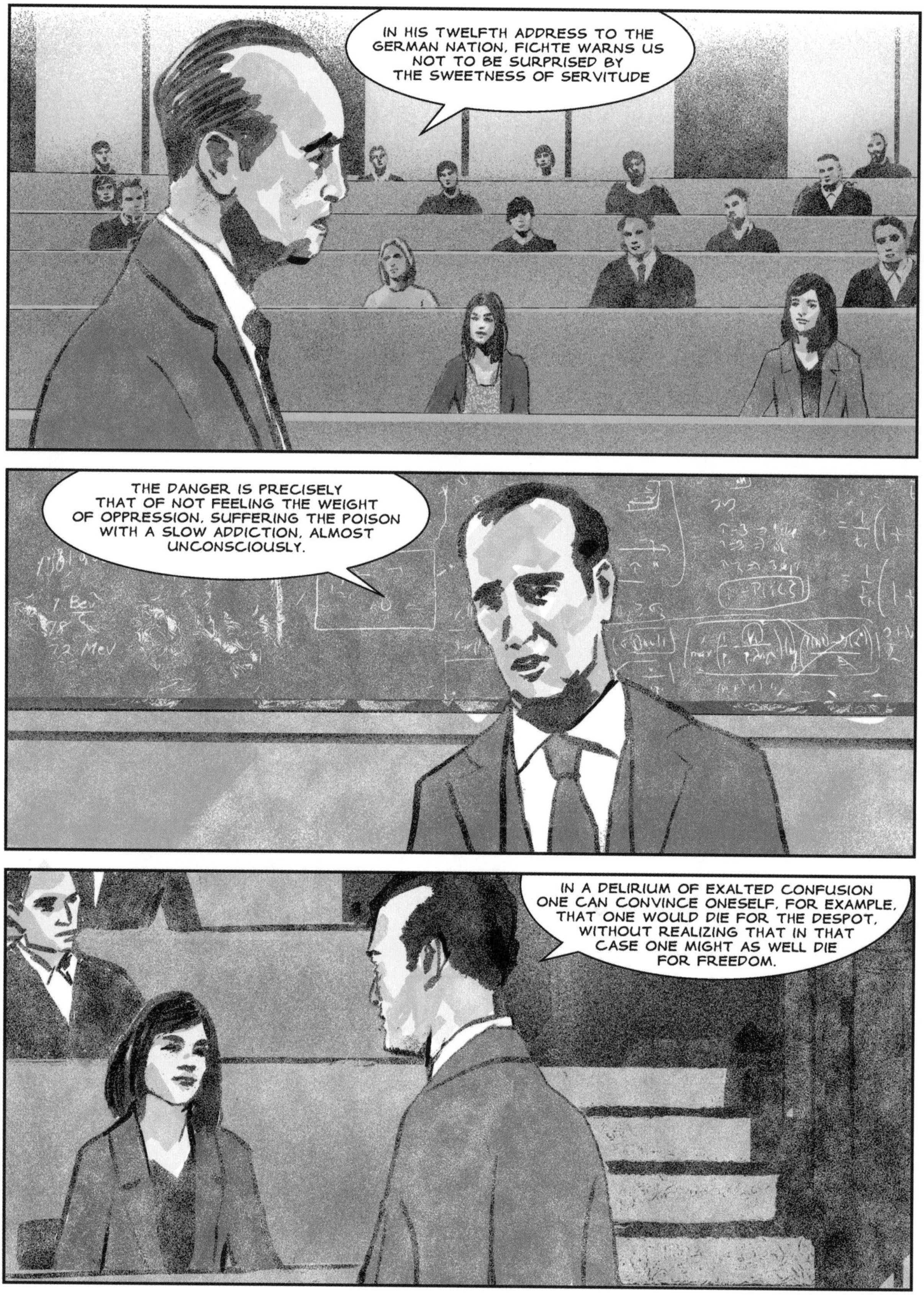
IN HIS TWELFTH ADDRESS TO THE GERMAN NATION, FICHTE WARNS US NOT TO BE SURPRISED BY THE SWEETNESS OF SERVITUDE
THE DANGER IS PRECISELY THAT OF NOT FEELING THE WEIGHT OF OPPRESSION, SUFFERING THE POISON WITH A SLOW ADDICTION, ALMOST UNCONSCIOUSLY.
IN A DELIRIUM OF EXALTED CONFUSION ONE CAN CONVINCE ONESELF, FOR EXAMPLE, THAT ONE WOULD DIE FOR THE DESPOT, WITHOUT REALIZING THAT IN THAT CASE ONE MIGHT AS WELL DIE FOR FREEDOM.

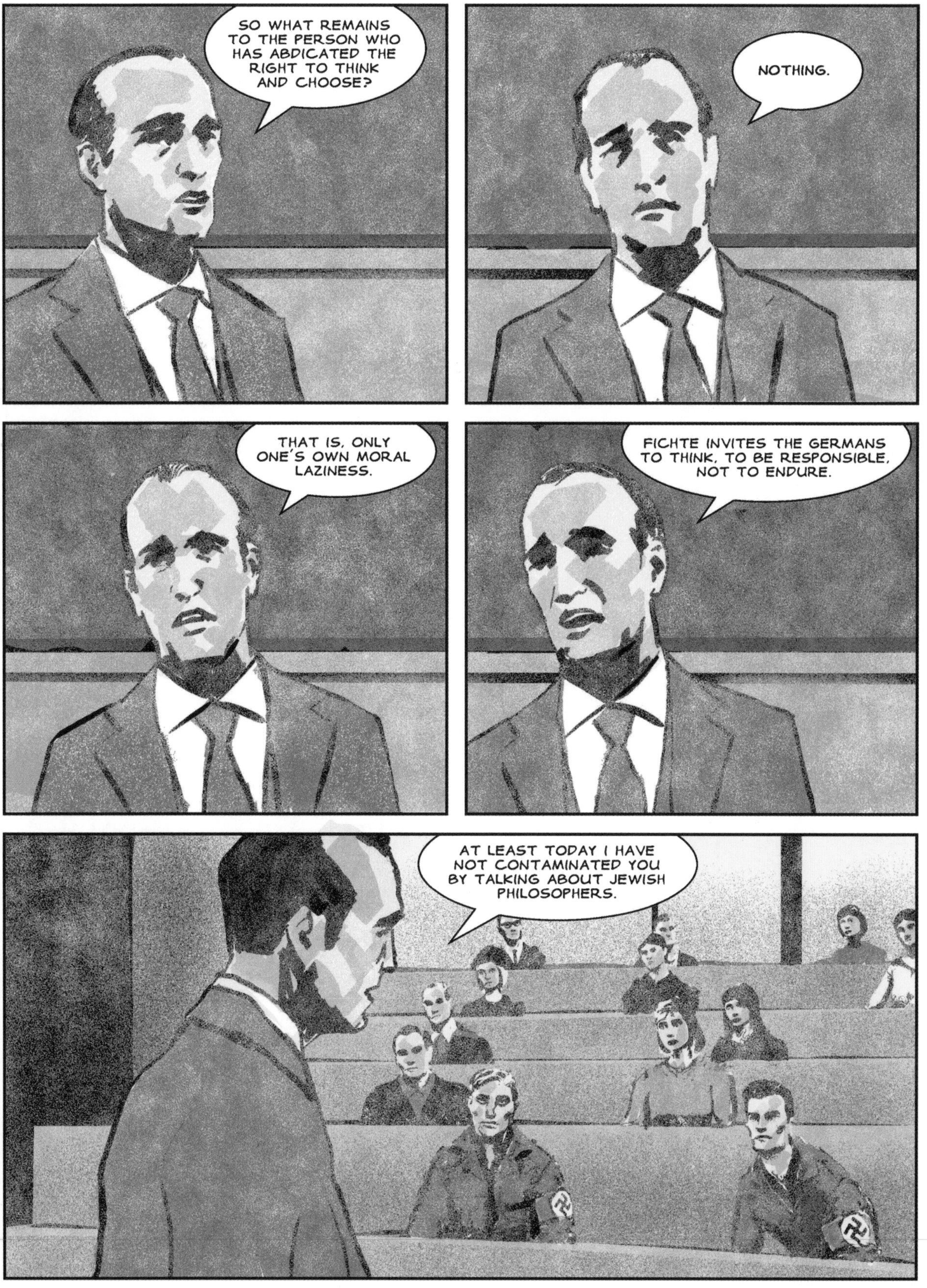
SO WHAT REMAINS TO THE PERSON WHO HAS ABDICATED THE RIGHT TO THINK AND CHOOSE?
NOTHING.
THAT IS, ONLY ONE'S OWN MORAL LAZINESS.
FICHTE INVITES THE GERMANS TO THINK, TO BE RESPONSIBLE, NOT TO ENDURE.
AT LEAST TODAY I HAVE NOT CONTAMINATED YOU BY TALKING ABOUT JEWISH PHILOSOPHERS.

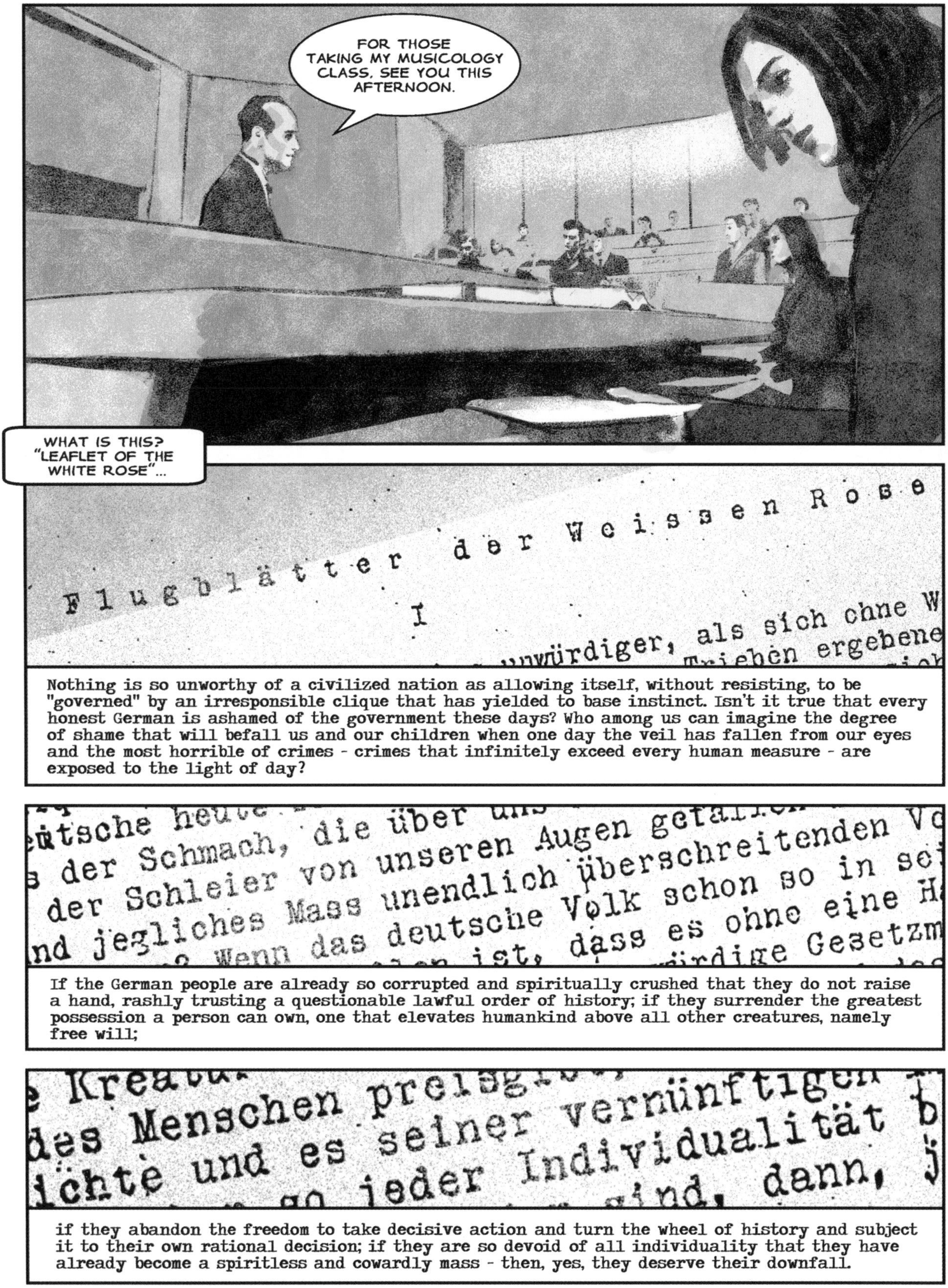
FOR THOSE TAKING MY MUSICOLOGY CLASS, SEE YOU THIS AFTERNOON.
WHAT IS THIS? "LEAFLET OF THE WHITE ROSE"...
Flugblätter der Weissen Rose
I
Nothing is so unworthy of a civilized nation as allowing itself, without resisting, to be "governed" by an irresponsible clique that has yielded to base instinct. Isn't it true that every honest German is ashamed of the government these days? Who among us can imagine the degree of shame that will befall us and our children when one day the veil has fallen from our eyes and the most horrible of crimes - crimes that infinitely exceed every human measure - are exposed to the light of day?
If the German people are already so corrupted and spiritually crushed that they do not raise a hand, rashly trusting a questionable lawful order of history; if they surrender the greatest possession a person can own, one that elevates humankind above all other creatures, namely free will;
if they abandon the freedom to take decisive action and turn the wheel of history and subject it to their own rational decision; if they are so devoid of all individuality that they have already become a spiritless and cowardly mass - then, yes, they deserve their downfall.

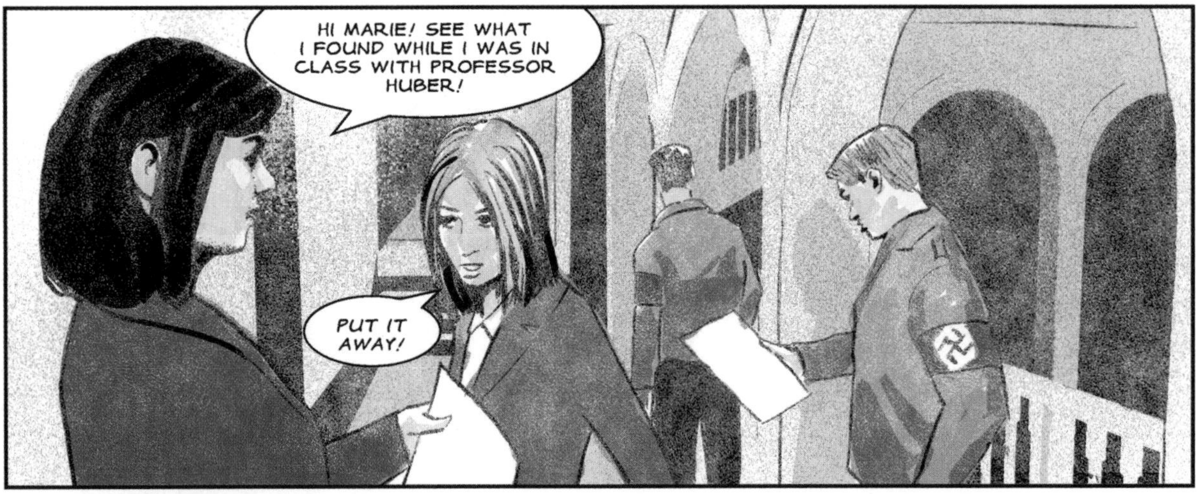
HI MARIE! SEE WHAT I FOUND WHILE I WAS IN CLASS WITH PROFESSOR HUBER!
PUT IT AWAY!

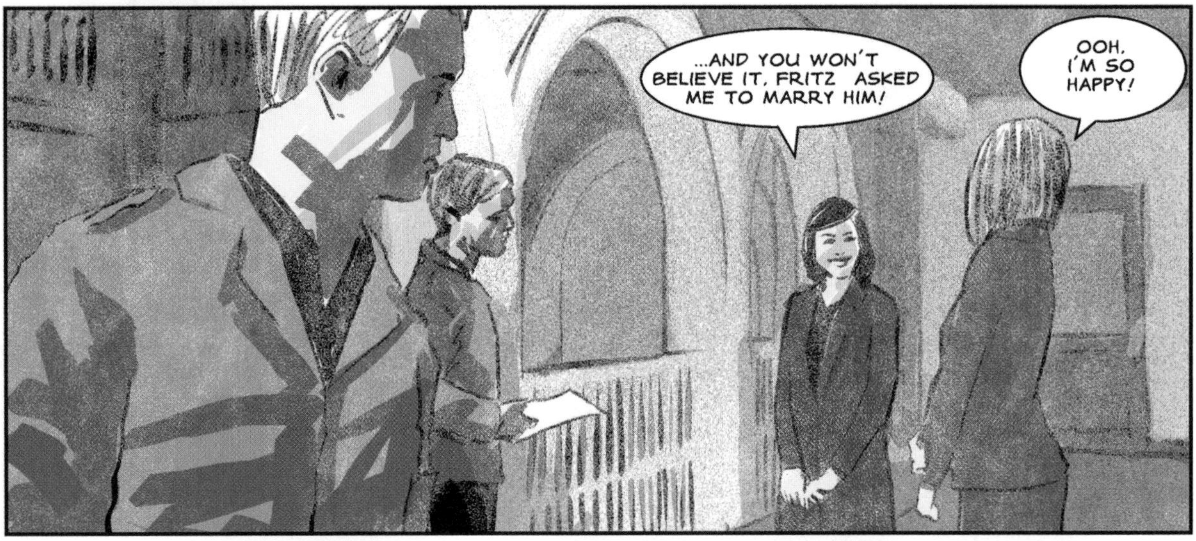
...AND YOU WON'T BELIEVE IT, FRITZ ASKED ME TO MARRY HIM!
OOH, I'M SO HAPPY!

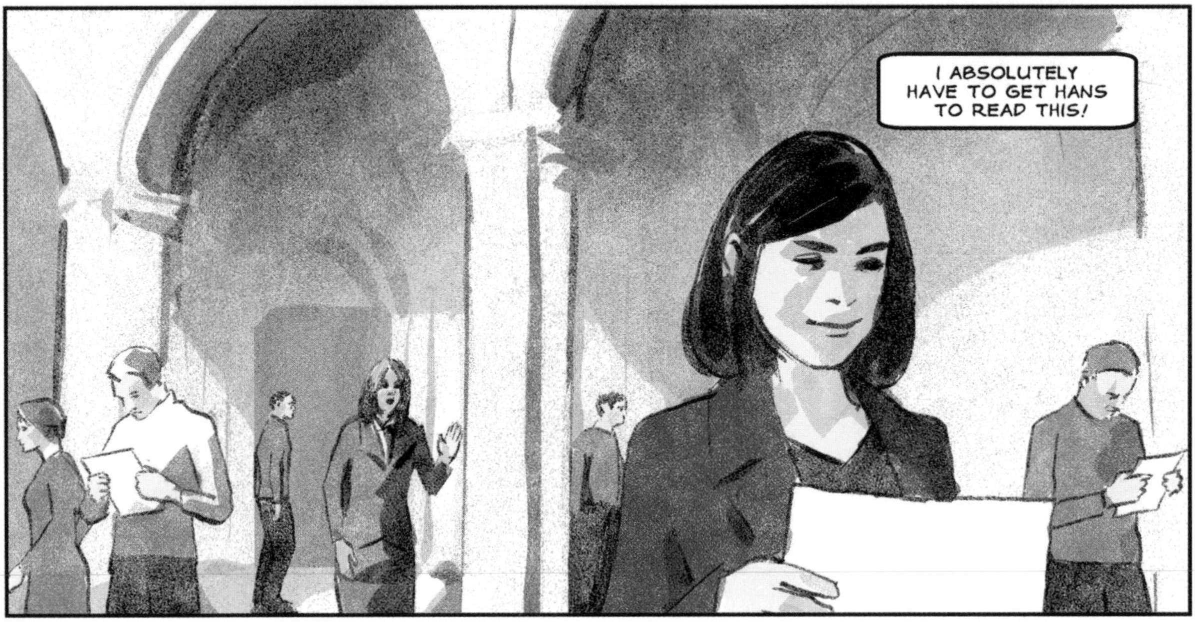
I ABSOLUTELY HAVE TO GET HANS TO READ THIS!

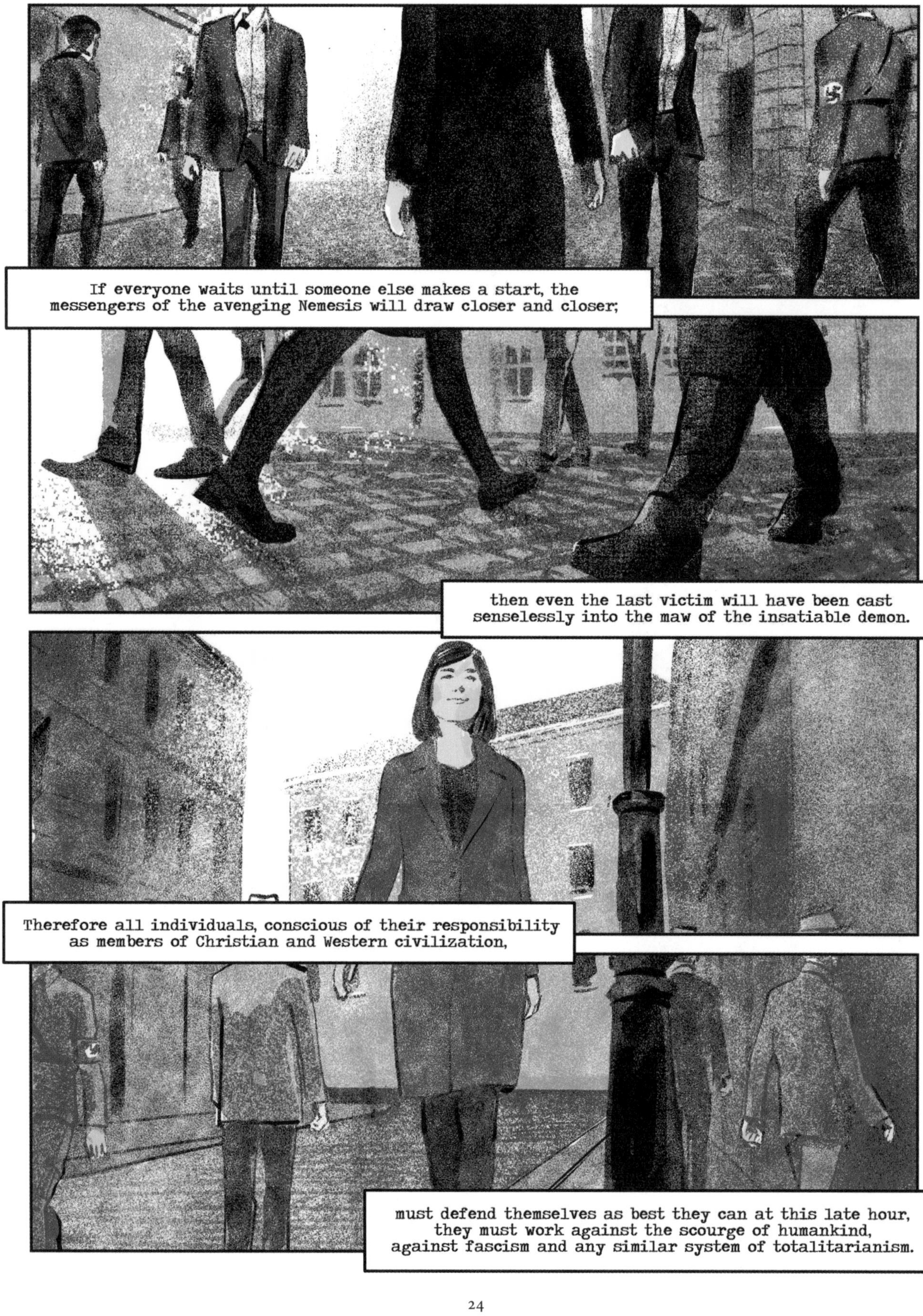
If everyone waits until someone else makes a start, the messengers of the avenging Nemesis will draw closer and closer;
then even the last victim will have been cast senselessly into the maw of the insatiable demon.
Therefore all individuals, conscious of their responsibility as members of Christian and Western civilization,
must defend themselves as best they can at this late hour, they must work against the scourge of humankind, against fascism and any similar system of totalitarianism.

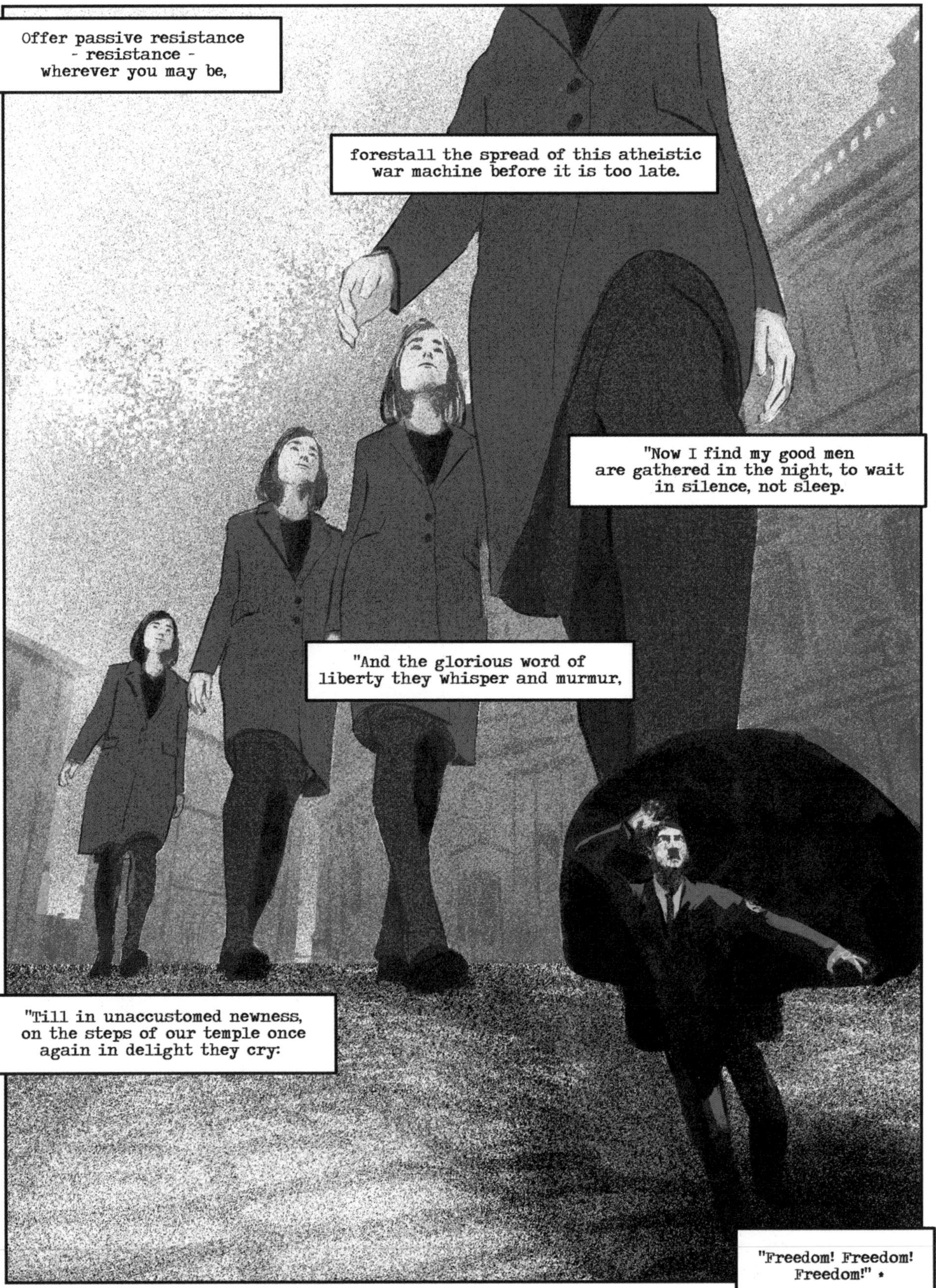
Offer passive resistance - resistance - wherever you may be,
forestall the spread of this atheistic war machine before it is too late.
"Now I find my good men are gathered in the night, to wait in silence, not sleep.
"And the glorious word of liberty they whisper and murmur,
"Till in unaccustomed newness, on the steps of our temple once again in delight they cry:
"Freedom! Freedom! Freedom!" *

*JOHANN WOLFGANG VON GOETHE, "THE AWAKENING OF EPIMENIDES" (1815)

HANS SCHOLL'S APARTMENT

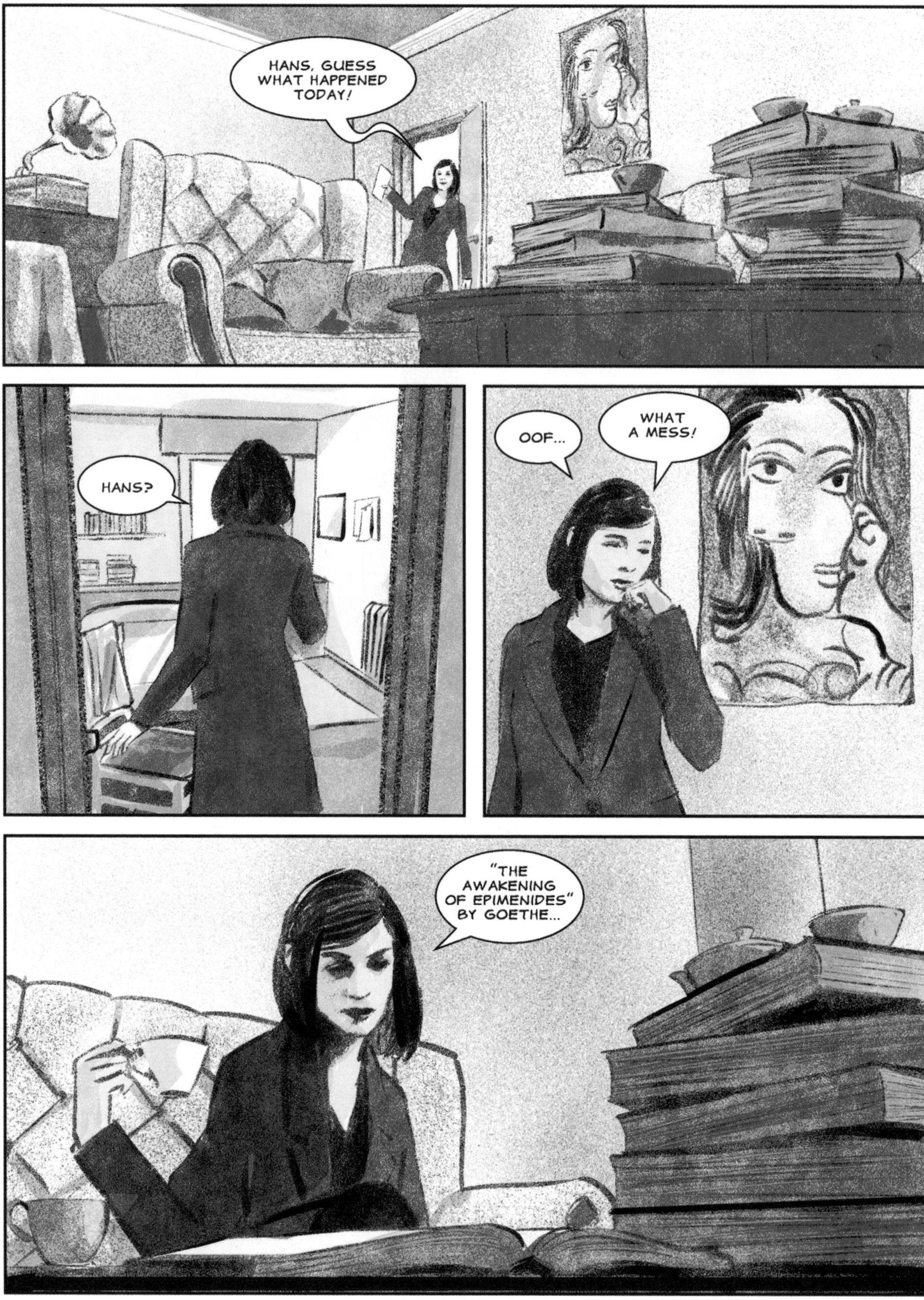
HANS, GUESS WHAT HAPPENED TODAY!
HANS?
OOF...
WHAT A MESS!
"THE AWAKENING OF EPIMENIDES" BY GOETHE...

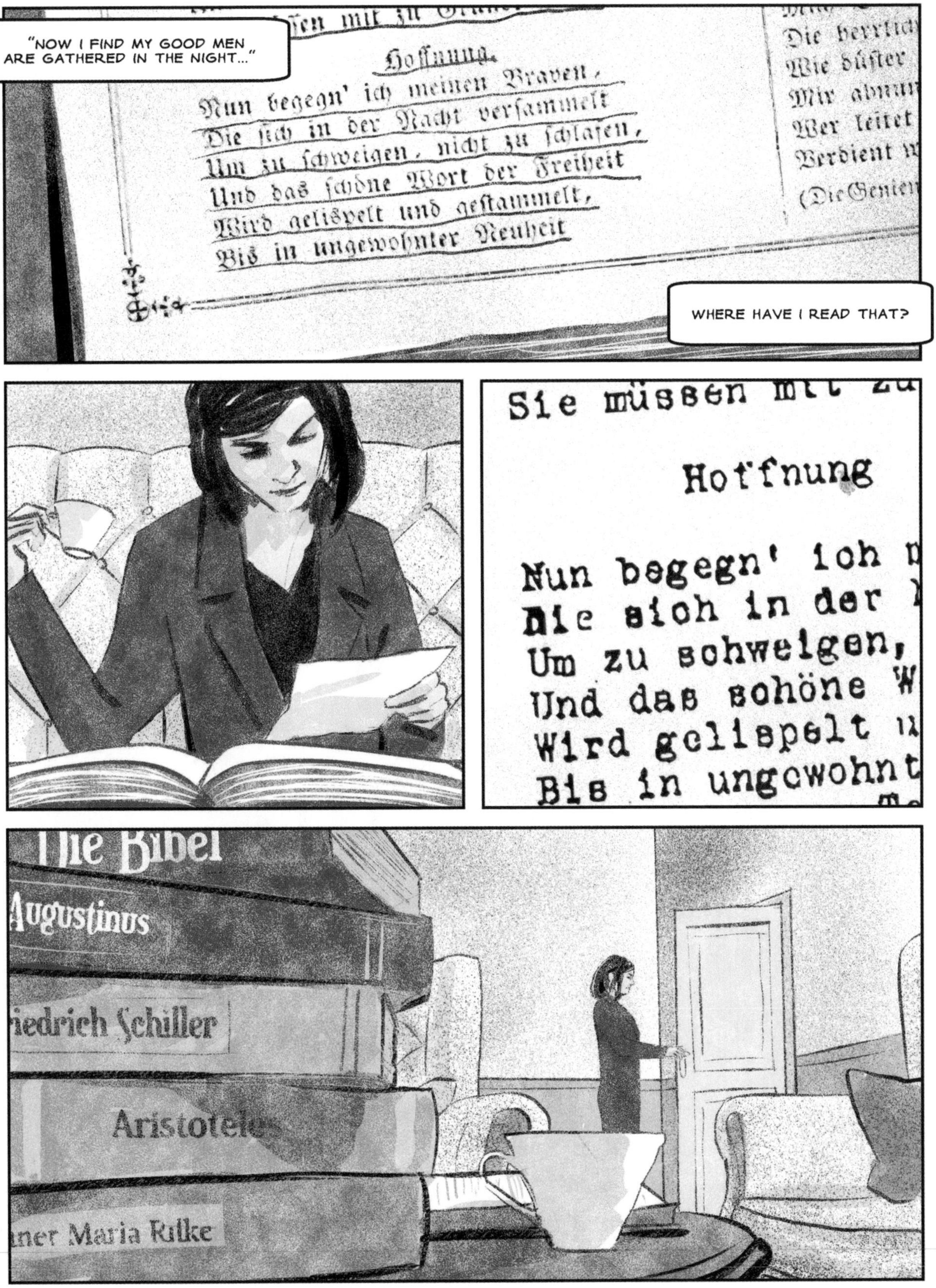
"NOW I FIND MY GOOD MEN ARE GATHERED IN THE NIGHT..."
Hoffnung.
Nun begegn' ich meinen Braven,
Die sich in der Nacht versammelt
Um zu schweigen, nicht zu schlafen,
Und das schöne Wort der Freiheit
Wird gelispelt und gestammelt,
Bis in ungewohnter Neuheit
WHERE HAVE I READ THAT?
Hoffnung
Augustinus

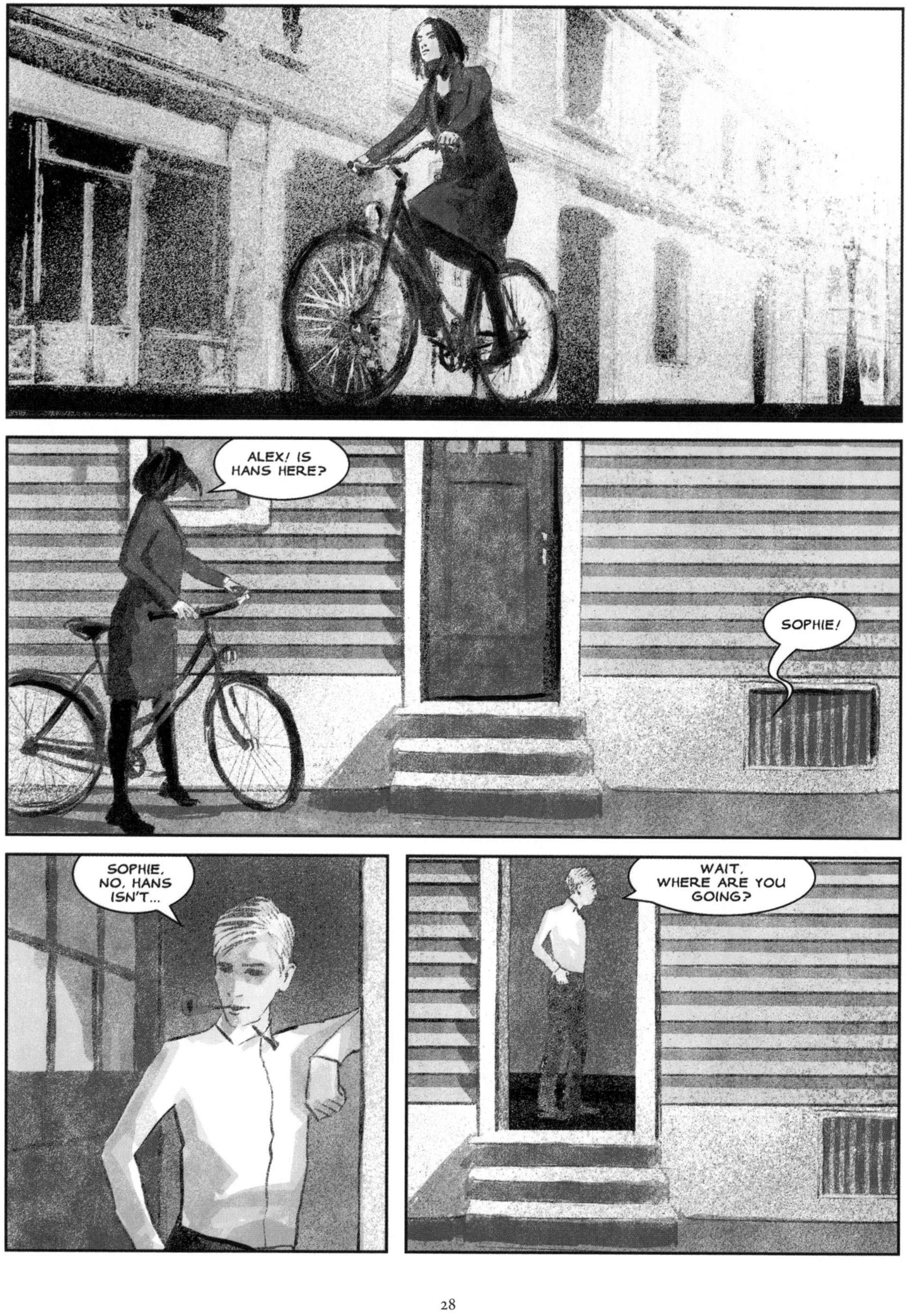
ALEX! IS HANS HERE?
SOPHIE!
SOPHIE, NO, HANS ISN'T...
WAIT, WHERE ARE YOU GOING?

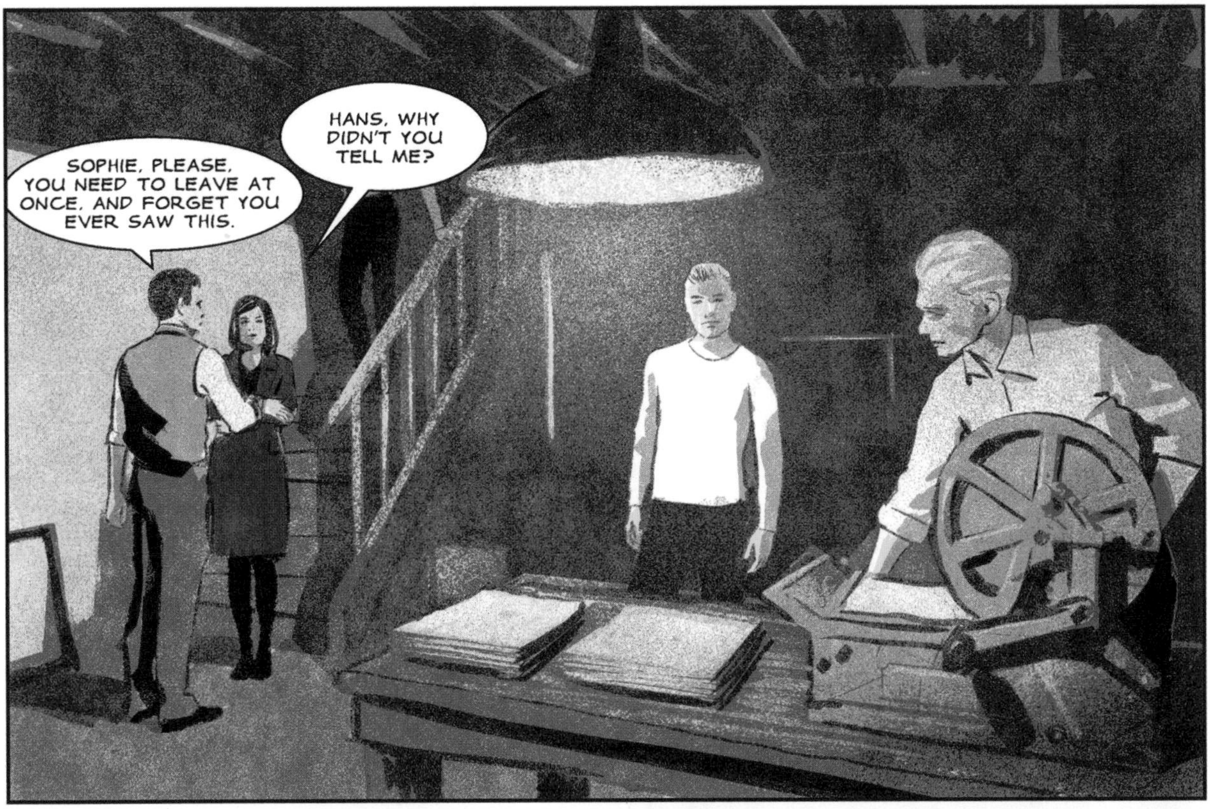
SOPHIE, PLEASE, YOU NEED TO LEAVE AT ONCE, AND FORGET YOU EVER SAW THIS.
HANS, WHY DIDN'T YOU TELL ME?

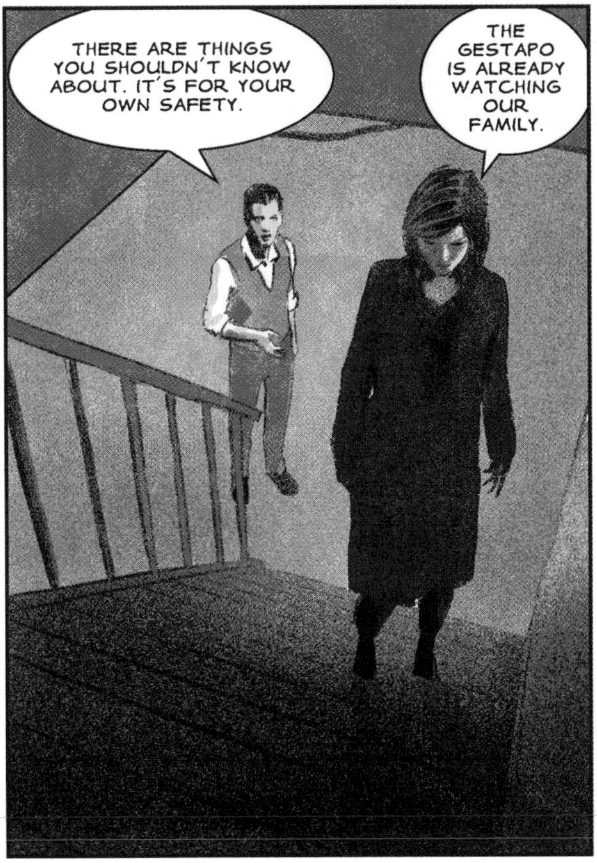
THERE ARE THINGS YOU SHOULDN'T KNOW ABOUT. IT'S FOR YOUR OWN SAFETY.
THE GESTAPO IS ALREADY WATCHING OUR FAMILY.

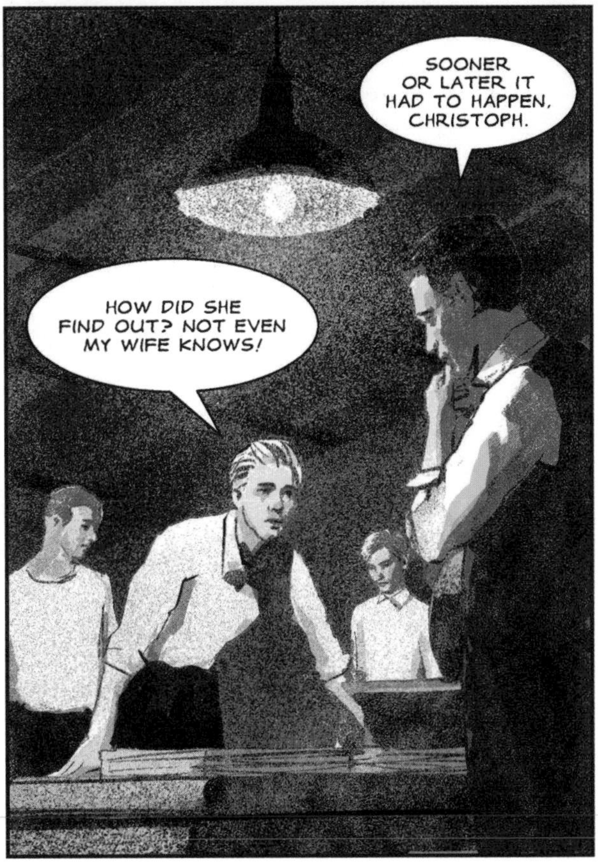
SOONER OR LATER IT HAD TO HAPPEN, CHRISTOPH.
HOW DID SHE FIND OUT? NOT EVEN MY WIFE KNOWS!

SOPHIE SCHOLL'S APARTMENT

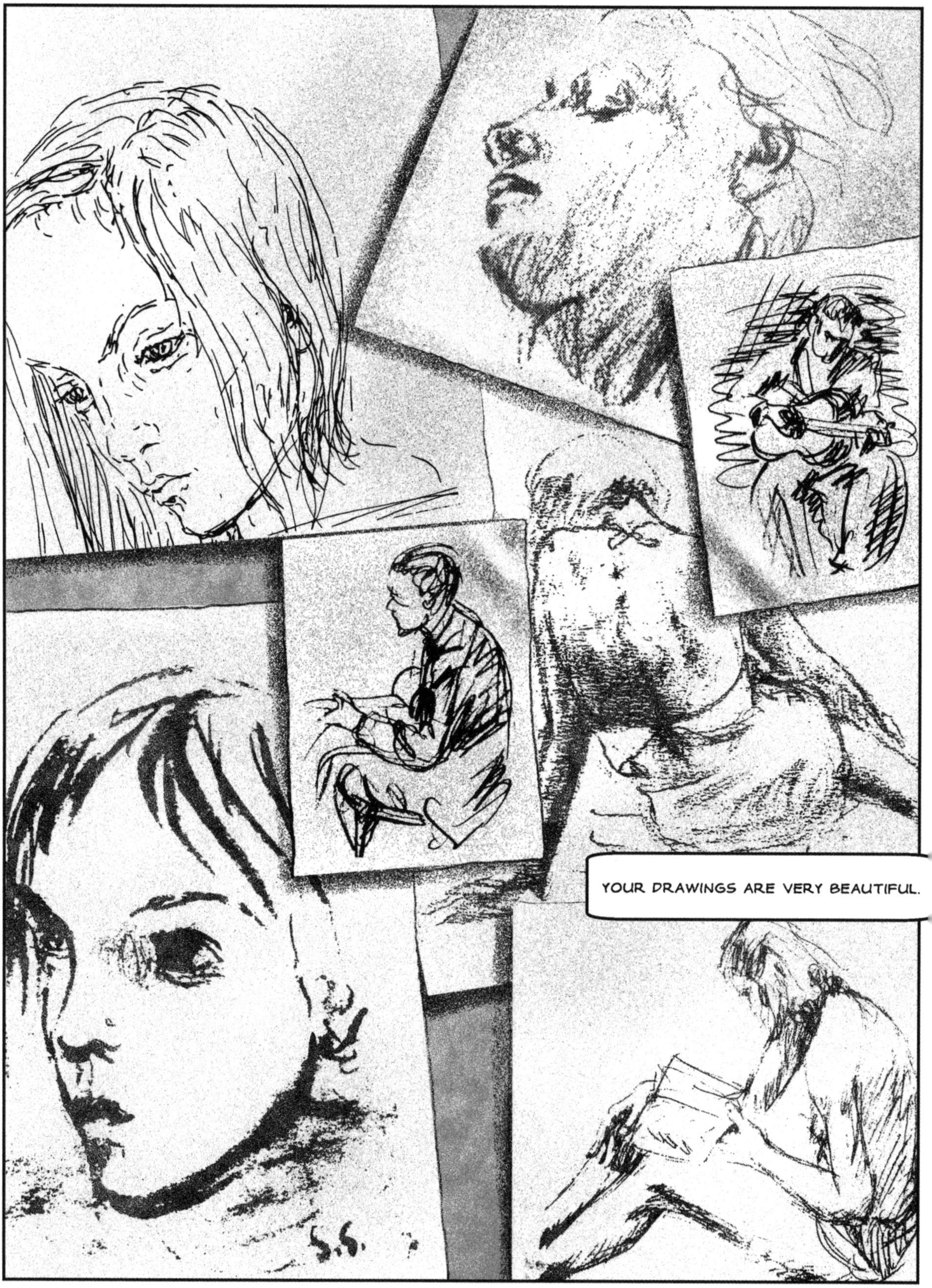

YOUR DRAWINGS ARE VERY BEAUTIFUL.
S.S.

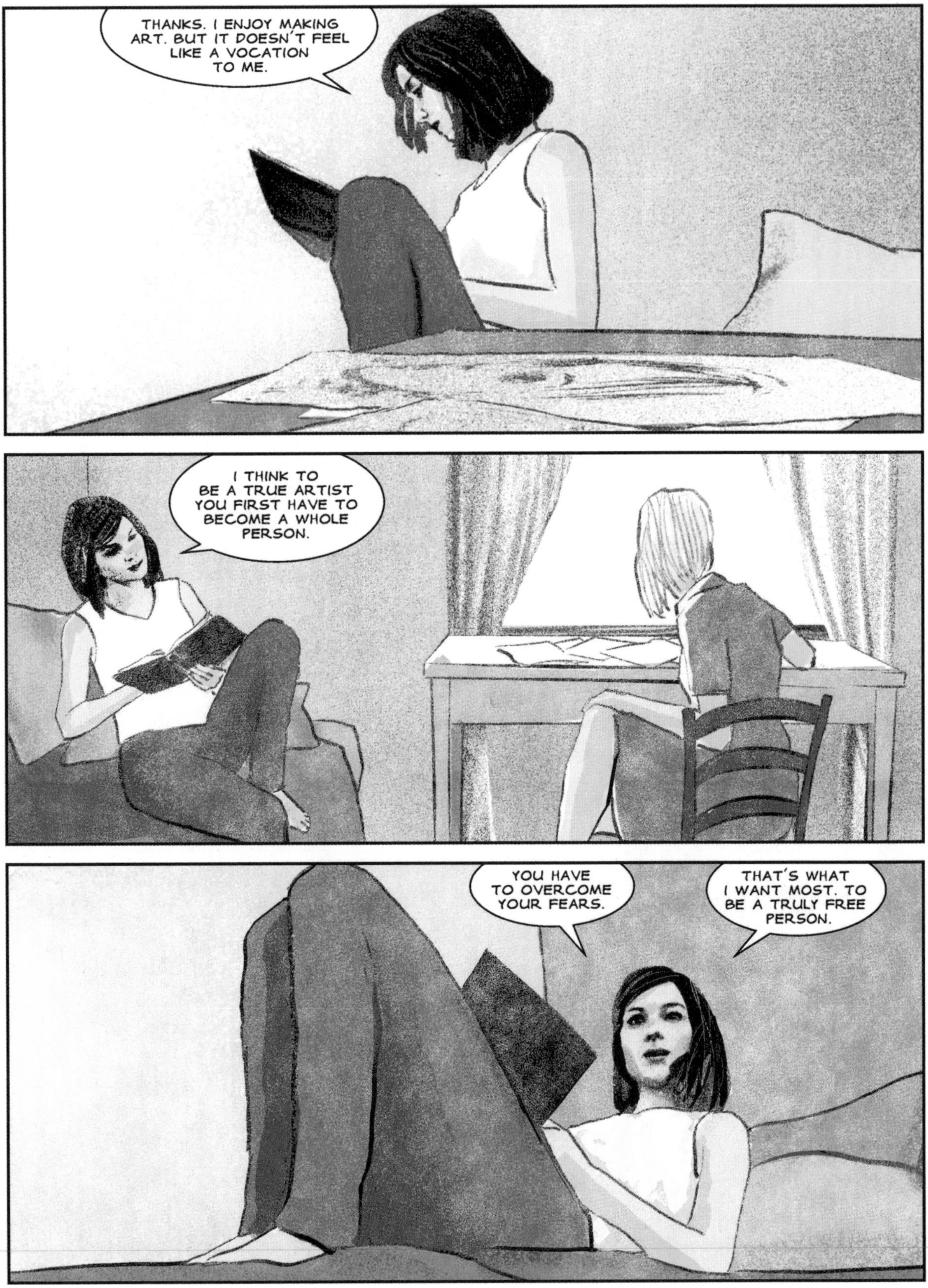
THANKS. I ENJOY MAKING ART. BUT IT DOESN'T FEEL LIKE A VOCATION TO ME.
I THINK TO BE A TRUE ARTIST YOU FIRST HAVE TO BECOME A WHOLE PERSON.
YOU HAVE TO OVERCOME YOUR FEARS.
THAT'S WHAT I WANT MOST. TO BE A TRULY FREE PERSON.

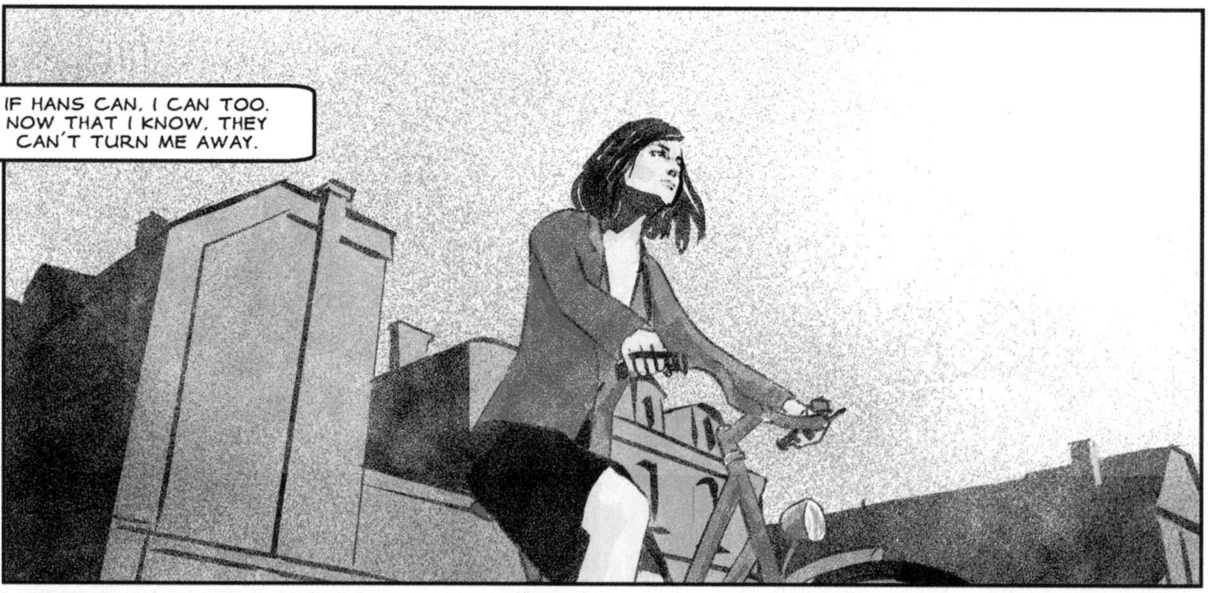
IF HANS CAN, I CAN TOO. NOW THAT I KNOW, THEY CAN'T TURN ME AWAY.

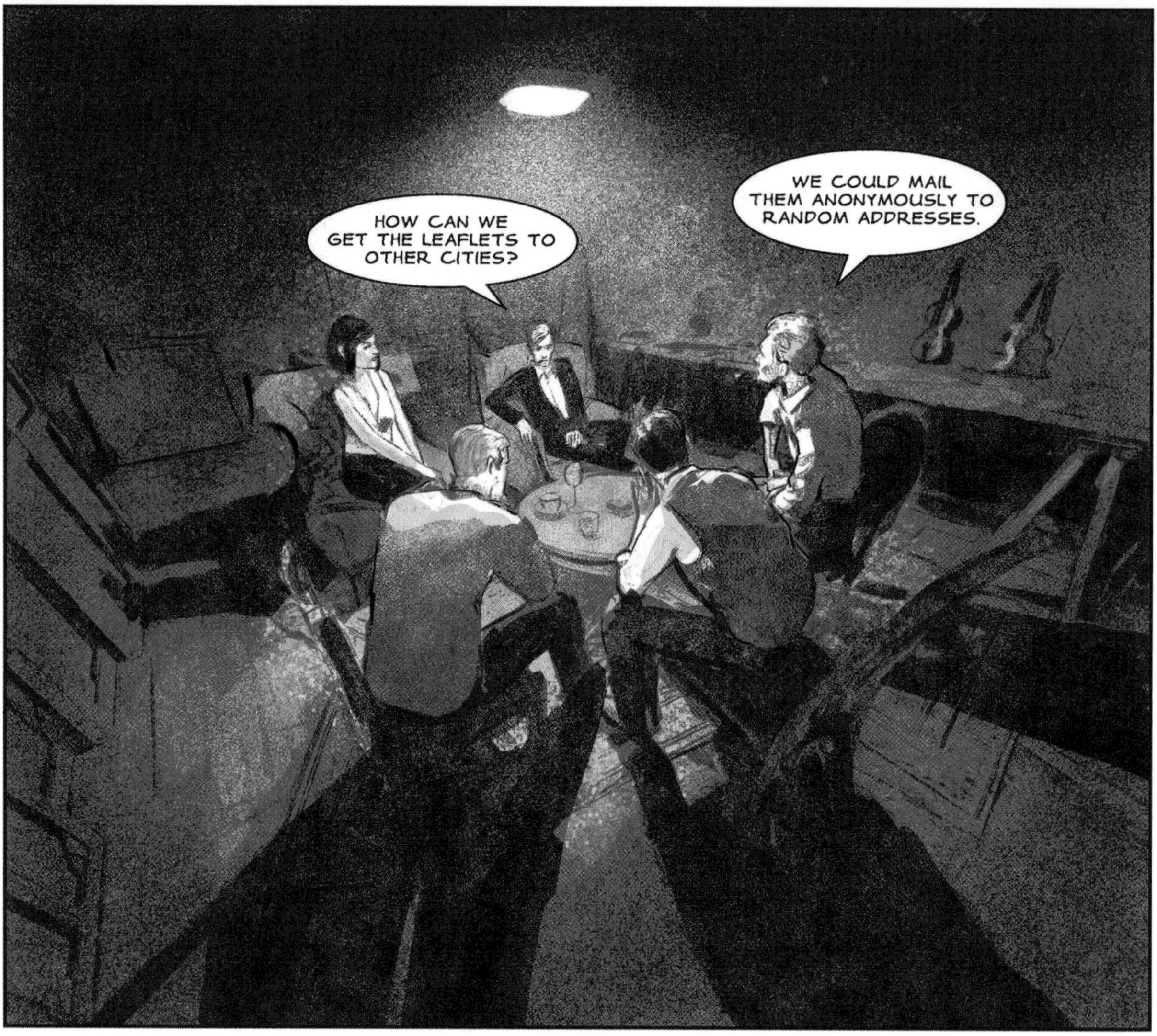
HOW CAN WE GET THE LEAFLETS TO OTHER CITIES?
WE COULD MAIL THEM ANONYMOUSLY TO RANDOM ADDRESSES.

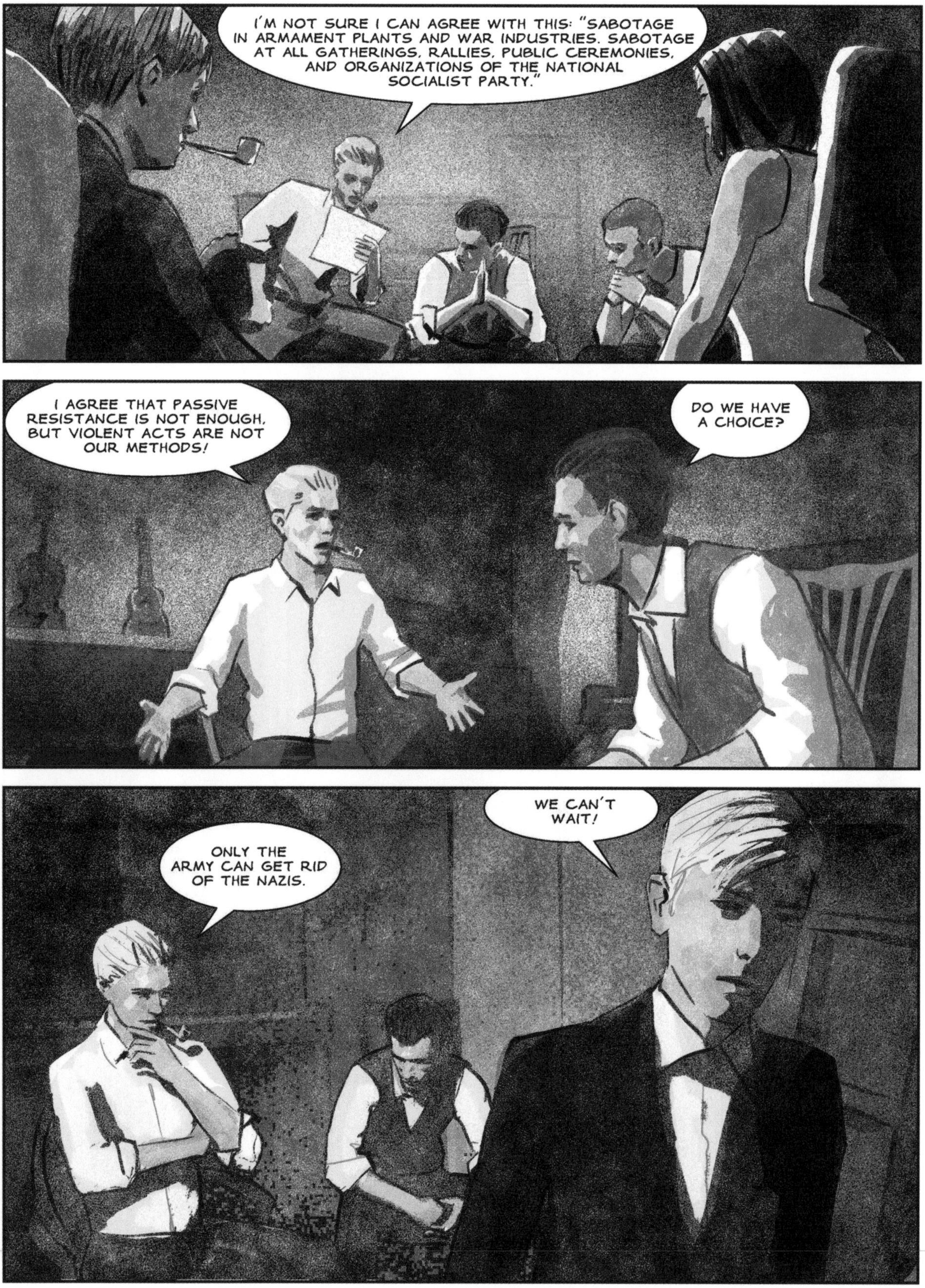
I'M NOT SURE I CAN AGREE WITH THIS: "SABOTAGE IN ARMAMENT PLANTS AND WAR INDUSTRIES. SABOTAGE AT ALL GATHERINGS, RALLIES, PUBLIC CEREMONIES, AND ORGANIZATIONS OF THE NATIONAL SOCIALIST PARTY."
I AGREE THAT PASSIVE RESISTANCE IS NOT ENOUGH, BUT VIOLENT ACTS ARE NOT OUR METHODS!
DO WE HAVE A CHOICE?
WE CAN'T WAIT!
ONLY THE ARMY CAN GET RID OF THE NAZIS.

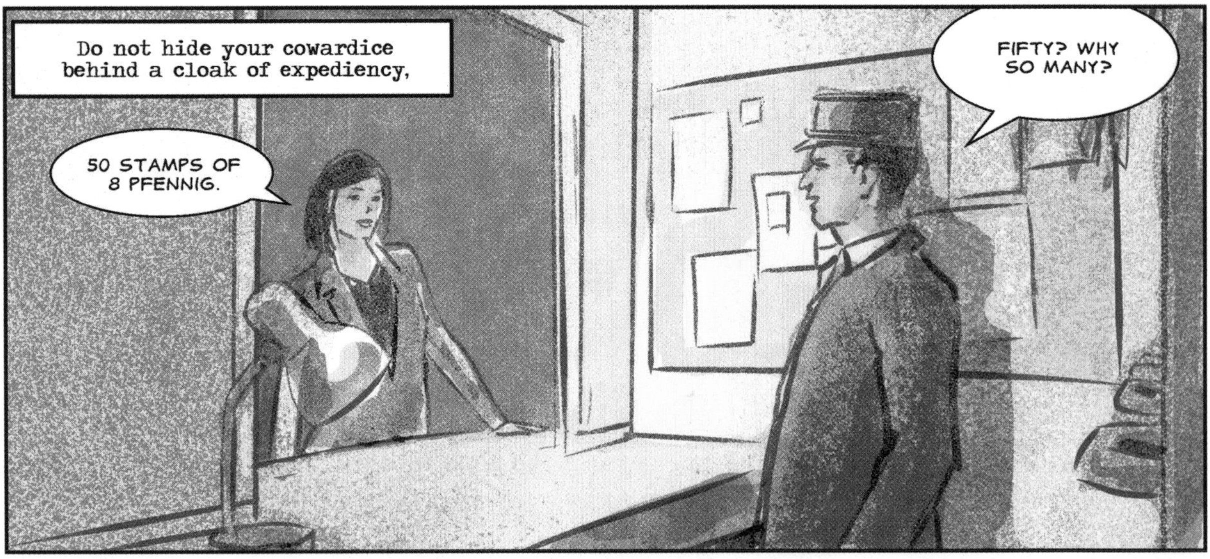
Do not hide your cowardice behind a cloak of expediency,
50 STAMPS OF 8 PFENNIG.
FIFTY? WHY SO MANY?

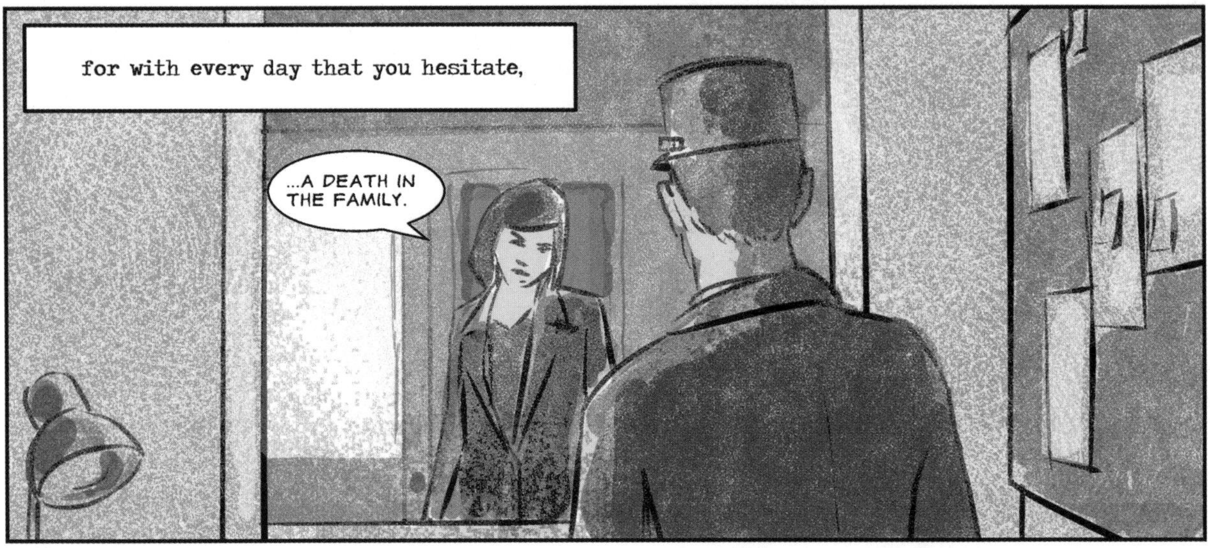
for with every day that you hesitate,
...A DEATH IN THE FAMILY.

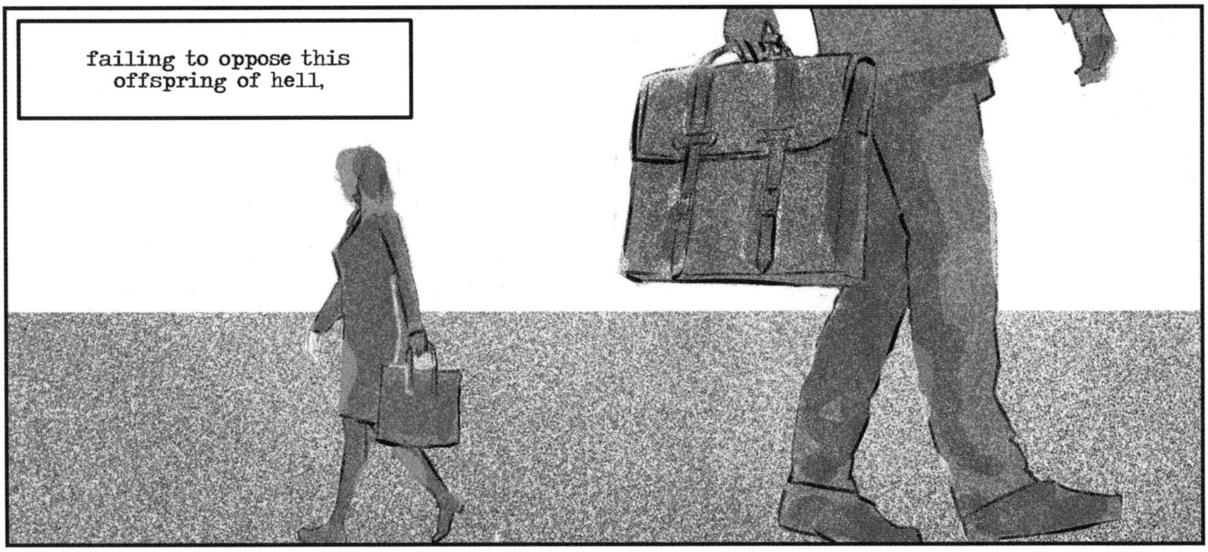
failing to oppose this offspring of hell,

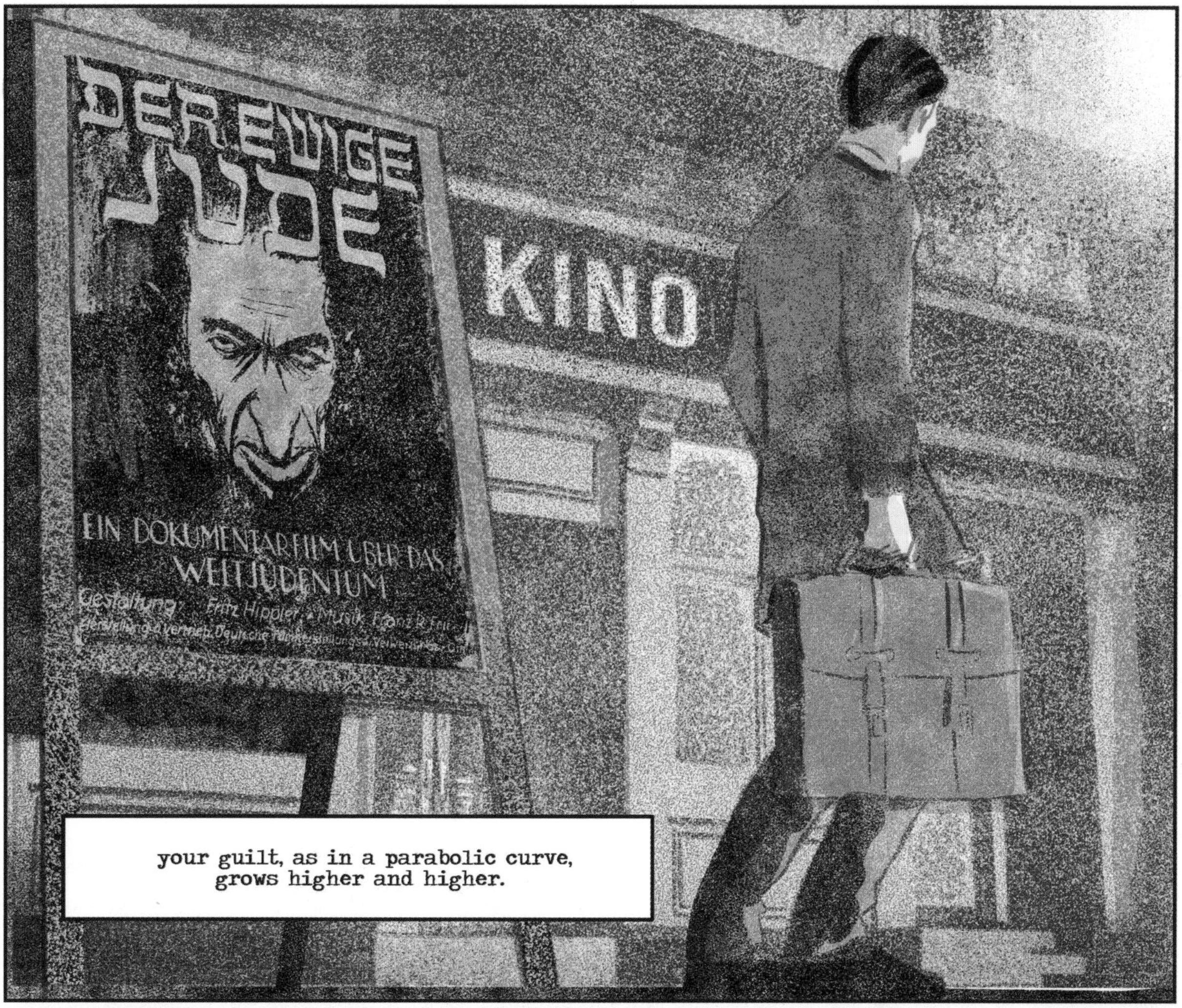
DER EWIGE JUDE
EIN DOKUMENTARFILM ÜBER DAS WELTJUDENTUM
Fritz Hippler
KINO
your guilt, as in a parabolic curve,
grows higher and higher.

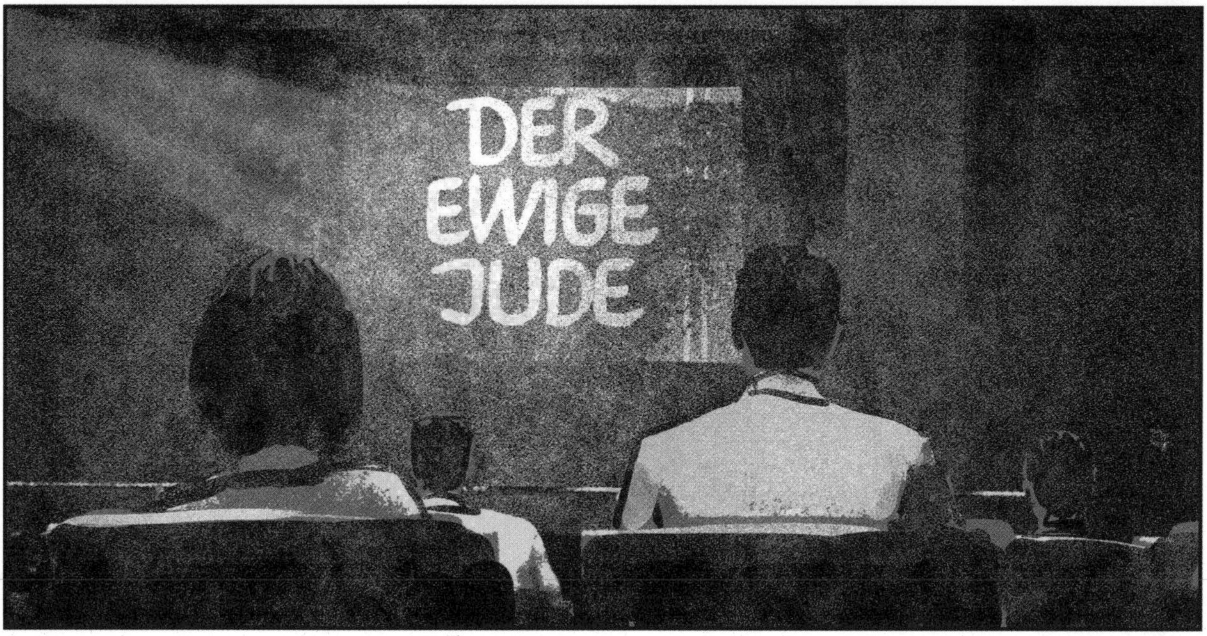
DER EWIGE JUDE

THE "CIVILIZED" JEWS WE KNOW IN GERMANY GIVE US A DISTORTED AND INCOMPLETE PICTURE OF THEIR TRUE NATURE AND THEIR RACIAL CHARACTERISTICS.

THIS FILM SHOWS CURRENT IMAGES OF POLISH GHETTOS. IT SHOWS THE JEWS AS THEY REALLY ARE BEFORE THEY INFILTRATE US AND HIDE BEHIND THE MASK OF THE CIVILIZED EUROPEAN.

RICHARD WAGNER ONCE SAID THAT JEWS ARE THE DEVIL BEHIND THE CORRUPTION AND DEGRADATION OF HUMANKIND.

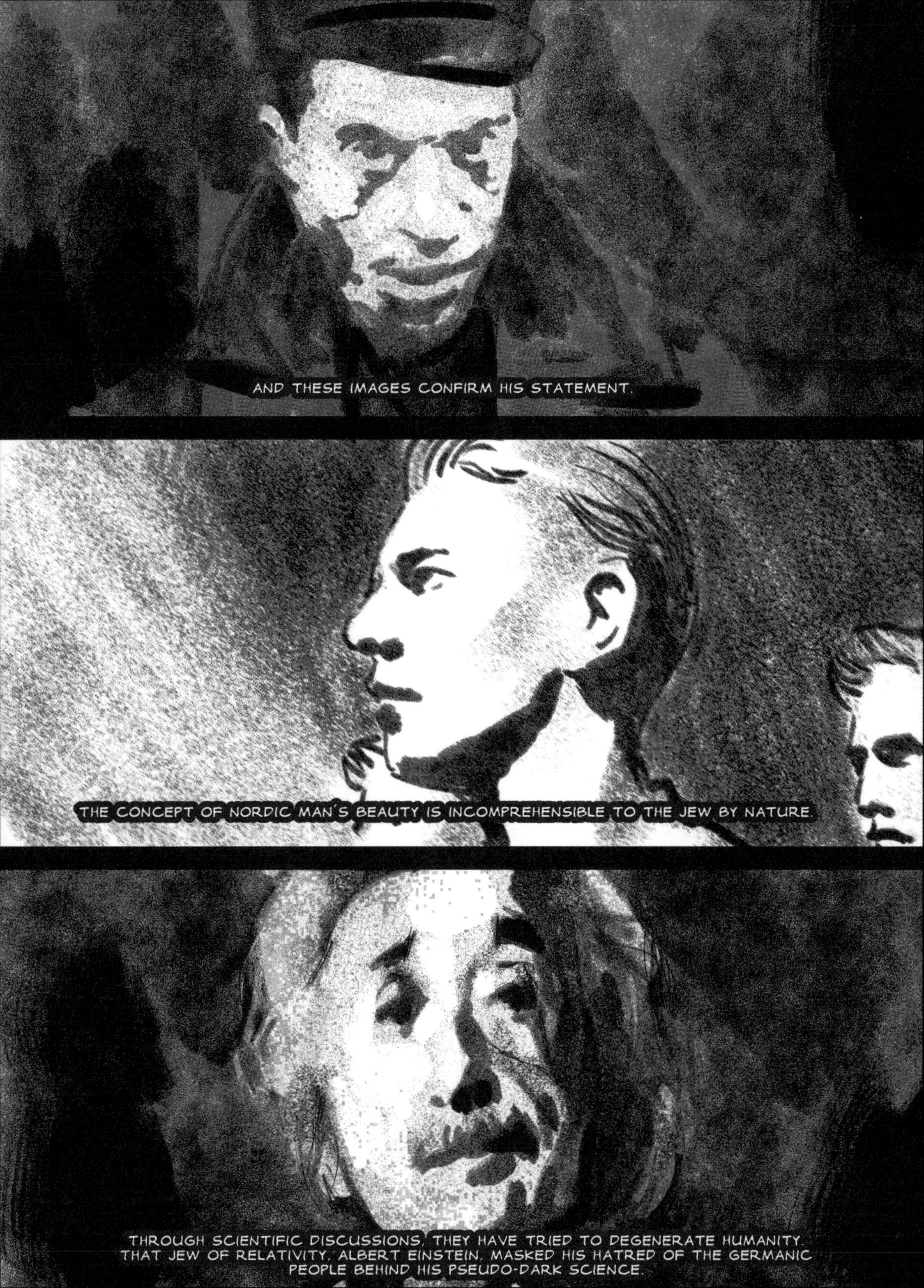
AND THESE IMAGES CONFIRM HIS STATEMENT.
THE CONCEPT OF NORDIC MAN'S BEAUTY IS INCOMPREHENSIBLE TO THE JEW BY NATURE.
THROUGH SCIENTIFIC DISCUSSIONS, THEY HAVE TRIED TO DEGENERATE HUMANITY. THAT JEW OF RELATIVITY, ALBERT EINSTEIN, MASKED HIS HATRED OF THE GERMANIC PEOPLE BEHIND HIS PSEUDO-DARK SCIENCE.

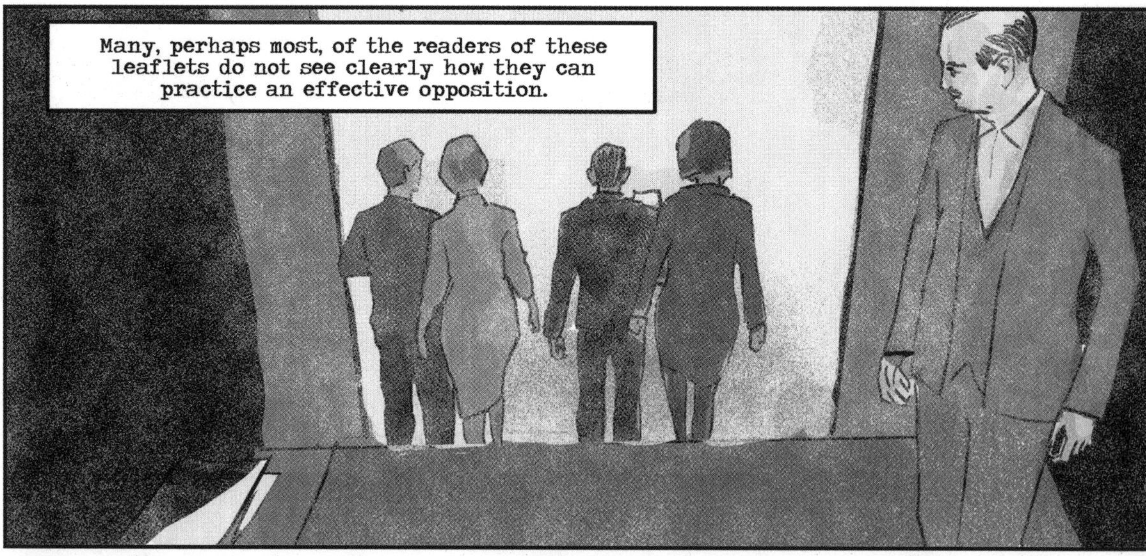
Many, perhaps most, of the readers of these leaflets do not see clearly how they can practice an effective opposition.

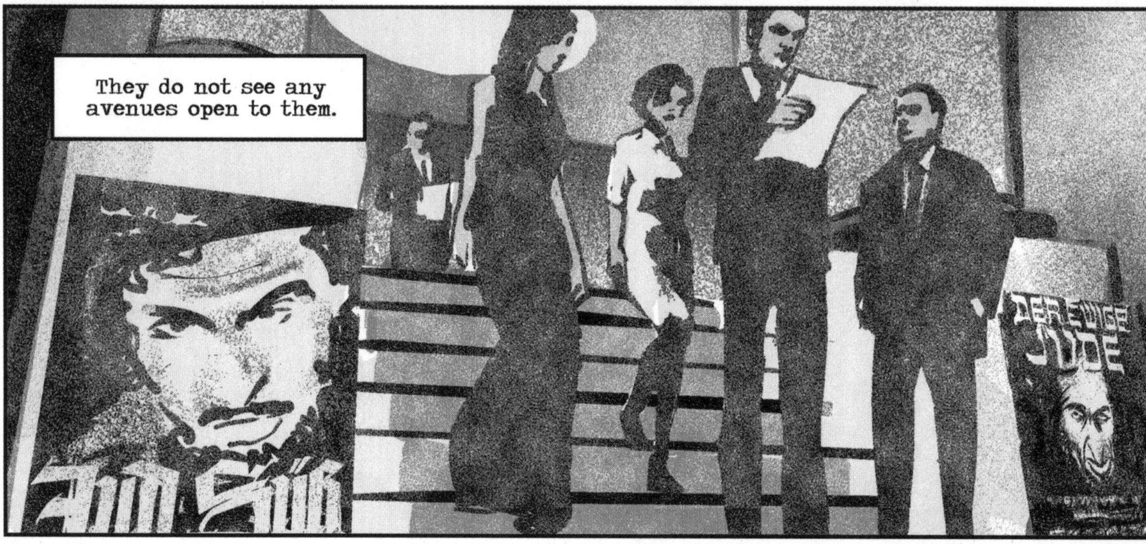
They do not see any avenues open to them.
DER EWIGE JUDE

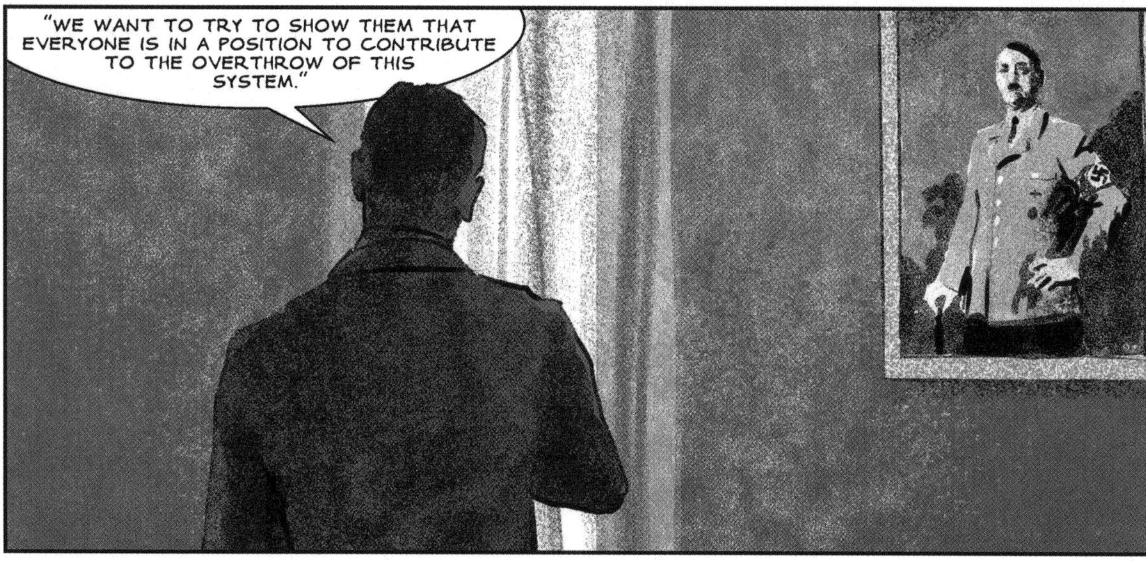
"WE WANT TO TRY TO SHOW THEM THAT EVERYONE IS IN A POSITION TO CONTRIBUTE TO THE OVERTHROW OF THIS SYSTEM."

GESTAPO HEADQUARTERS, MUNICH

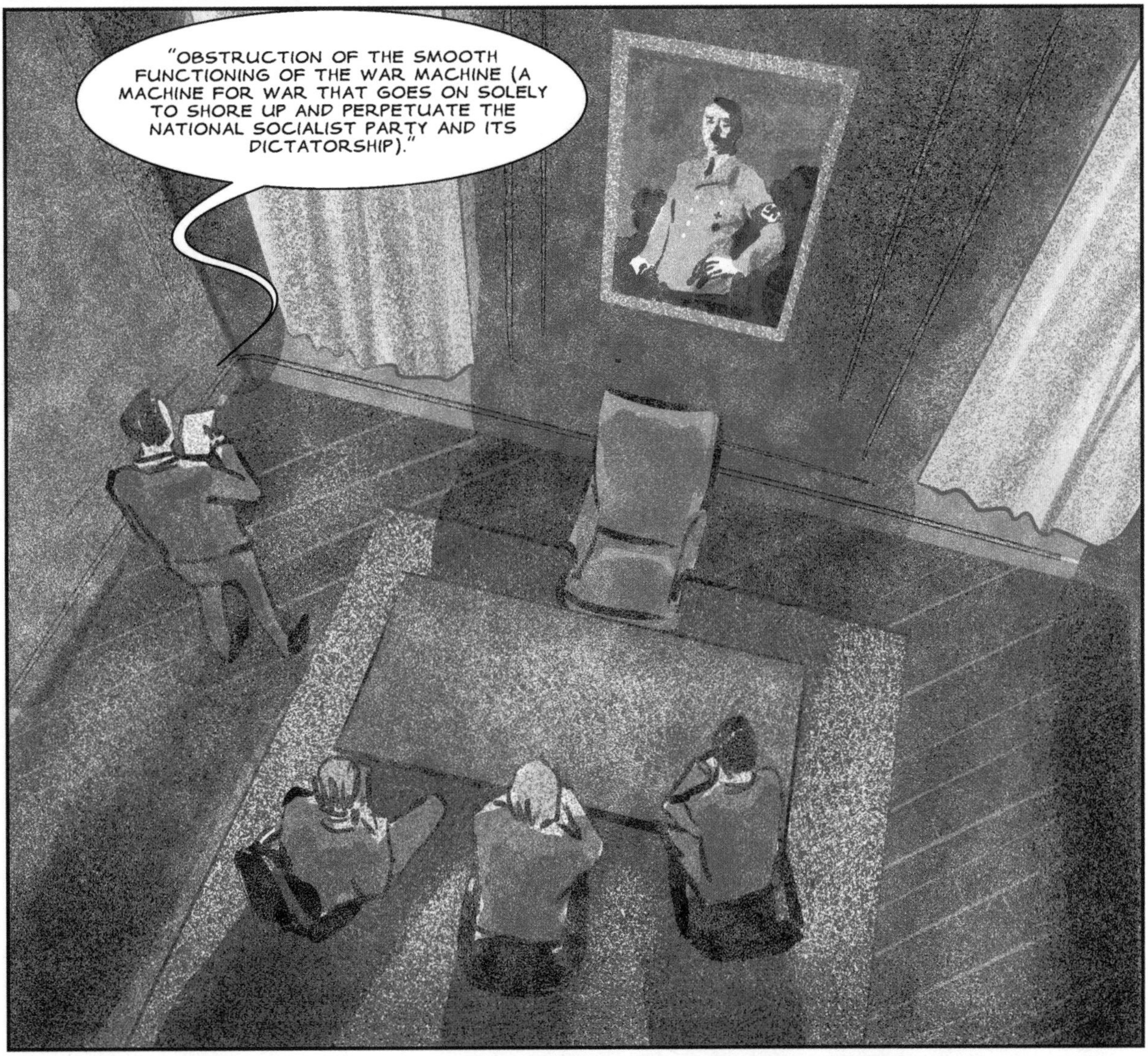
"OBSTRUCTION OF THE SMOOTH FUNCTIONING OF THE WAR MACHINE (A MACHINE FOR WAR THAT GOES ON SOLELY TO SHORE UP AND PERPETUATE THE NATIONAL SOCIALIST PARTY AND ITS DICTATORSHIP)."

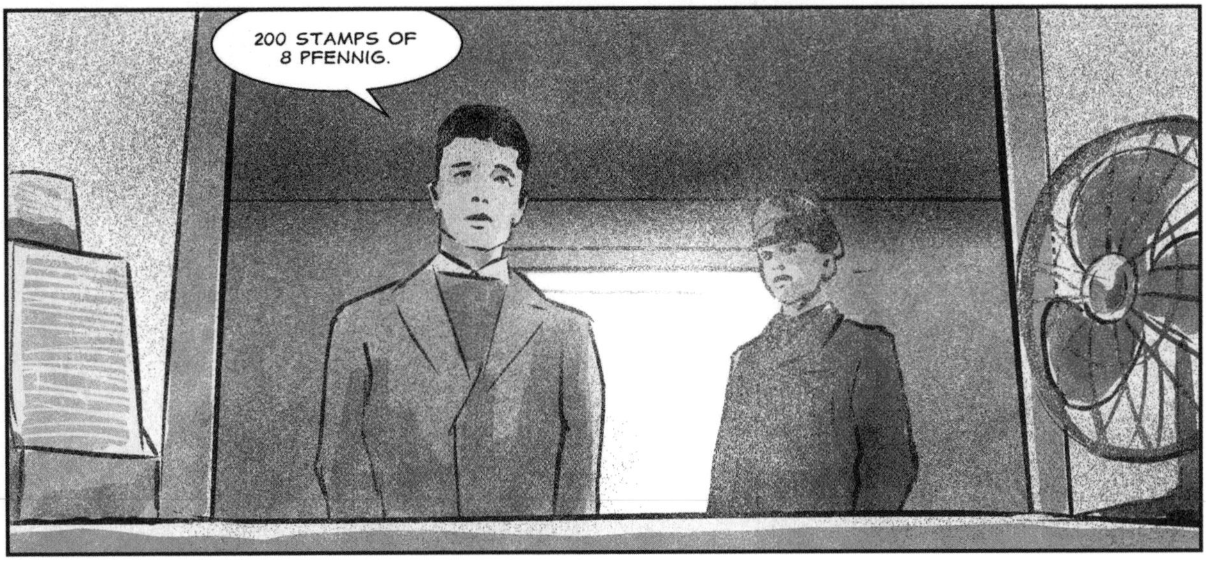
200 STAMPS OF 8 PFENNIG.

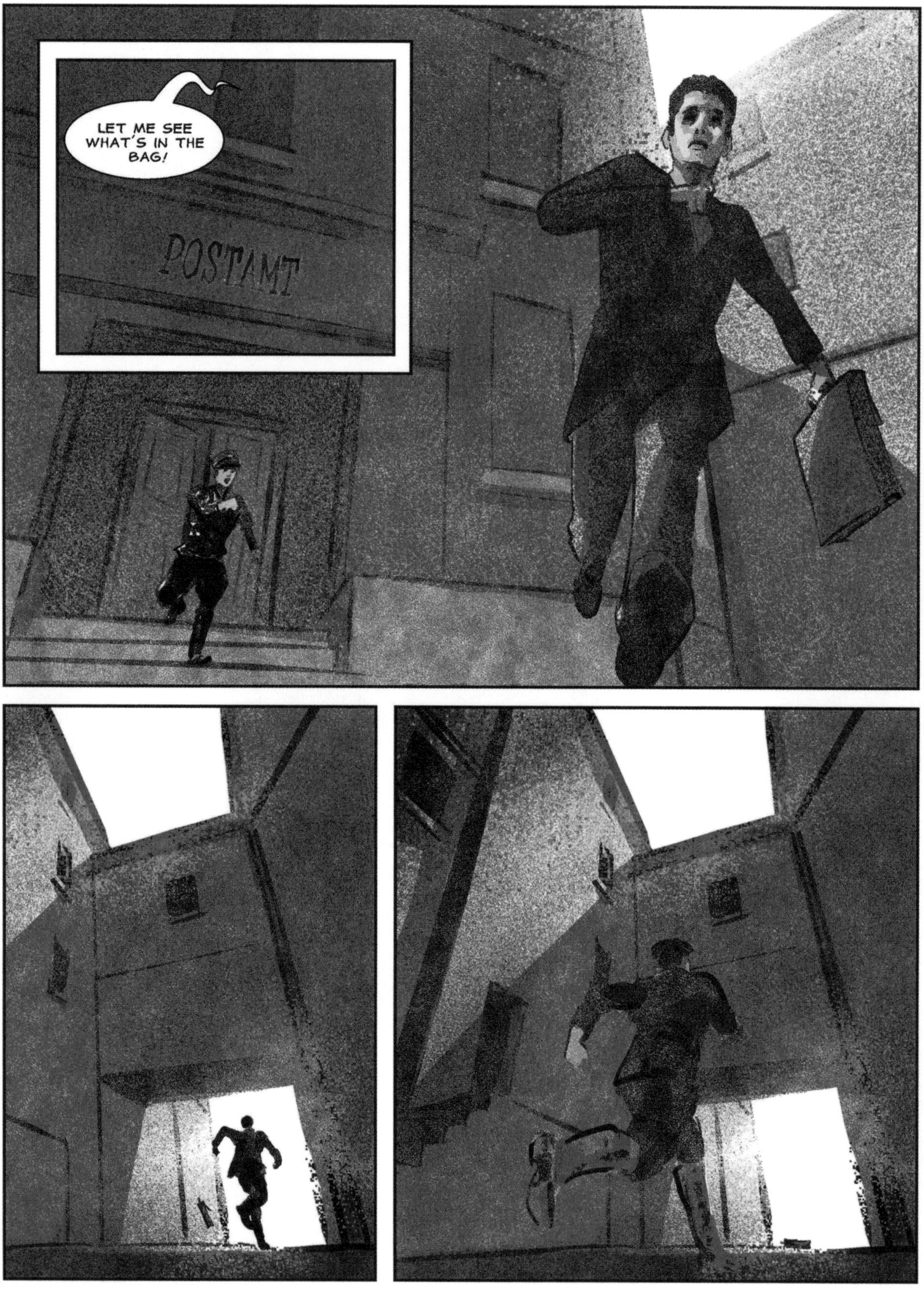
LET ME SEE WHAT'S IN THE BAG!
POSTAMT

GESTAPO HEADQUARTERS

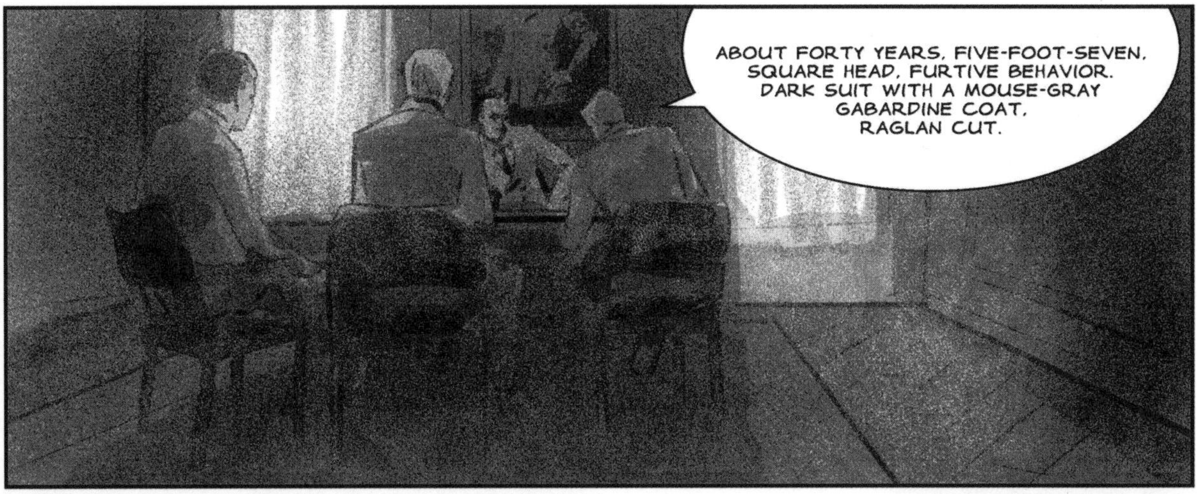
ABOUT FORTY YEARS, FIVE-FOOT-SEVEN, SQUARE HEAD, FURTIVE BEHAVIOR. DARK SUIT WITH A MOUSE-GRAY GABARDINE COAT, RAGLAN CUT.

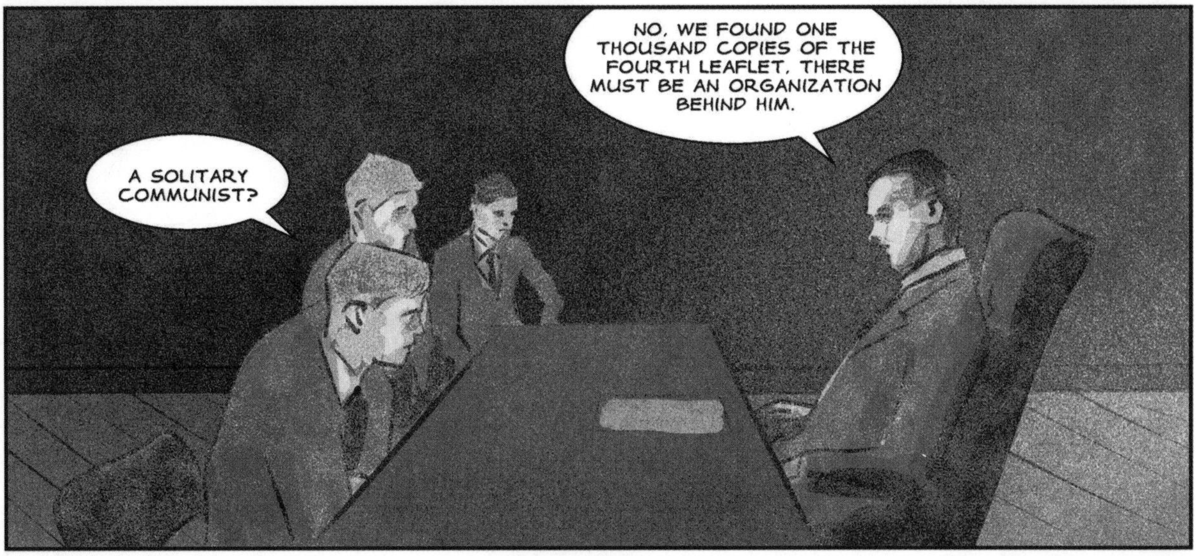
A SOLITARY COMMUNIST?
NO, WE FOUND ONE THOUSAND COPIES OF THE FOURTH LEAFLET, THERE MUST BE AN ORGANIZATION BEHIND HIM.

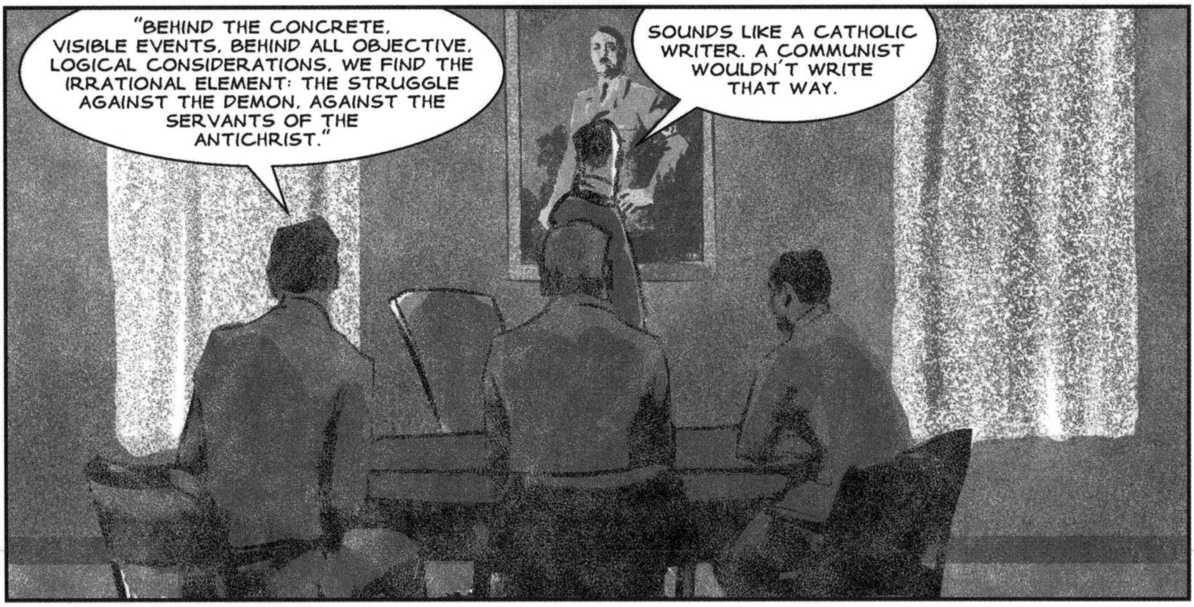
"BEHIND THE CONCRETE, VISIBLE EVENTS, BEHIND ALL OBJECTIVE, LOGICAL CONSIDERATIONS, WE FIND THE IRRATIONAL ELEMENT: THE STRUGGLE AGAINST THE DEMON, AGAINST THE SERVANTS OF THE ANTICHRIST."
SOUNDS LIKE A CATHOLIC WRITER. A COMMUNIST WOULDN'T WRITE THAT WAY.

SCHOLL FAMILY HOME, ULM

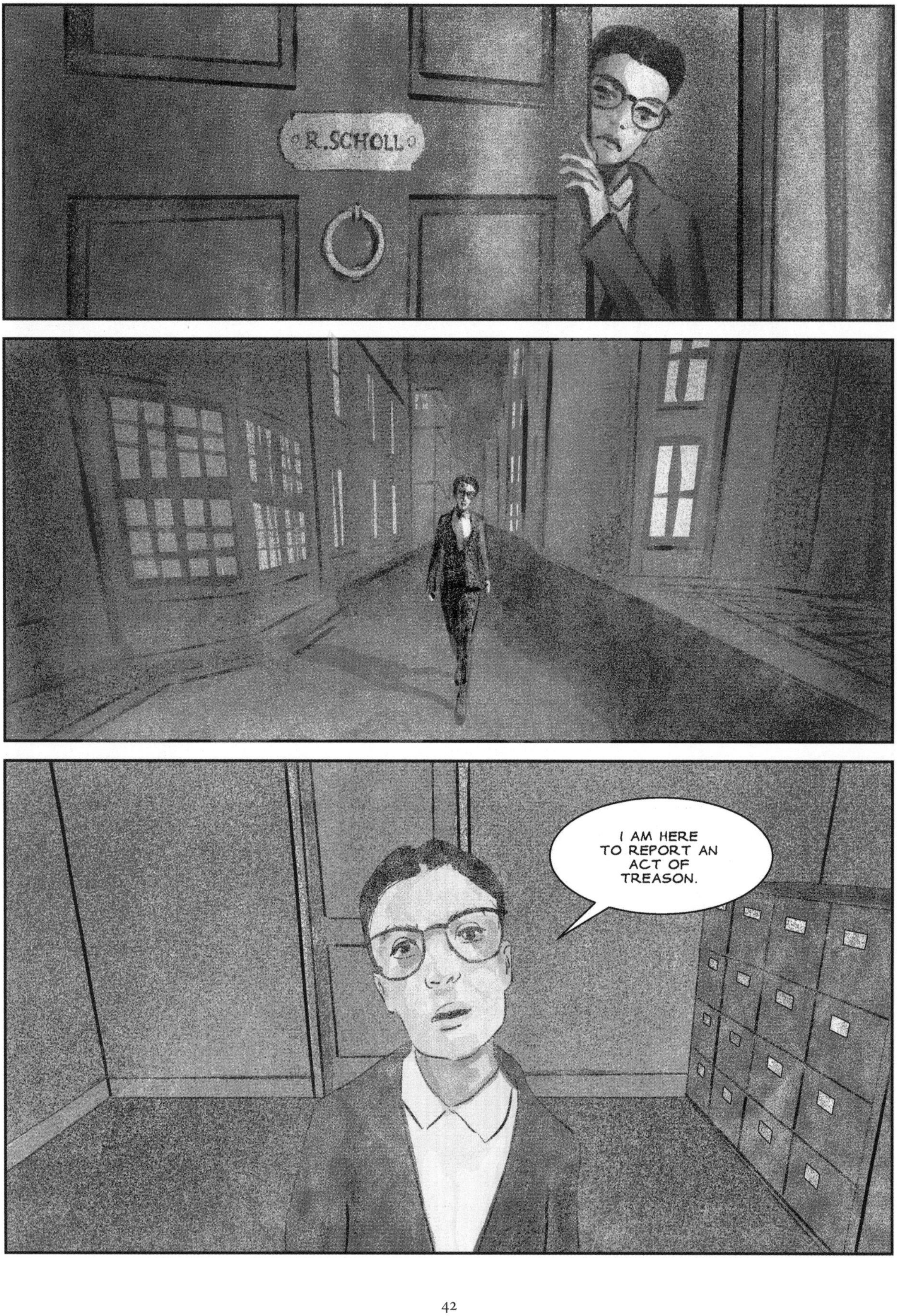
R.SCHOLL
I AM HERE TO REPORT AN ACT OF TREASON.

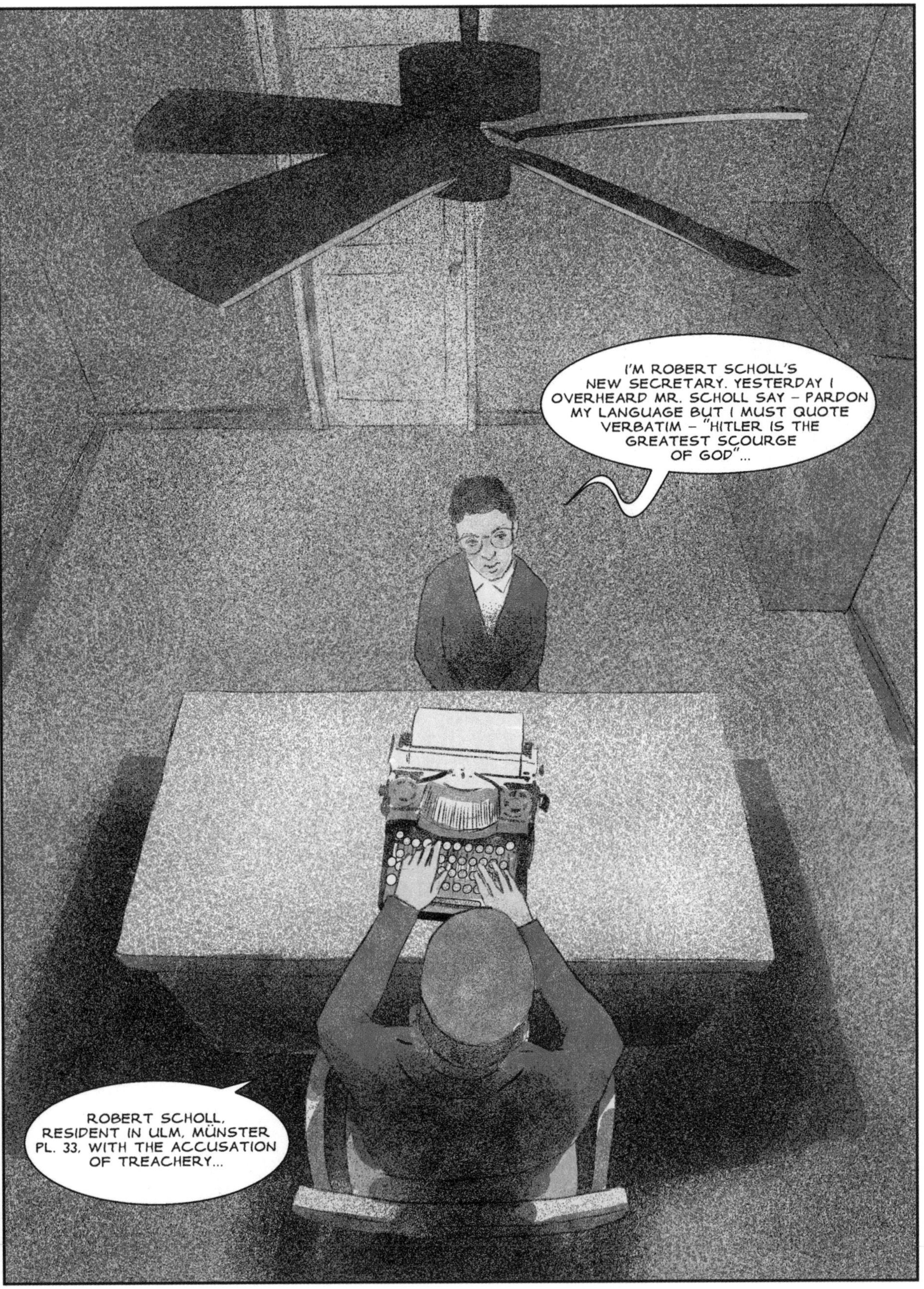
I'M ROBERT SCHOLL'S NEW SECRETARY. YESTERDAY I OVERHEARD MR. SCHOLL SAY – PARDON MY LANGUAGE BUT I MUST QUOTE VERBATIM – "HITLER IS THE GREATEST SCOURGE OF GOD"...
ROBERT SCHOLL, RESIDENT IN ULM, MÜNSTER PL. 33, WITH THE ACCUSATION OF TREACHERY...

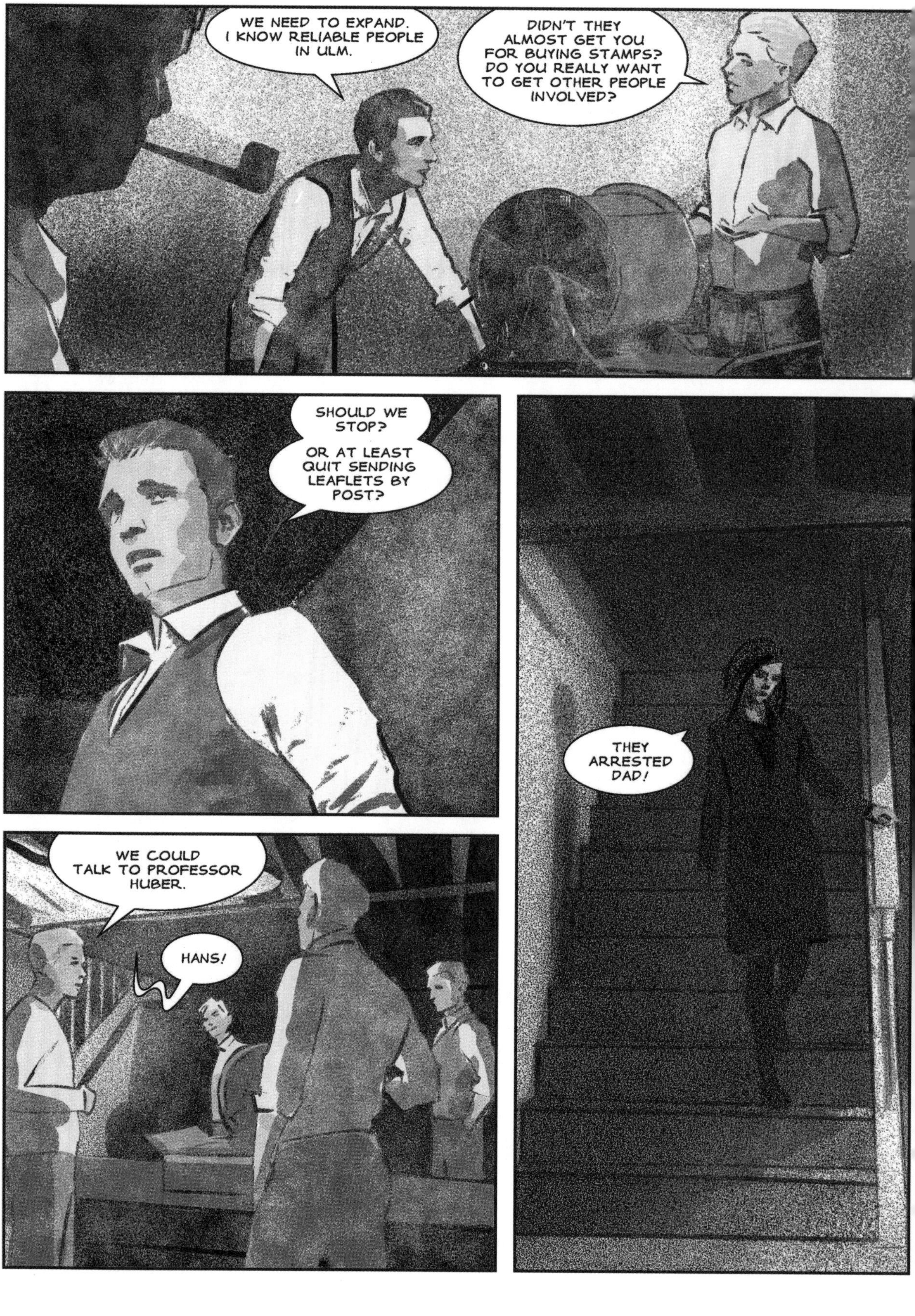
WE NEED TO EXPAND. I KNOW RELIABLE PEOPLE IN ULM.
DIDN'T THEY ALMOST GET YOU FOR BUYING STAMPS? DO YOU REALLY WANT TO GET OTHER PEOPLE INVOLVED?
SHOULD WE STOP?
OR AT LEAST QUIT SENDING LEAFLETS BY POST?
WE COULD TALK TO PROFESSOR HUBER.
HANS!
THEY ARRESTED DAD!

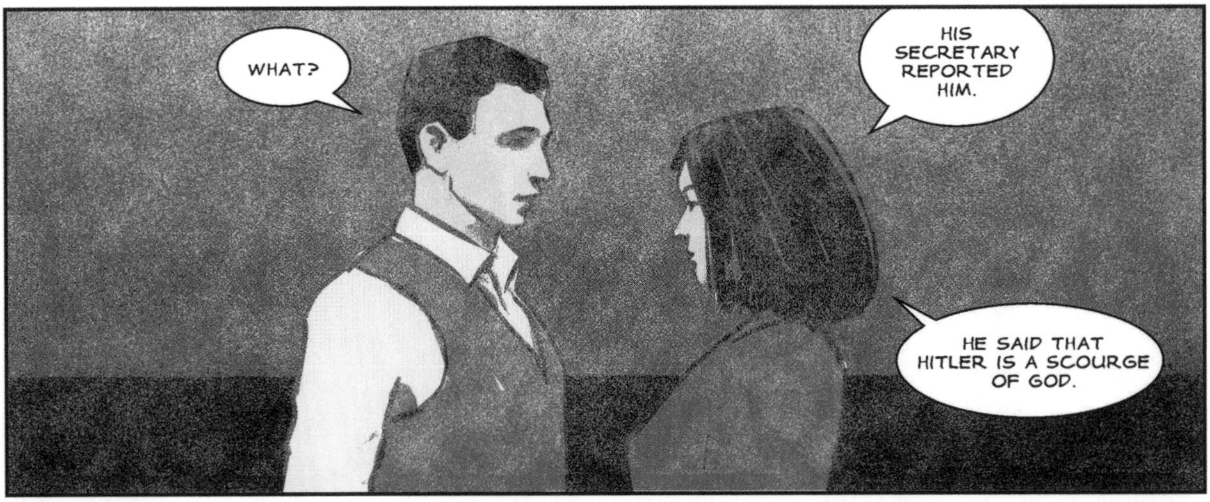
WHAT?
HIS SECRETARY REPORTED HIM.
HE SAID THAT HITLER IS A SCOURGE OF GOD.

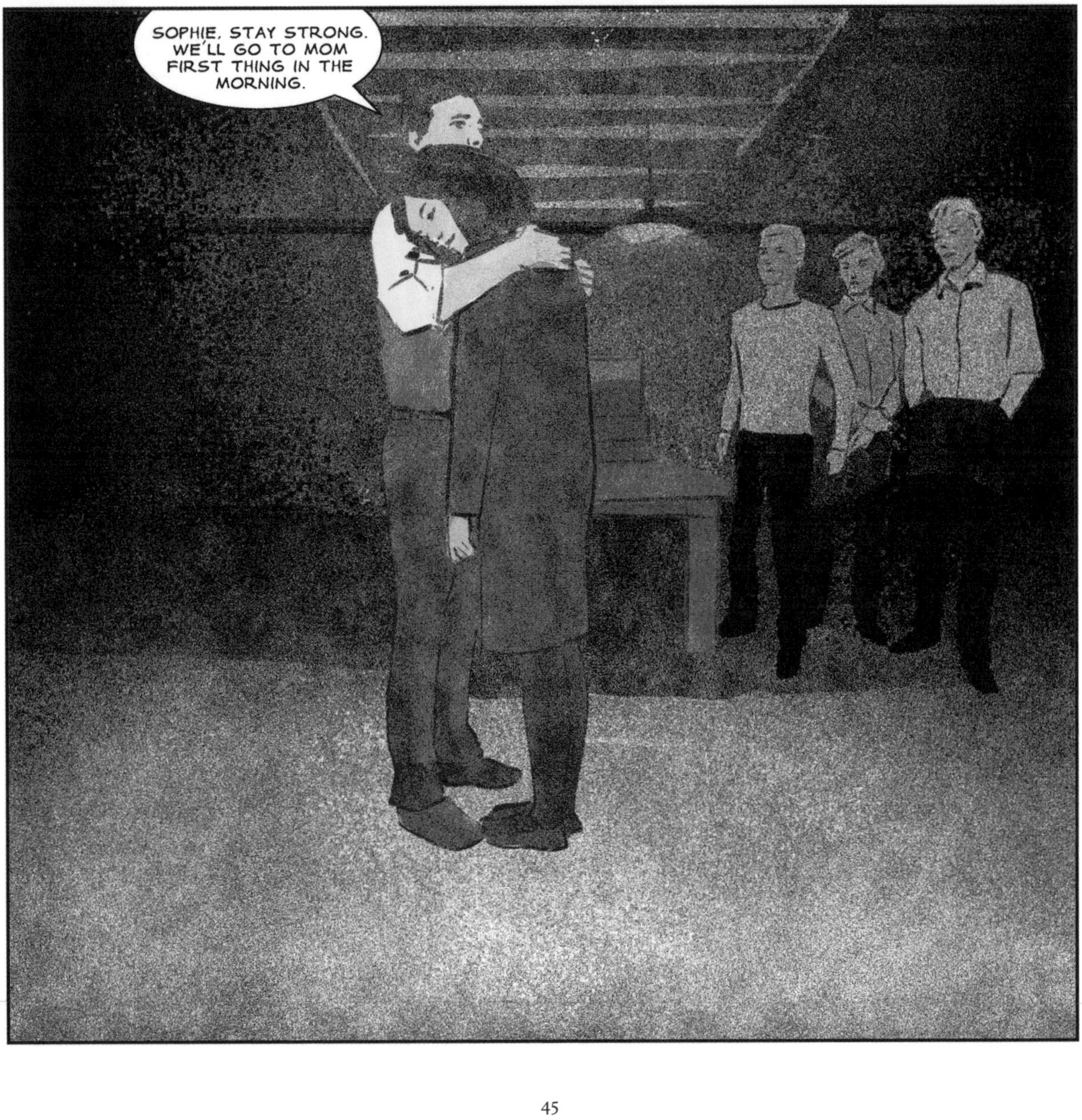
SOPHIE, STAY STRONG. WE'LL GO TO MOM FIRST THING IN THE MORNING.

SCHOLL FAMILY HOME, ULM, JULY 1942

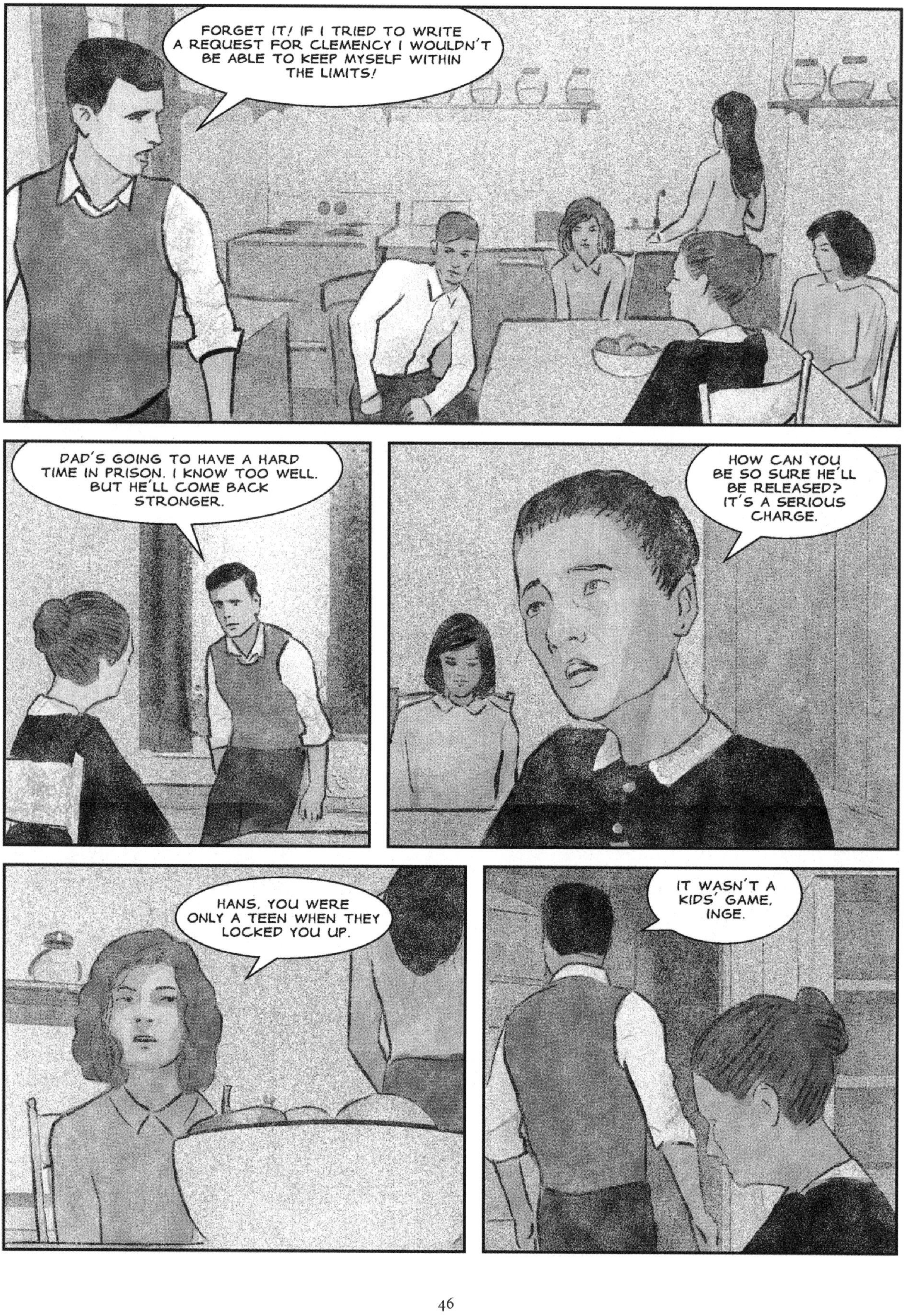
FORGET IT! IF I TRIED TO WRITE A REQUEST FOR CLEMENCY I WOULDN'T BE ABLE TO KEEP MYSELF WITHIN THE LIMITS!
DAD'S GOING TO HAVE A HARD TIME IN PRISON. I KNOW TOO WELL. BUT HE'LL COME BACK STRONGER.
HOW CAN YOU BE SO SURE HE'LL BE RELEASED? IT'S A SERIOUS CHARGE.
HANS, YOU WERE ONLY A TEEN WHEN THEY LOCKED YOU UP.
IT WASN'T A KIDS' GAME, INGE.

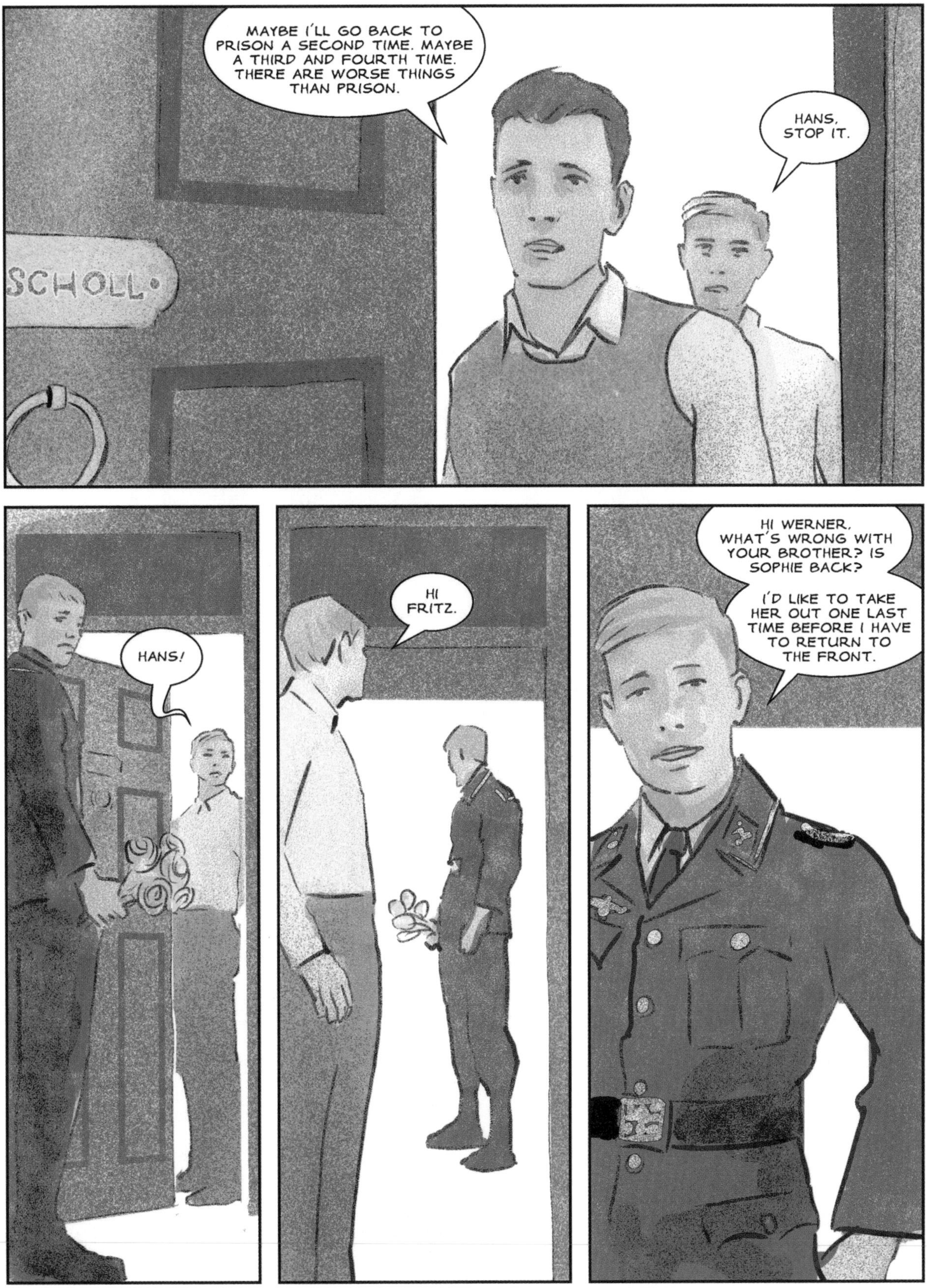
MAYBE I'LL GO BACK TO PRISON A SECOND TIME. MAYBE A THIRD AND FOURTH TIME. THERE ARE WORSE THINGS THAN PRISON.
HANS, STOP IT.
SCHOLL
HANS!
HI FRITZ.
HI WERNER, WHAT'S WRONG WITH YOUR BROTHER? IS SOPHIE BACK?
I'D LIKE TO TAKE HER OUT ONE LAST TIME BEFORE I HAVE TO RETURN TO THE FRONT.

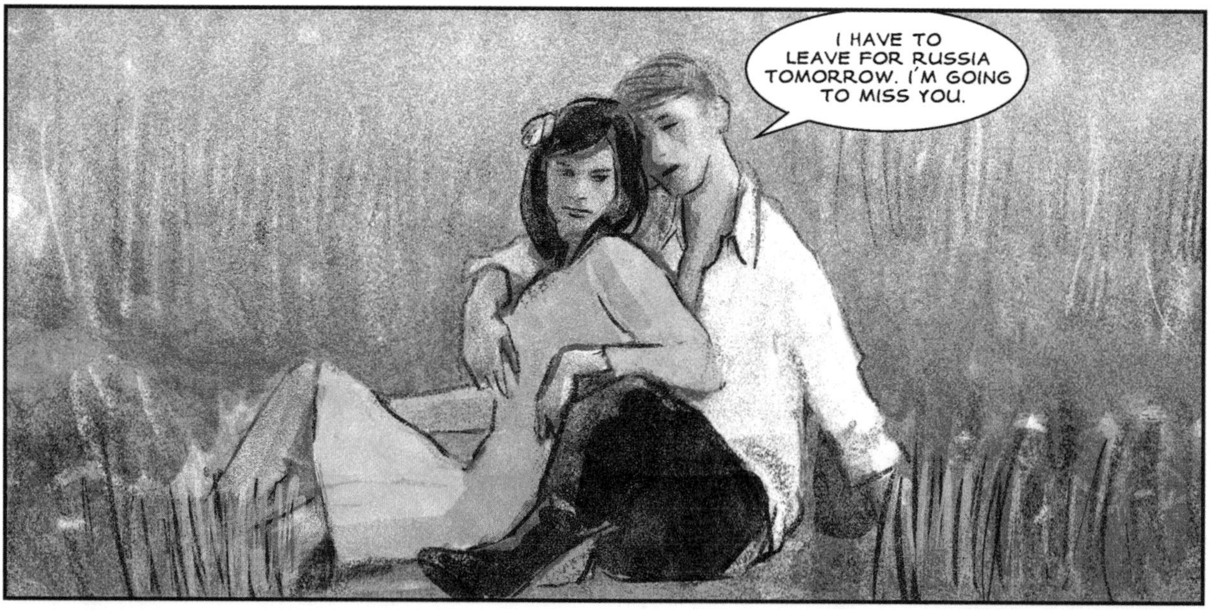
I HAVE TO LEAVE FOR RUSSIA TOMORROW. I'M GOING TO MISS YOU.

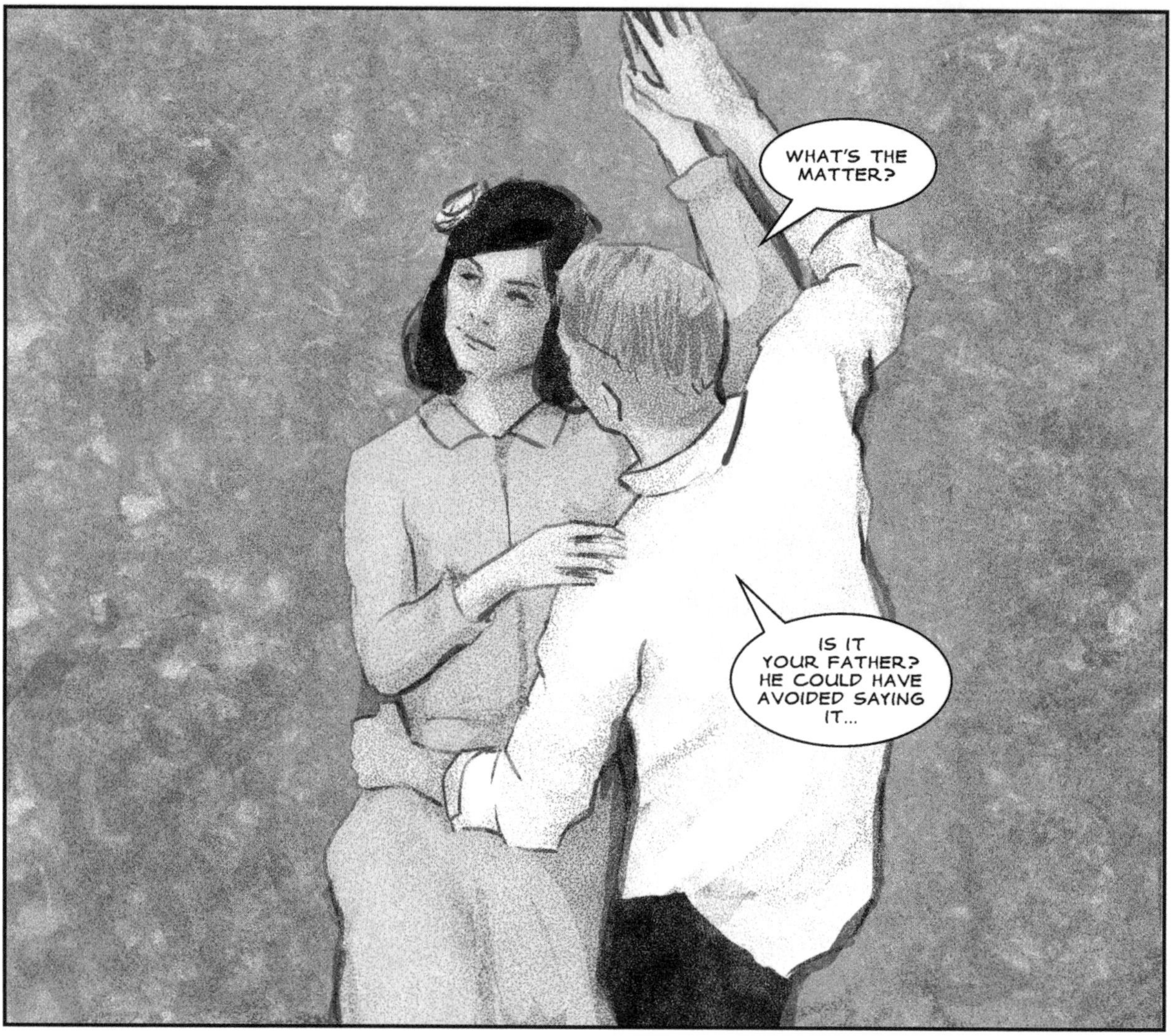
WHAT'S THE MATTER?
IS IT YOUR FATHER? HE COULD HAVE AVOIDED SAYING IT...

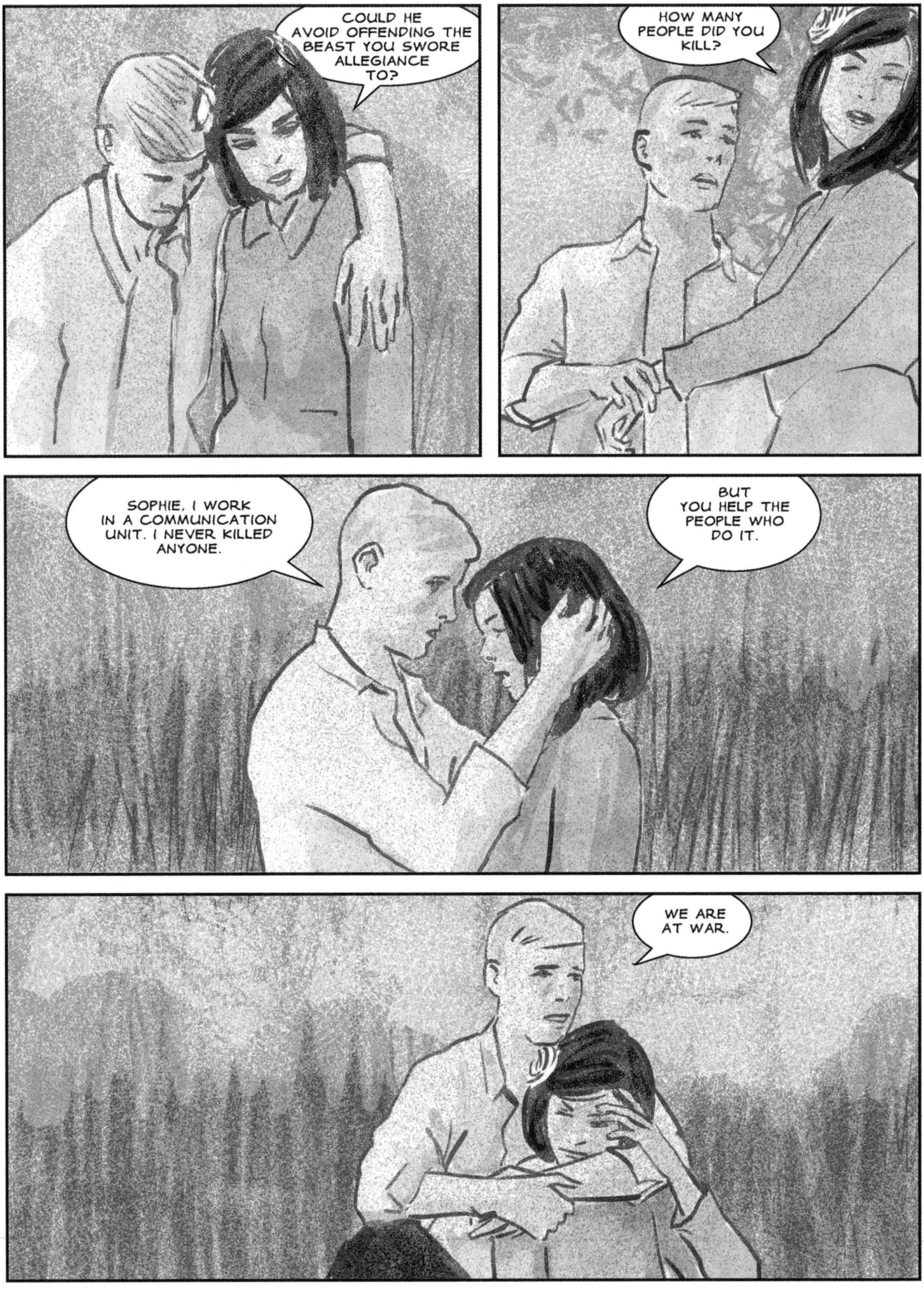
COULD HE AVOID OFFENDING THE BEAST YOU SWORE ALLEGIANCE TO?
HOW MANY PEOPLE DID YOU KILL?
SOPHIE, I WORK IN A COMMUNICATION UNIT. I NEVER KILLED ANYONE.
BUT YOU HELP THE PEOPLE WHO DO IT.
WE ARE AT WAR.

FAREWELL PARTY FOR HANS, WILLI, ALEX, AND OTHERS, JULY 22, 1942

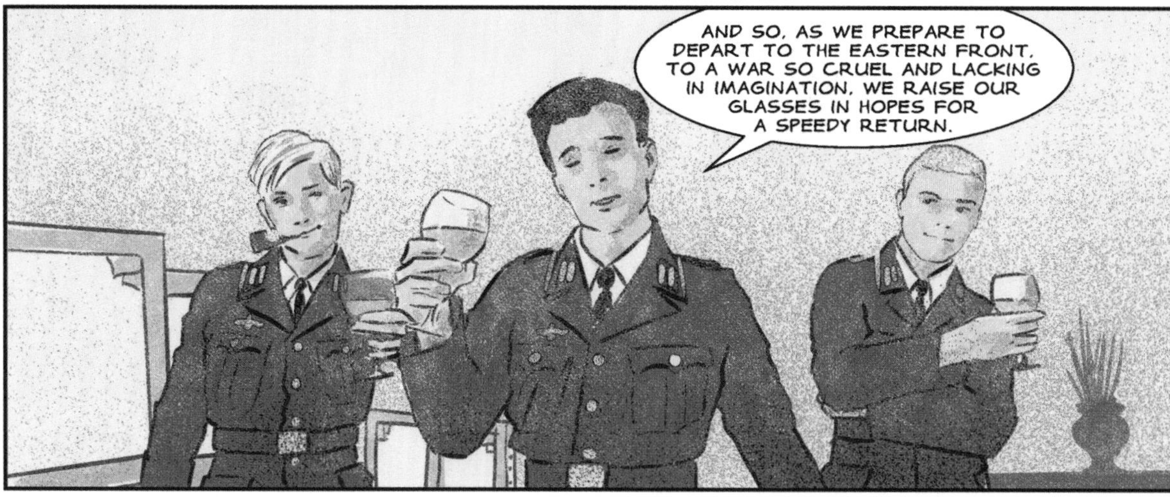
AND SO, AS WE PREPARE TO DEPART TO THE EASTERN FRONT, TO A WAR SO CRUEL AND LACKING IN IMAGINATION, WE RAISE OUR GLASSES IN HOPES FOR A SPEEDY RETURN.

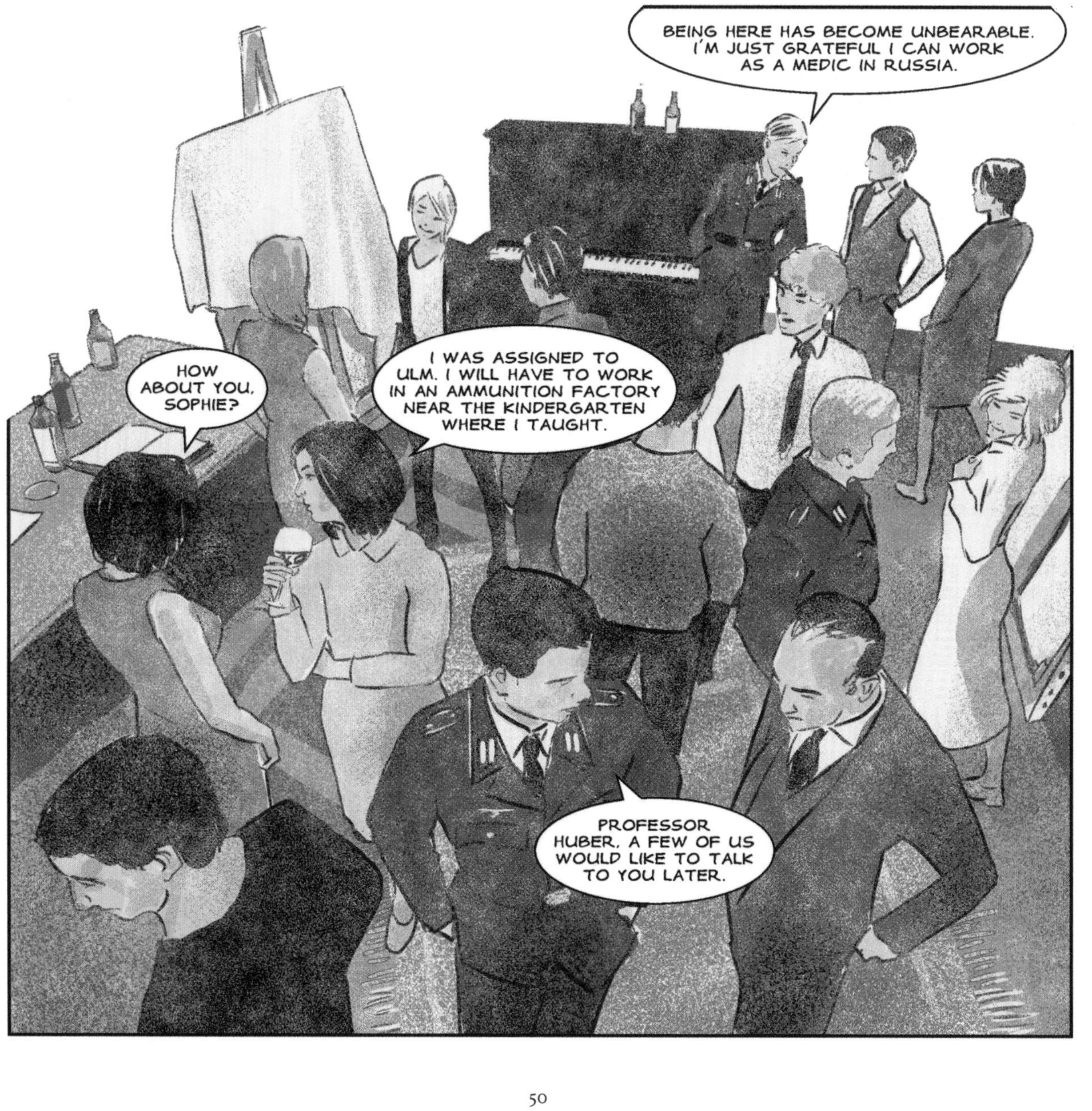
BEING HERE HAS BECOME UNBEARABLE. I'M JUST GRATEFUL I CAN WORK AS A MEDIC IN RUSSIA.
HOW ABOUT YOU, SOPHIE?
I WAS ASSIGNED TO ULM. I WILL HAVE TO WORK IN AN AMMUNITION FACTORY NEAR THE KINDERGARTEN WHERE I TAUGHT.
PROFESSOR HUBER, A FEW OF US WOULD LIKE TO TALK TO YOU LATER.

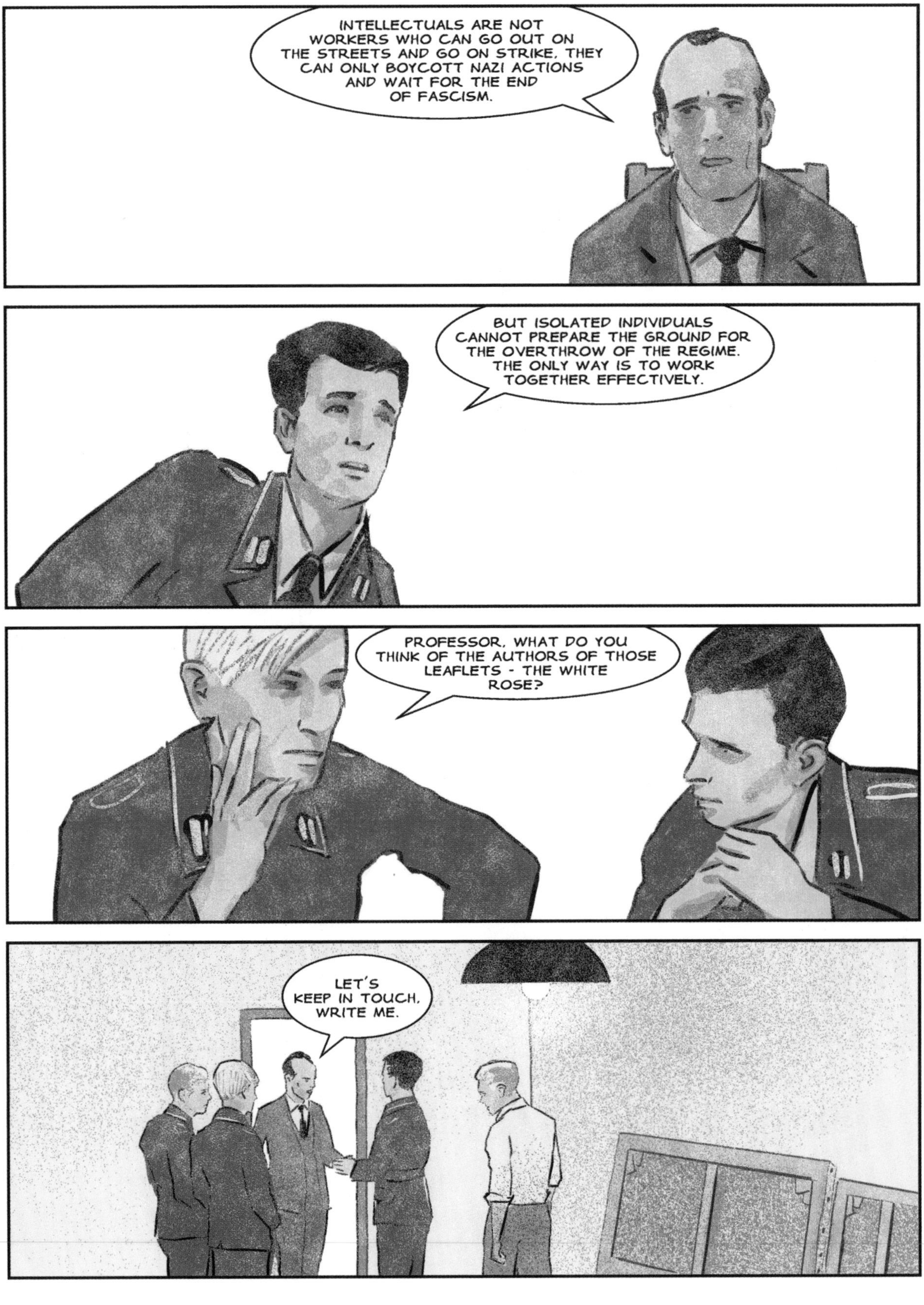
INTELLECTUALS ARE NOT WORKERS WHO CAN GO OUT ON THE STREETS AND GO ON STRIKE, THEY CAN ONLY BOYCOTT NAZI ACTIONS AND WAIT FOR THE END OF FASCISM.
BUT ISOLATED INDIVIDUALS CANNOT PREPARE THE GROUND FOR THE OVERTHROW OF THE REGIME. THE ONLY WAY IS TO WORK TOGETHER EFFECTIVELY.
PROFESSOR, WHAT DO YOU THINK OF THE AUTHORS OF THOSE LEAFLETS - THE WHITE ROSE?
LET'S KEEP IN TOUCH, WRITE ME.

MUNICH EAST TRAIN STATION, JULY 23, 1942

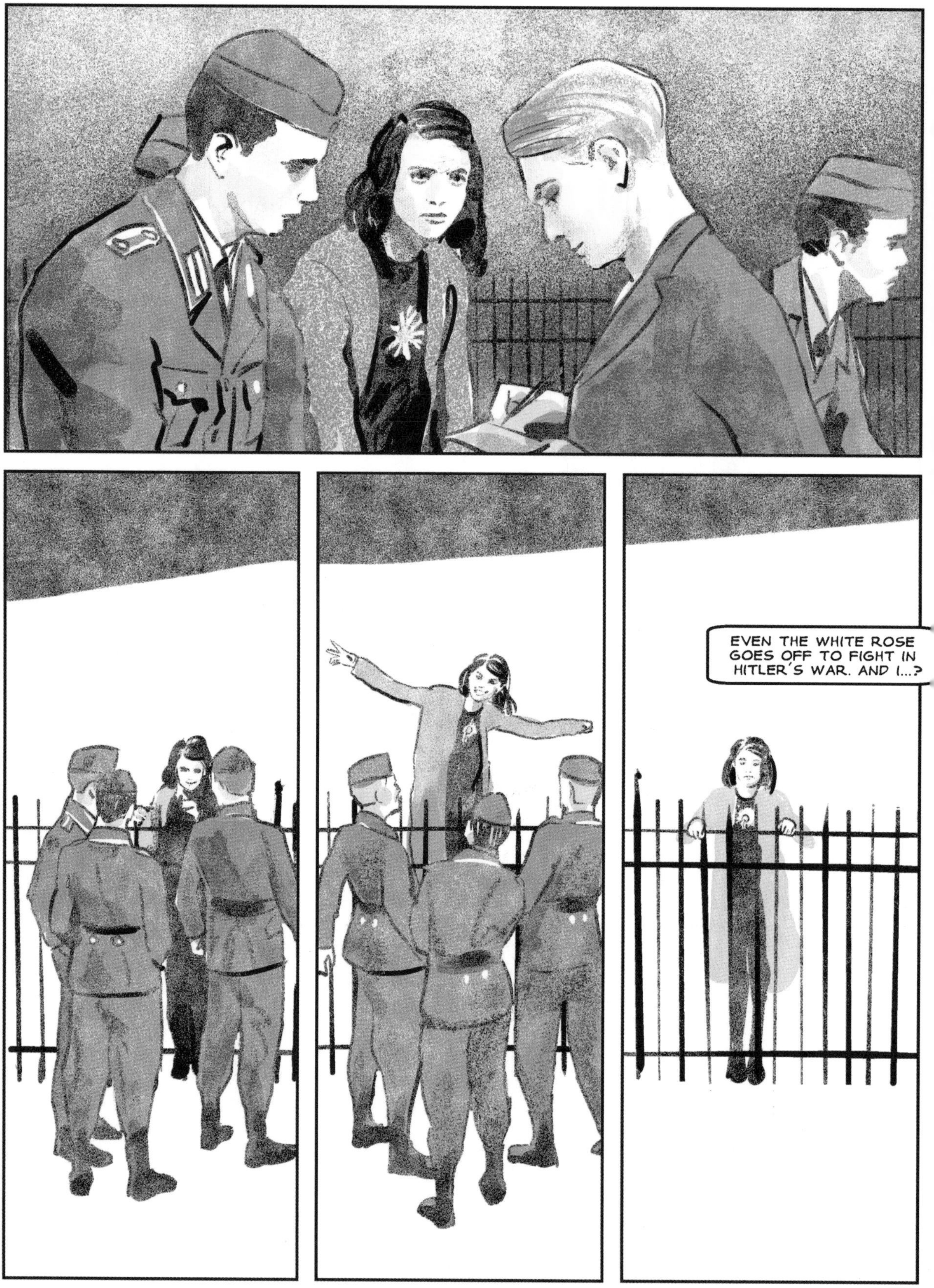
EVEN THE WHITE ROSE GOES OFF TO FIGHT IN HITLER'S WAR. AND I...?

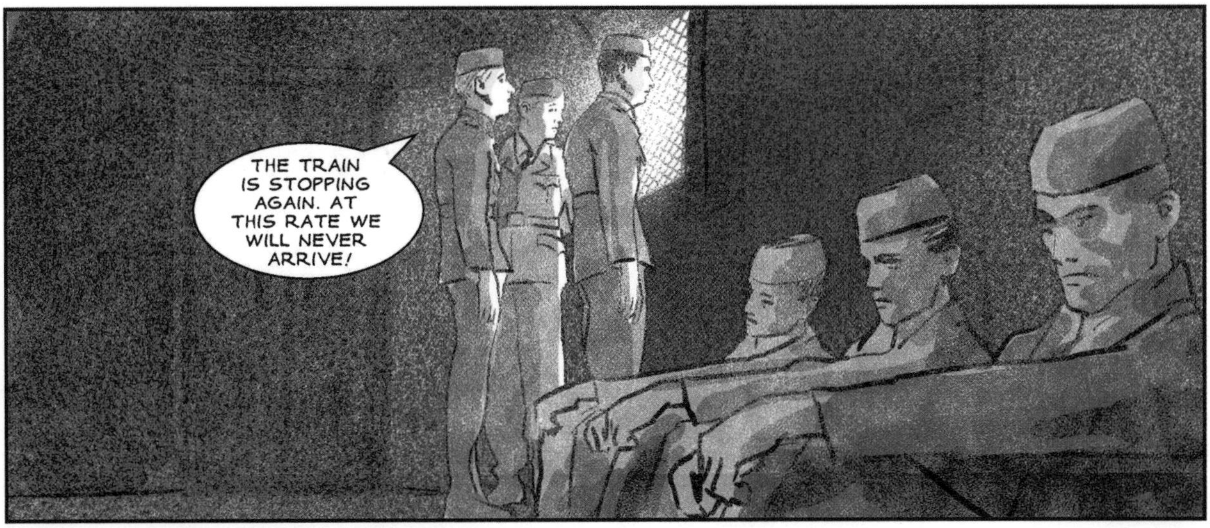
THE TRAIN IS STOPPING AGAIN. AT THIS RATE WE WILL NEVER ARRIVE!

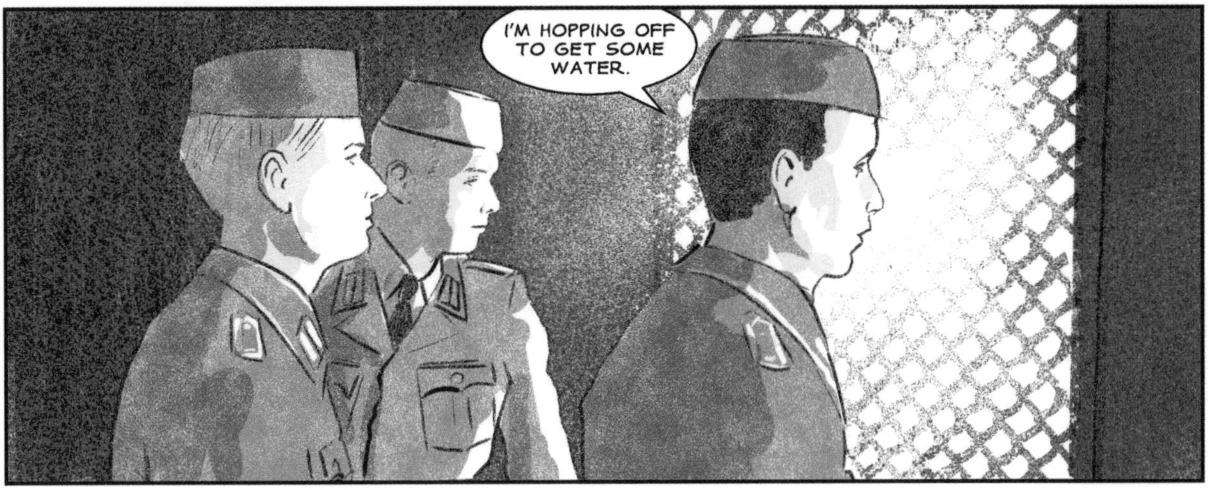
I'M HOPPING OFF TO GET SOME WATER.

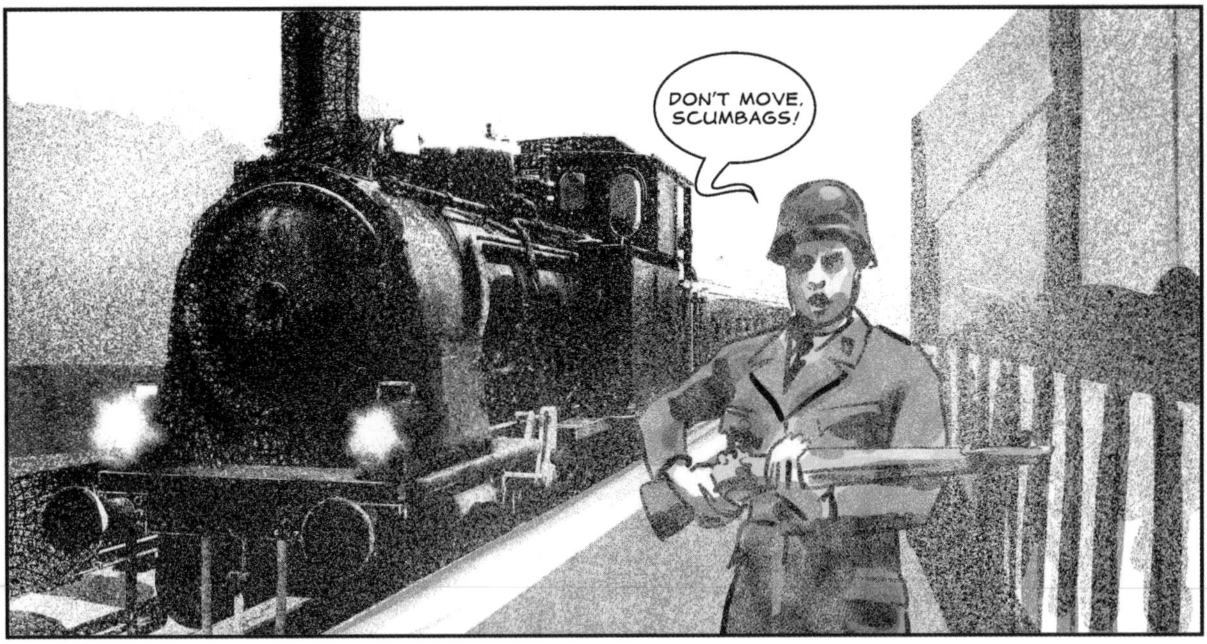
DON'T MOVE, SCUMBAGS!

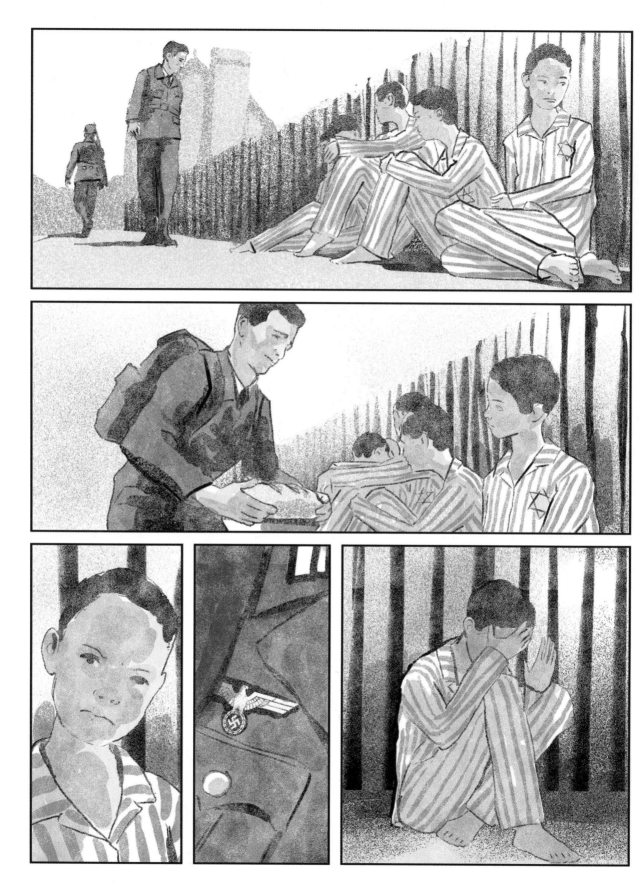

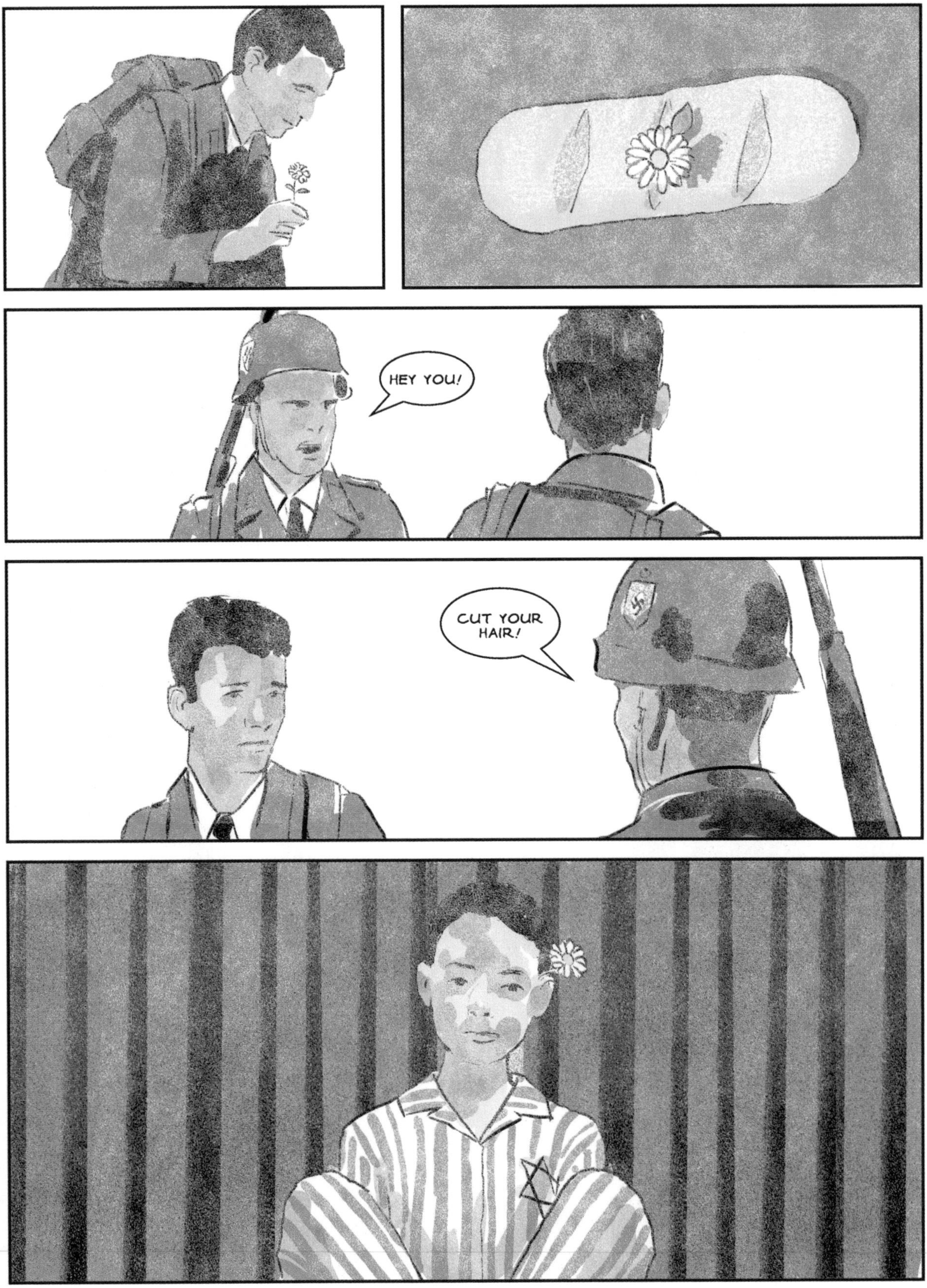
HEY YOU!
CUT YOUR HAIR!

MUNITIONS FACTORY, ULM, AUGUST 1942

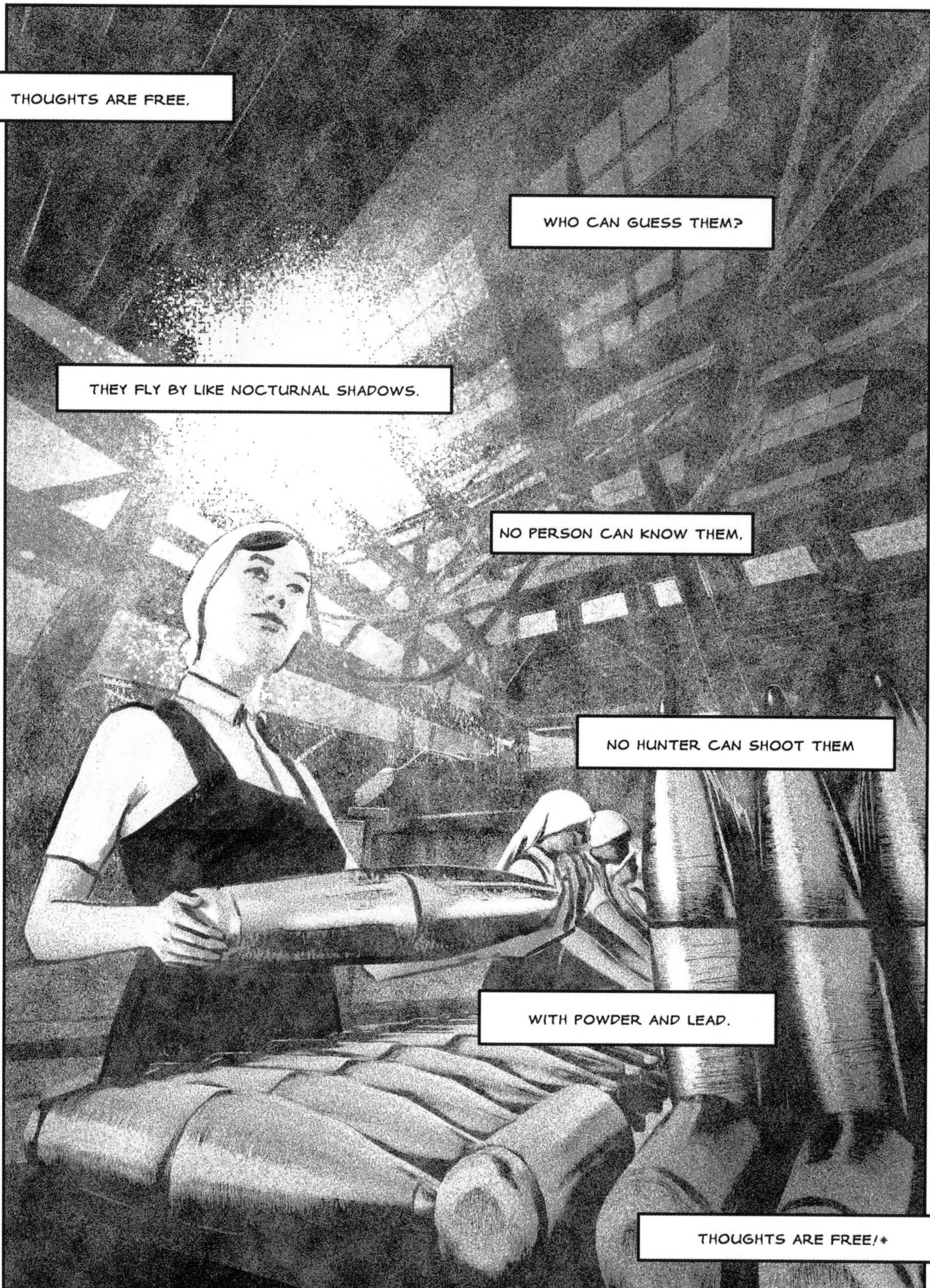

THOUGHTS ARE FREE.
WHO CAN GUESS THEM?
THEY FLY BY LIKE NOCTURNAL SHADOWS.
NO PERSON CAN KNOW THEM,
NO HUNTER CAN SHOOT THEM
WITH POWDER AND LEAD.
THOUGHTS ARE FREE!*

* "DIE GEDANKEN SIND FREI," TRADITIONAL REVOLUTIONARY SONG, FORBIDDEN DURING NAZISM.

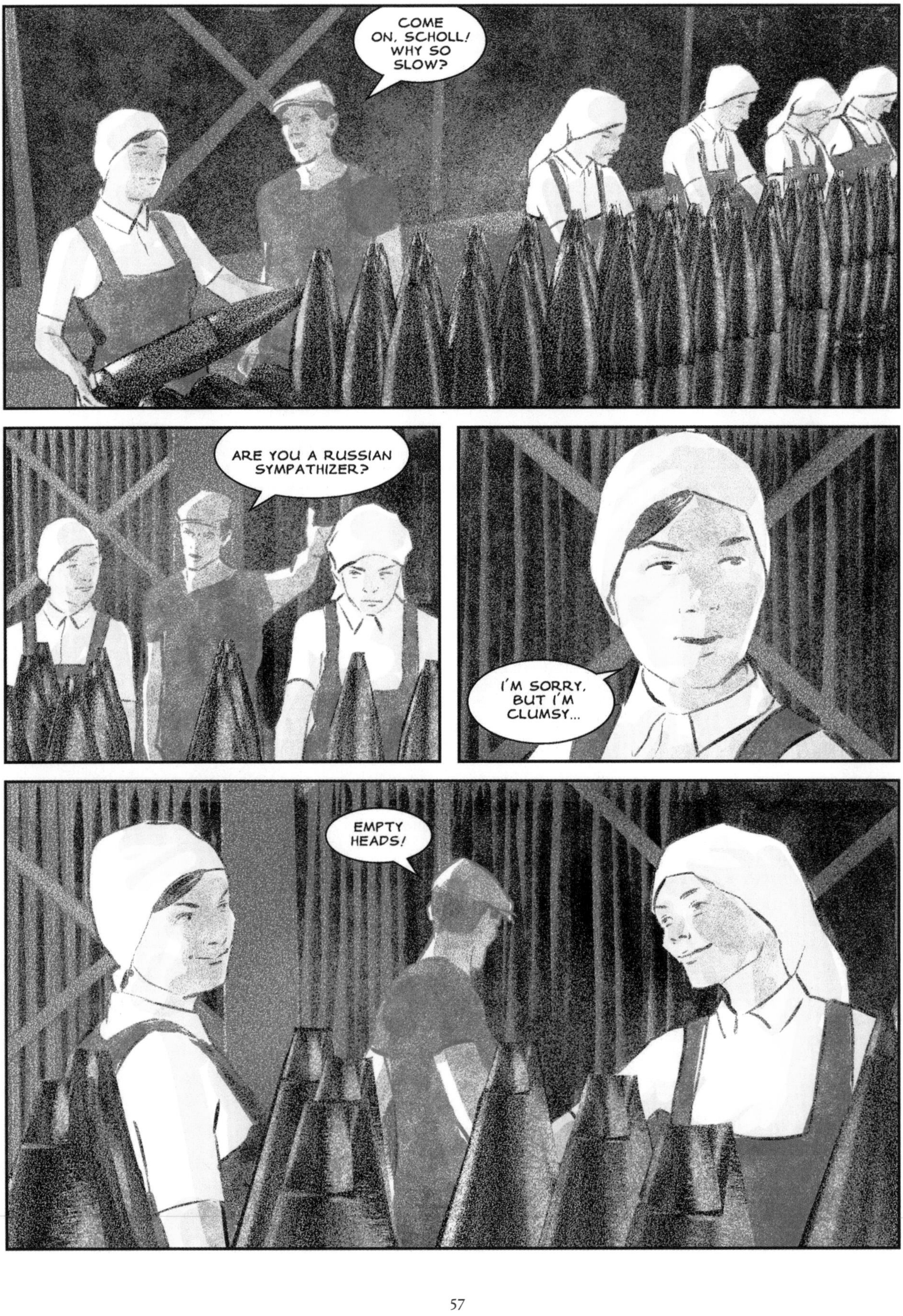
COME ON, SCHOLL! WHY SO SLOW?
ARE YOU A RUSSIAN SYMPATHIZER?
I'M SORRY, BUT I'M CLUMSY...
EMPTY HEADS!

DESTROYED VILLAGE NEAR RUSSIAN FRONT, NOVEMBER 1942

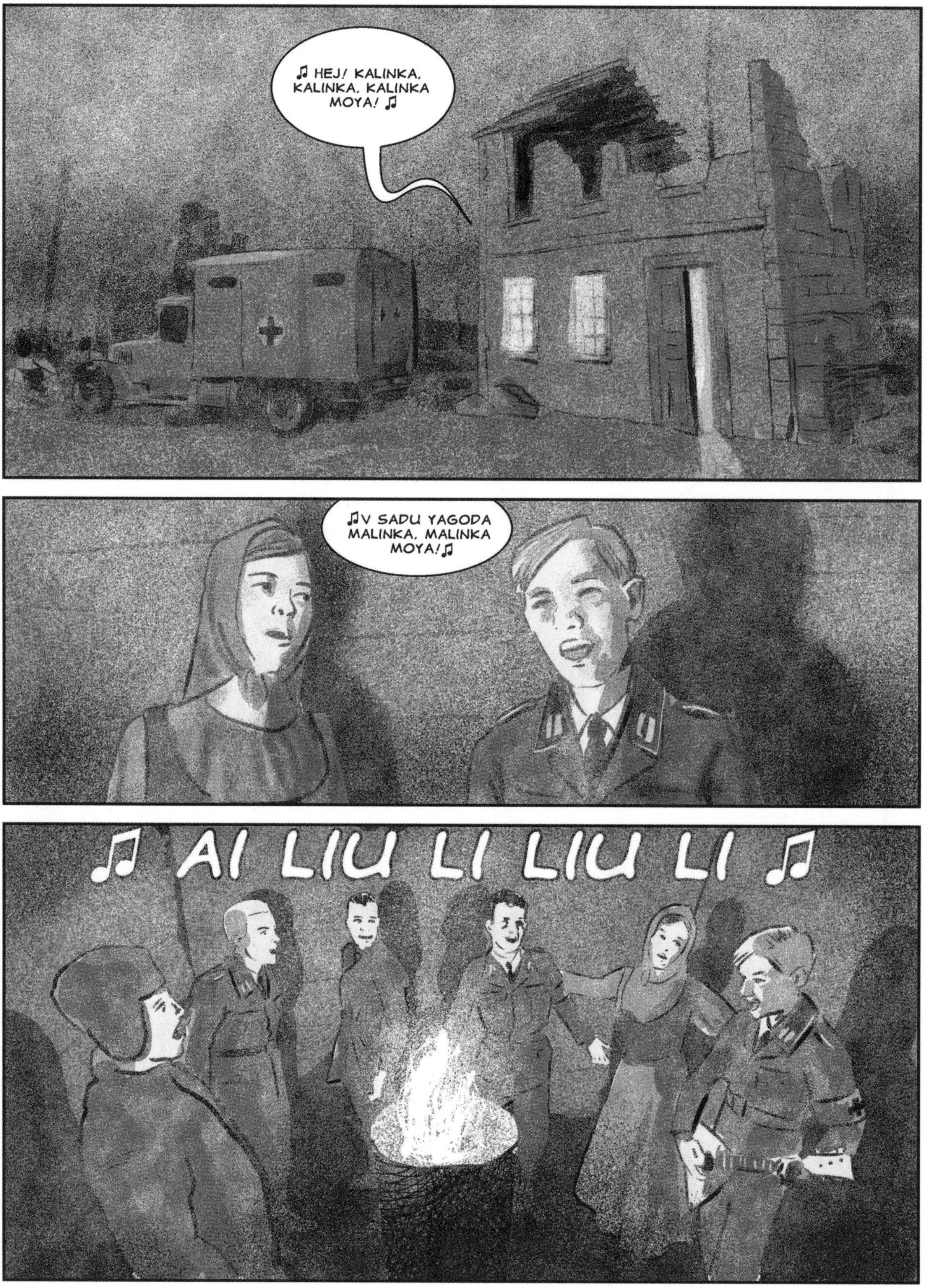
♫ HEJ! KALINKA, KALINKA, KALINKA MOYA! ♫
♫V SADU YAGODA MALINKA, MALINKA MOYA!♫
♫ AI LIU LI LIU LI ♫

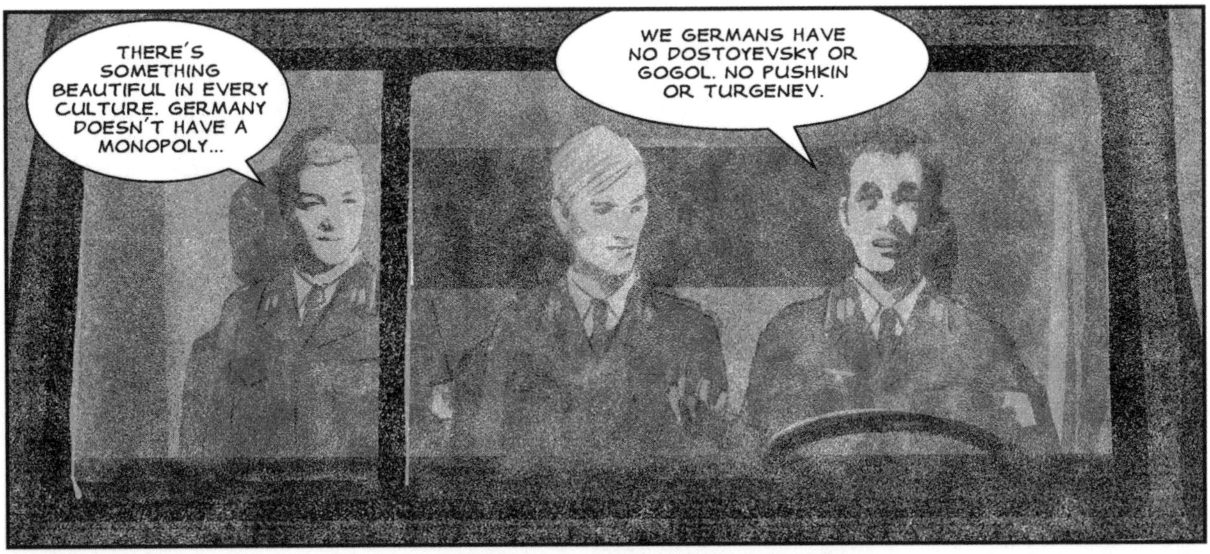
THERE'S SOMETHING BEAUTIFUL IN EVERY CULTURE. GERMANY DOESN'T HAVE A MONOPOLY...
WE GERMANS HAVE NO DOSTOYEVSKY OR GOGOL. NO PUSHKIN OR TURGENEV.

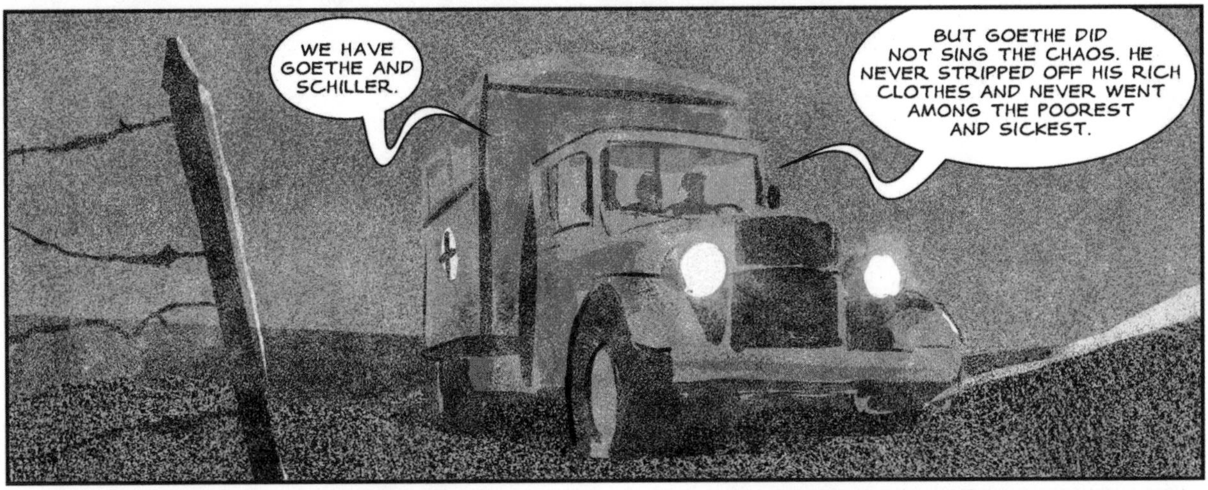
WE HAVE GOETHE AND SCHILLER.
BUT GOETHE DID NOT SING THE CHAOS. HE NEVER STRIPPED OFF HIS RICH CLOTHES AND NEVER WENT AMONG THE POOREST AND SICKEST.

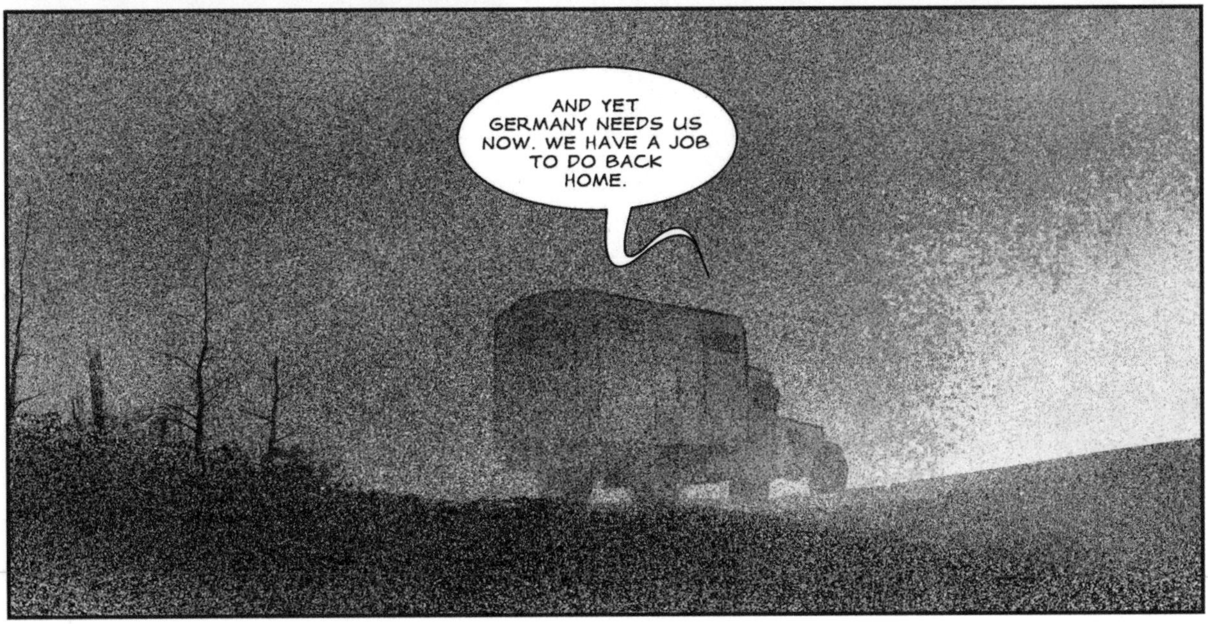
AND YET GERMANY NEEDS US NOW. WE HAVE A JOB TO DO BACK HOME.

HOME OF CHRISTOPH AND HERTA PROBST, RUHPOLDING, NOVEMBER 1942

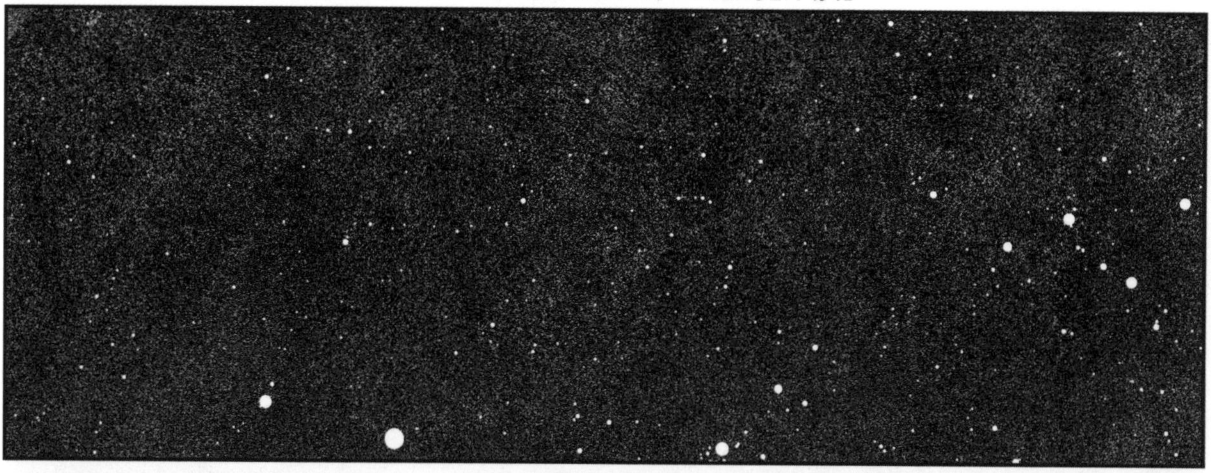

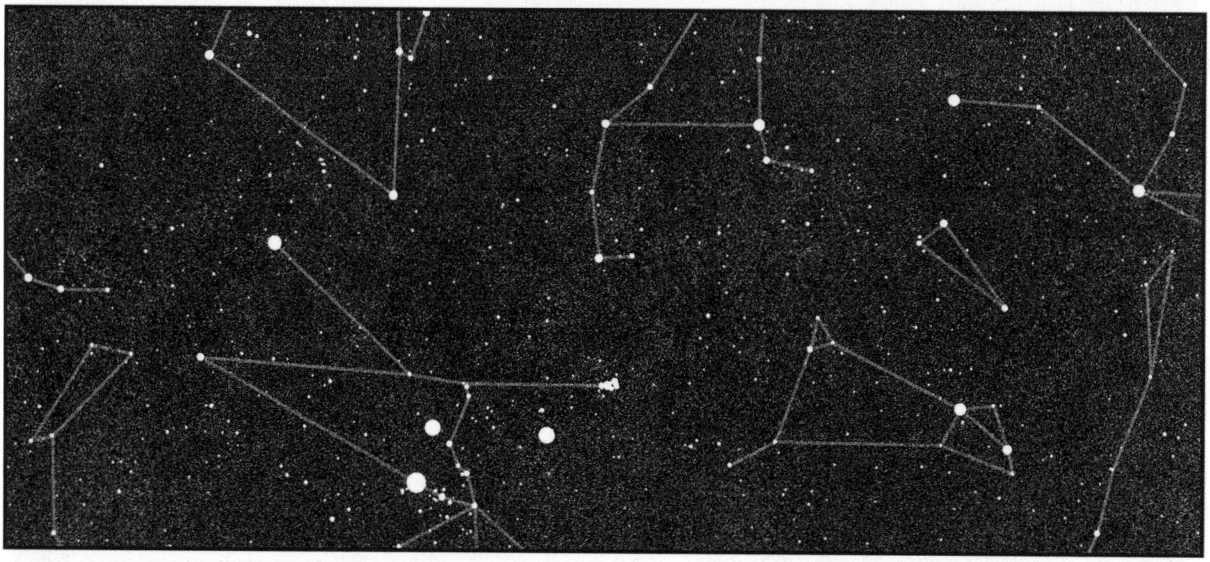

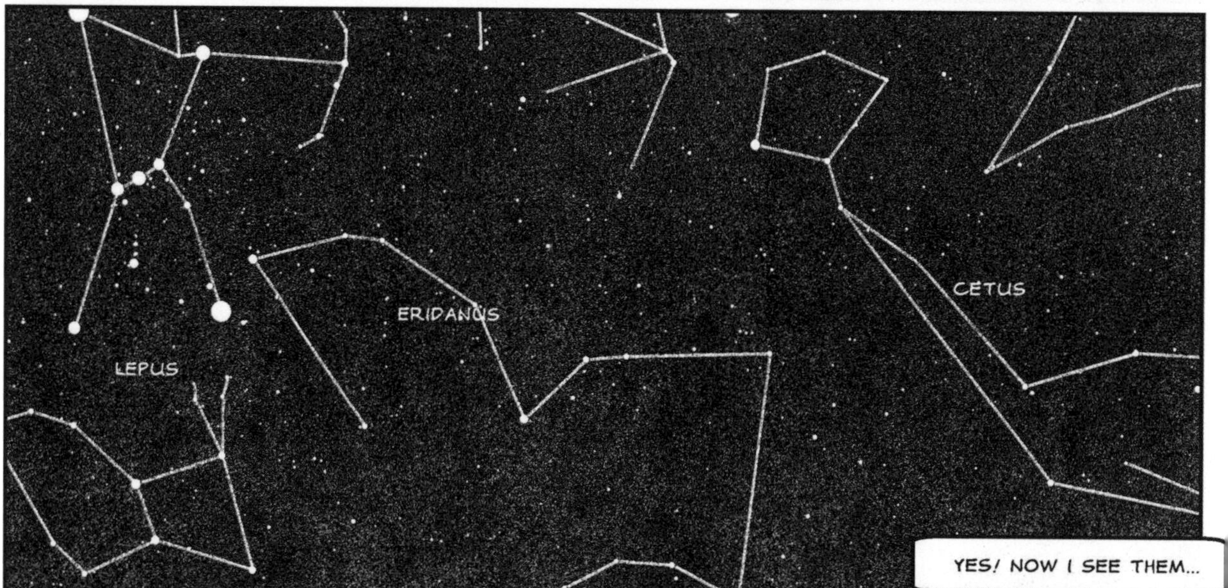
ERIDANUS
CETUS
LEPUS
YES! NOW I SEE THEM...

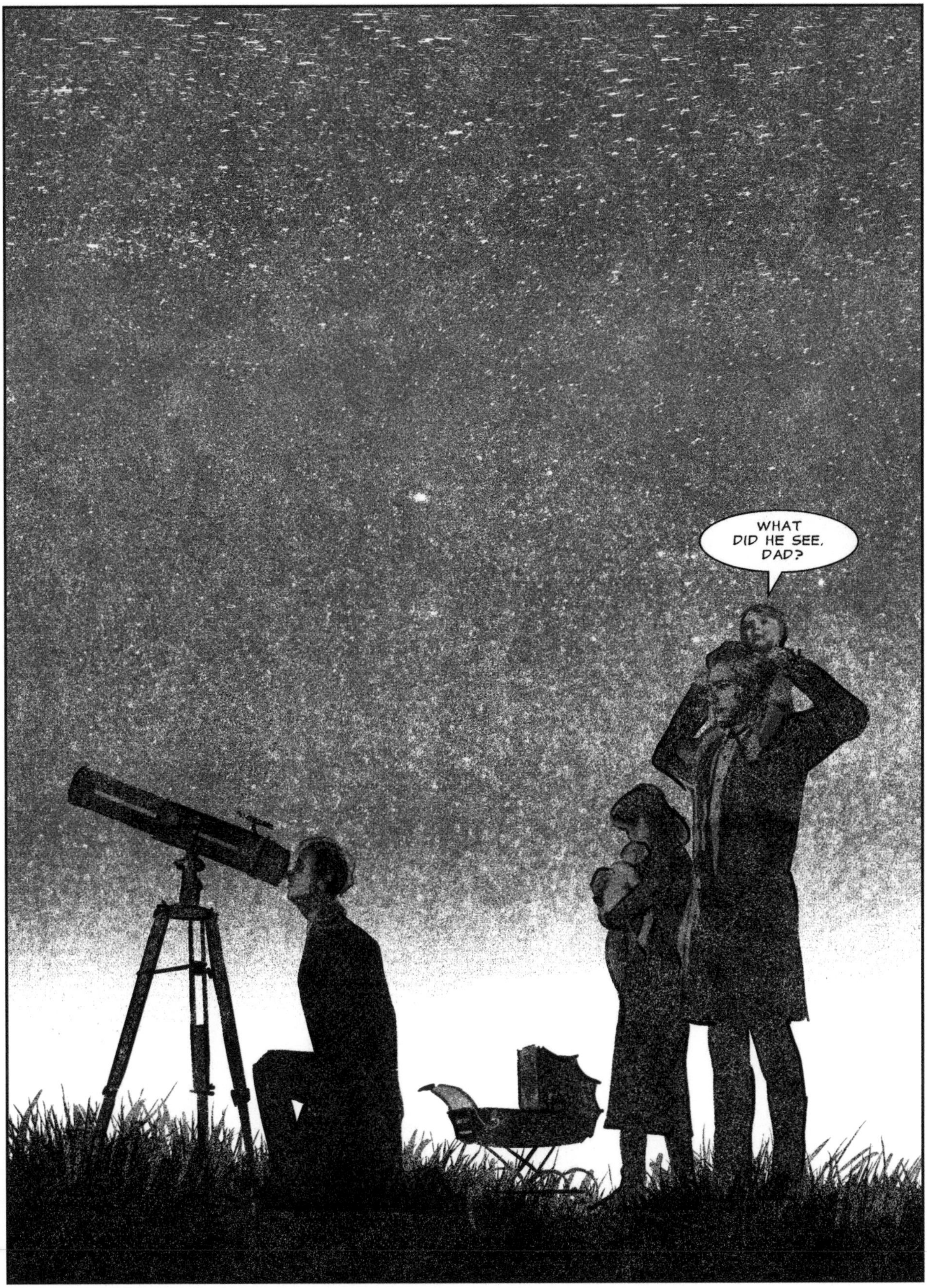
WHAT DID HE SEE, DAD?

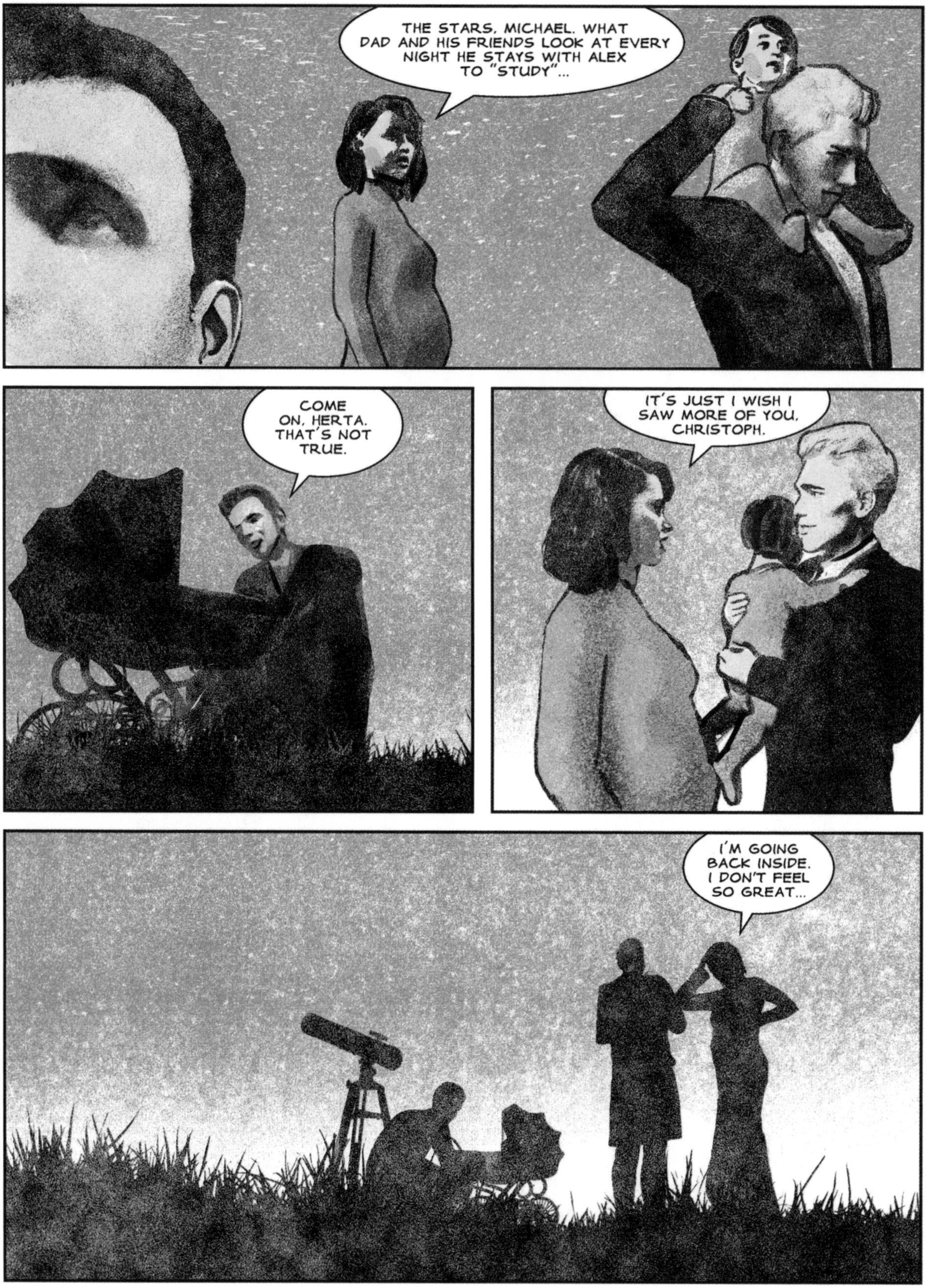
THE STARS, MICHAEL. WHAT DAD AND HIS FRIENDS LOOK AT EVERY NIGHT HE STAYS WITH ALEX TO "STUDY"...
COME ON, HERTA. THAT'S NOT TRUE.
IT'S JUST I WISH I SAW MORE OF YOU, CHRISTOPH.
I'M GOING BACK INSIDE. I DON'T FEEL SO GREAT...

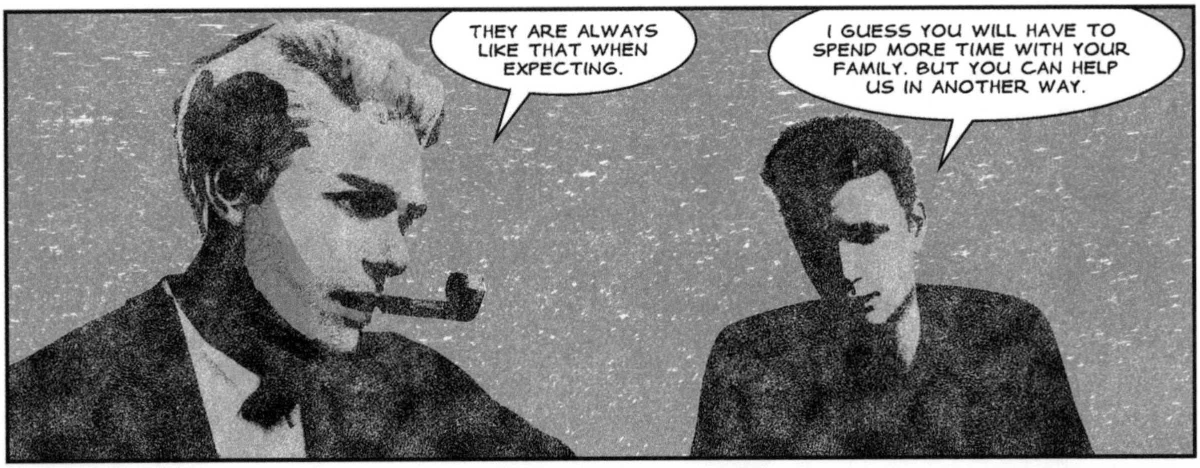
THEY ARE ALWAYS LIKE THAT WHEN EXPECTING.
I GUESS YOU WILL HAVE TO SPEND MORE TIME WITH YOUR FAMILY. BUT YOU CAN HELP US IN ANOTHER WAY.

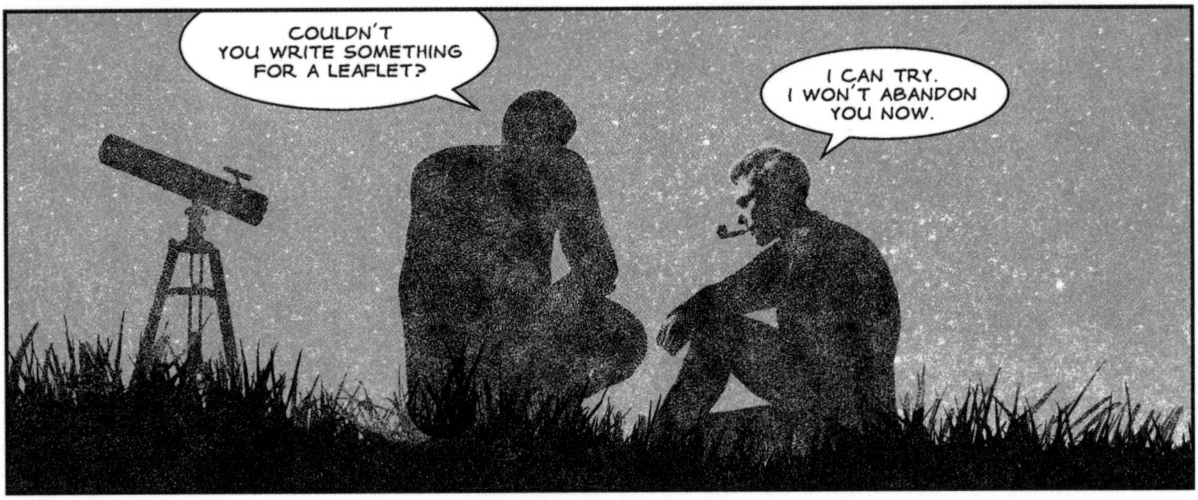
COULDN'T YOU WRITE SOMETHING FOR A LEAFLET?
I CAN TRY. I WON'T ABANDON YOU NOW.

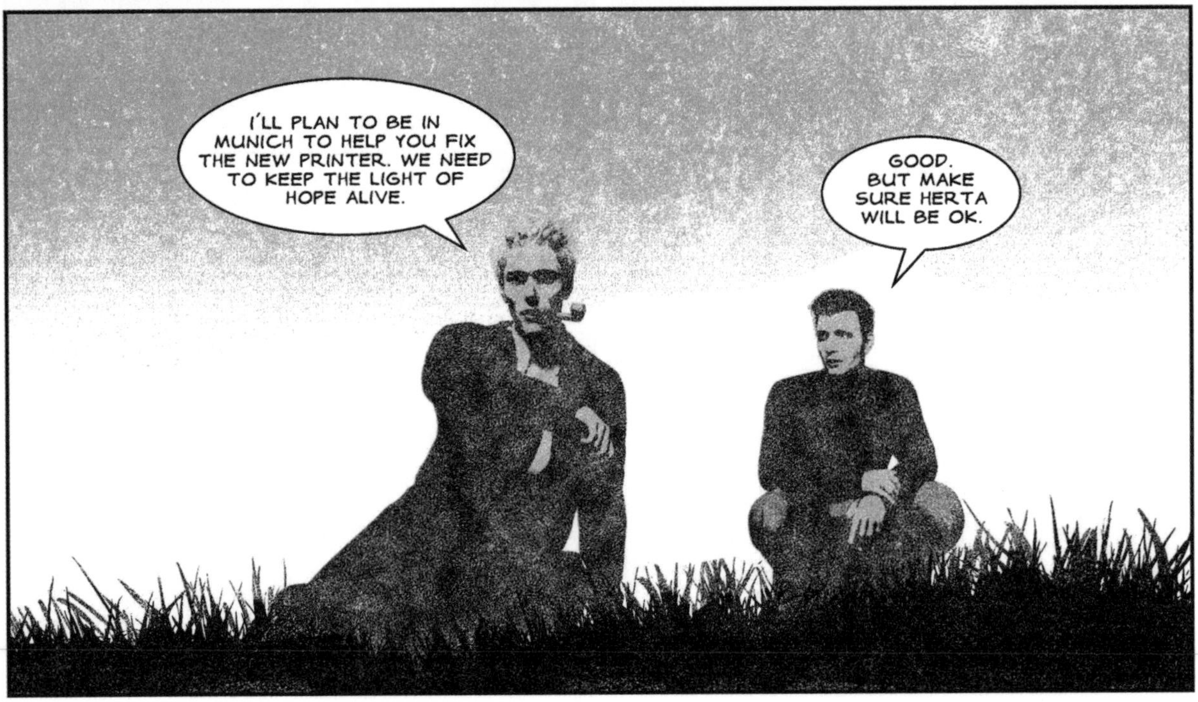
I'LL PLAN TO BE IN MUNICH TO HELP YOU FIX THE NEW PRINTER. WE NEED TO KEEP THE LIGHT OF HOPE ALIVE.
GOOD. BUT MAKE SURE HERTA WILL BE OK.

AUDITORIUM OF THE DEUTSCHE MUSEUM, MUNICH, JANUARY 13, 1943

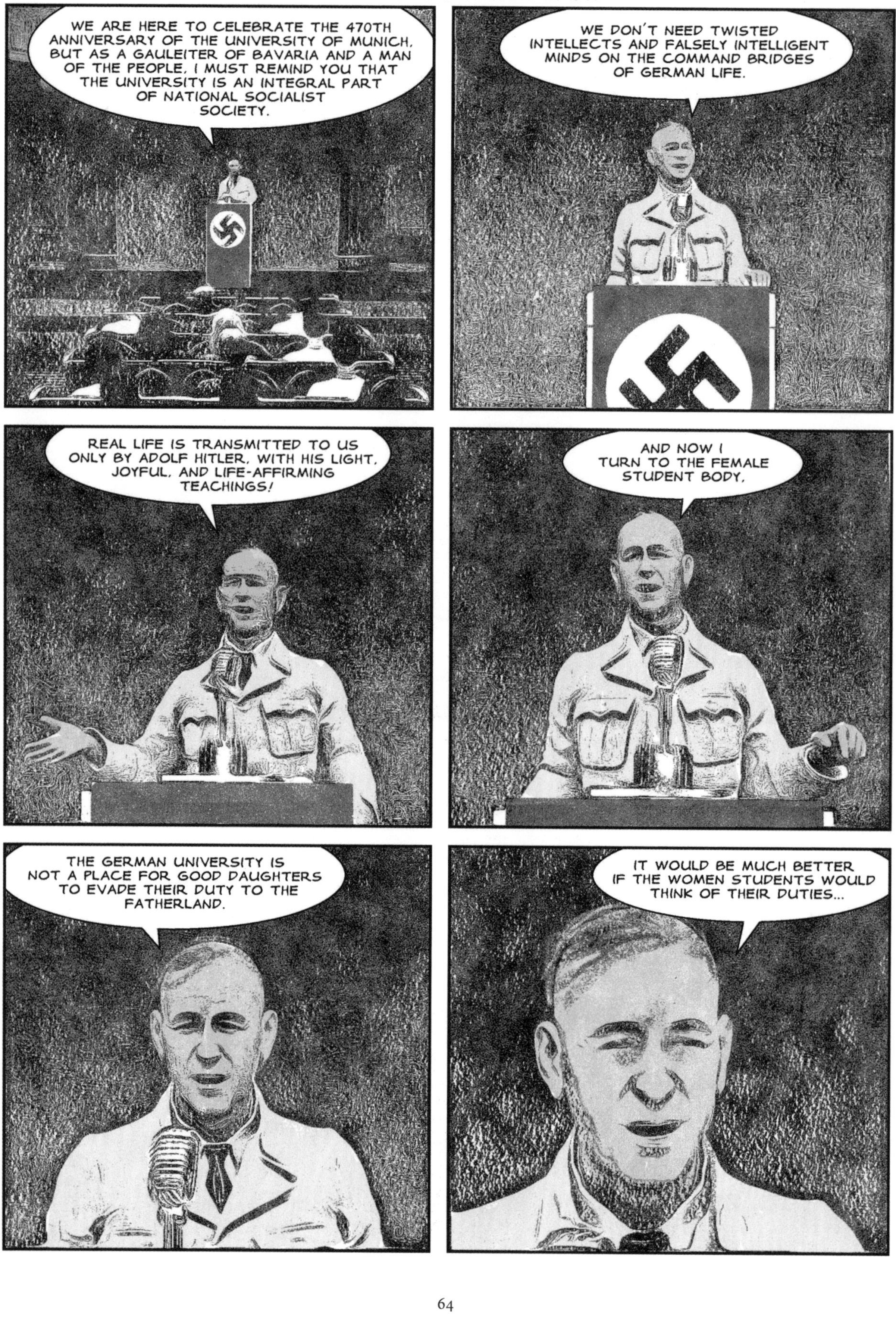
WE ARE HERE TO CELEBRATE THE 470TH ANNIVERSARY OF THE UNIVERSITY OF MUNICH, BUT AS A GAULEITER OF BAVARIA AND A MAN OF THE PEOPLE, I MUST REMIND YOU THAT THE UNIVERSITY IS AN INTEGRAL PART OF NATIONAL SOCIALIST SOCIETY.
WE DON'T NEED TWISTED INTELLECTS AND FALSELY INTELLIGENT MINDS ON THE COMMAND BRIDGES OF GERMAN LIFE.
REAL LIFE IS TRANSMITTED TO US ONLY BY ADOLF HITLER, WITH HIS LIGHT, JOYFUL, AND LIFE-AFFIRMING TEACHINGS!
AND NOW I TURN TO THE FEMALE STUDENT BODY,
THE GERMAN UNIVERSITY IS NOT A PLACE FOR GOOD DAUGHTERS TO EVADE THEIR DUTY TO THE FATHERLAND.
IT WOULD BE MUCH BETTER IF THE WOMEN STUDENTS WOULD THINK OF THEIR DUTIES...

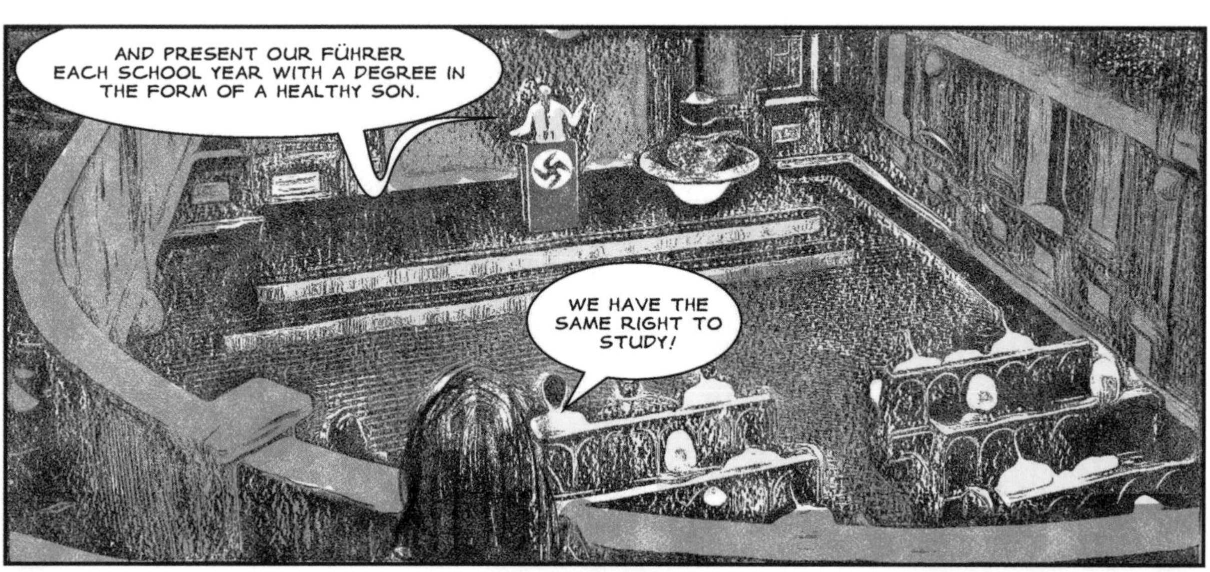
AND PRESENT OUR FÜHRER EACH SCHOOL YEAR WITH A DEGREE IN THE FORM OF A HEALTHY SON.
WE HAVE THE SAME RIGHT TO STUDY!

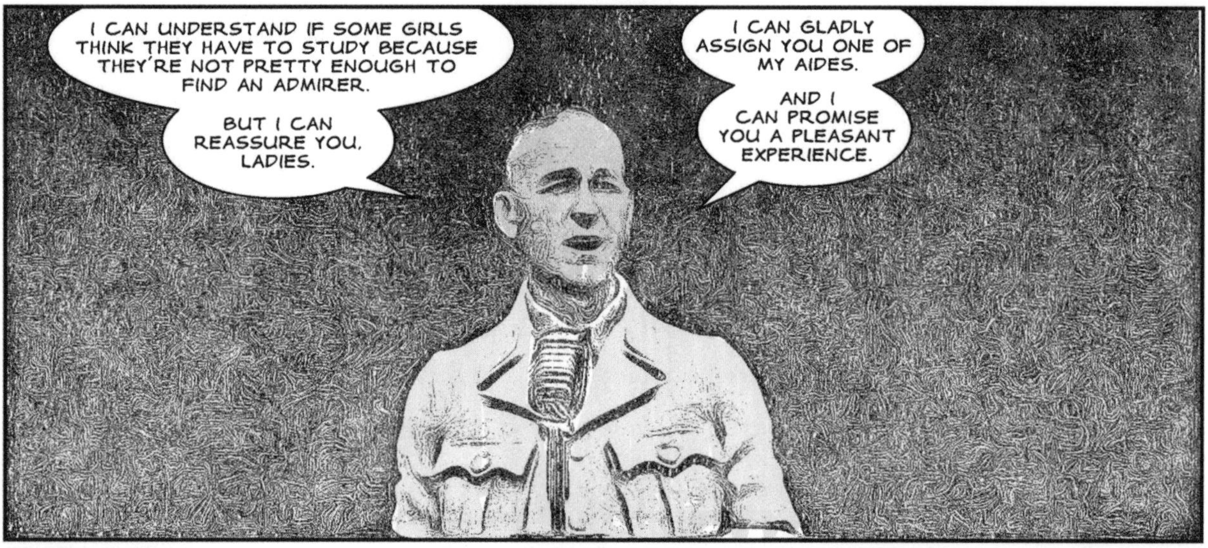
I CAN UNDERSTAND IF SOME GIRLS THINK THEY HAVE TO STUDY BECAUSE THEY'RE NOT PRETTY ENOUGH TO FIND AN ADMIRER.
BUT I CAN REASSURE YOU, LADIES.
I CAN GLADLY ASSIGN YOU ONE OF MY AIDES.
AND I CAN PROMISE YOU A PLEASANT EXPERIENCE.

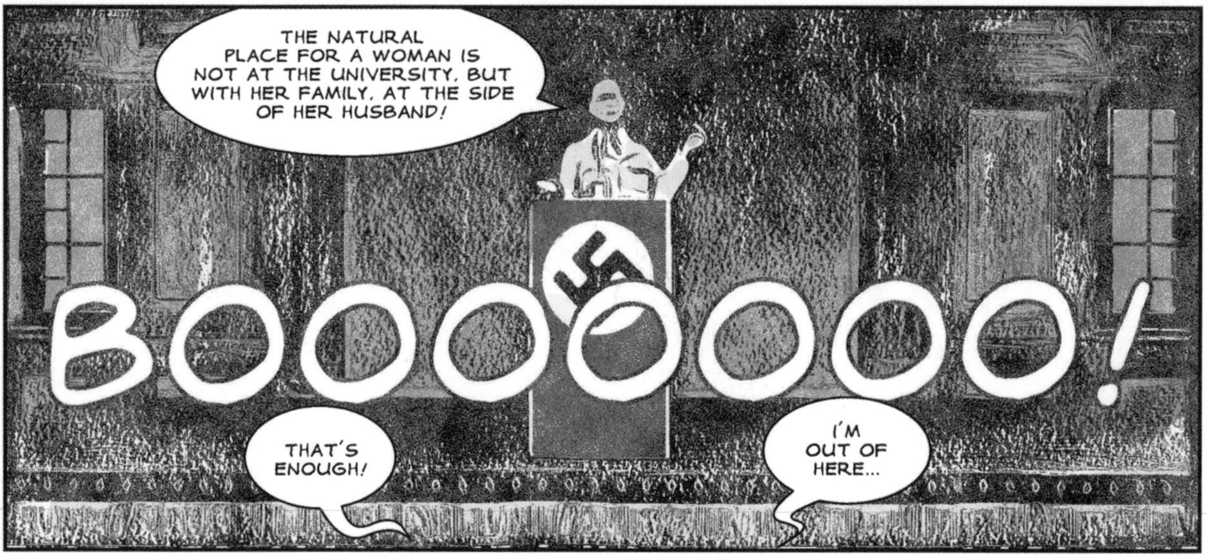
THE NATURAL PLACE FOR A WOMAN IS NOT AT THE UNIVERSITY, BUT WITH HER FAMILY, AT THE SIDE OF HER HUSBAND!
BOOOOOOO!
THAT'S ENOUGH!
I'M OUT OF HERE...

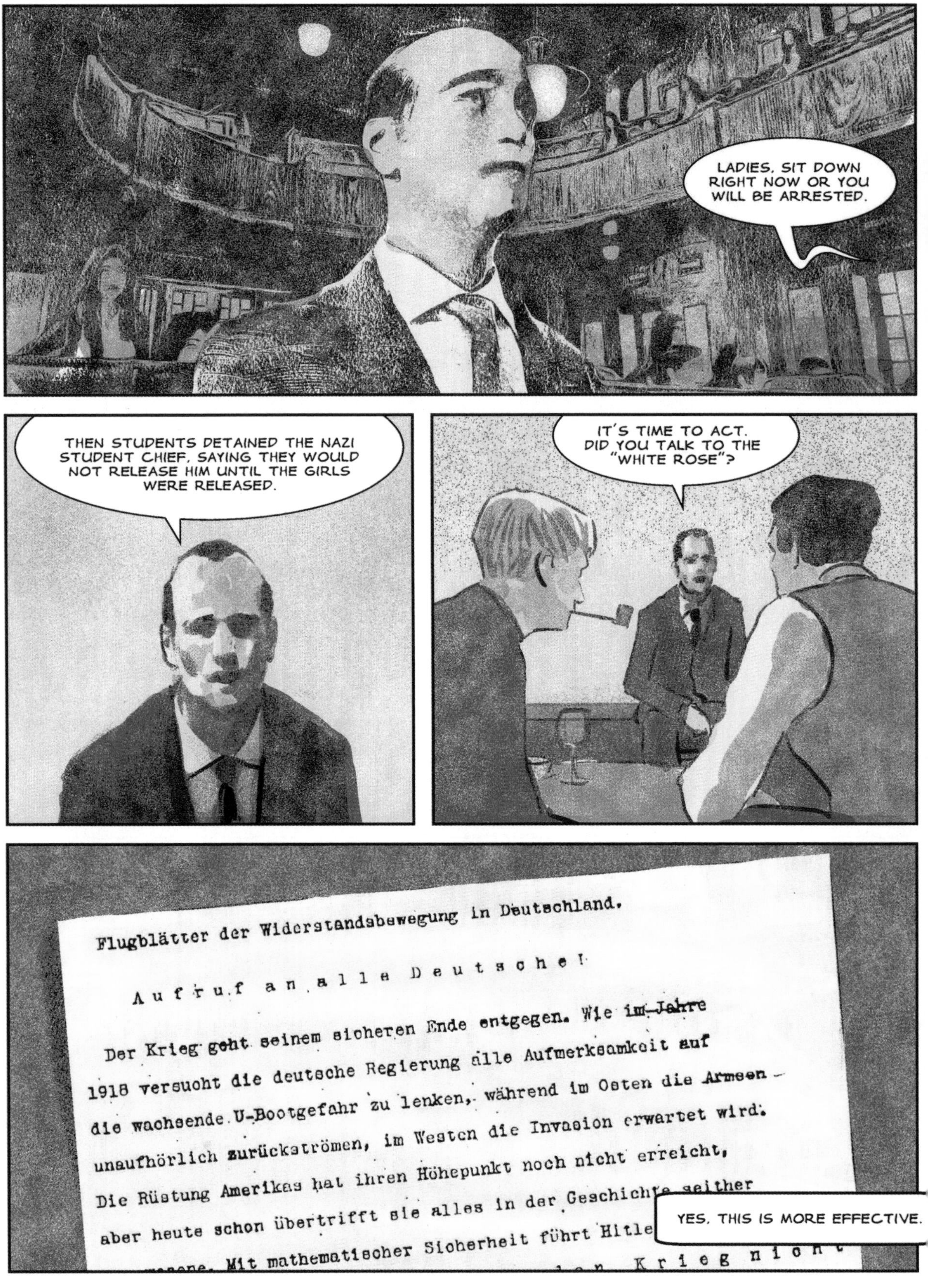
LADIES, SIT DOWN RIGHT NOW OR YOU WILL BE ARRESTED.
THEN STUDENTS DETAINED THE NAZI STUDENT CHIEF, SAYING THEY WOULD NOT RELEASE HIM UNTIL THE GIRLS WERE RELEASED.
IT'S TIME TO ACT. DID YOU TALK TO THE "WHITE ROSE"?
Flugblätter der Widerstandsbewegung in Deutschland.
Aufruf an alle Deutsche!
Der Krieg geht seinem sicheren Ende entgegen. Wie im Jahre
1918 versucht die deutsche Regierung alle Aufmerksamkeit auf
die wachsende U-Bootgefahr zu lenken, während im Osten die Armeen
unaufhörlich zurückströmen, im Westen die Invasion erwartet wird.
Die Rüstung Amerikas hat ihren Höhepunkt noch nicht erreicht,
aber heute schon übertrifft sie alles in der Geschicht
Mit mathematischer Sicherheit führt Hitle
YES, THIS IS MORE EFFECTIVE.

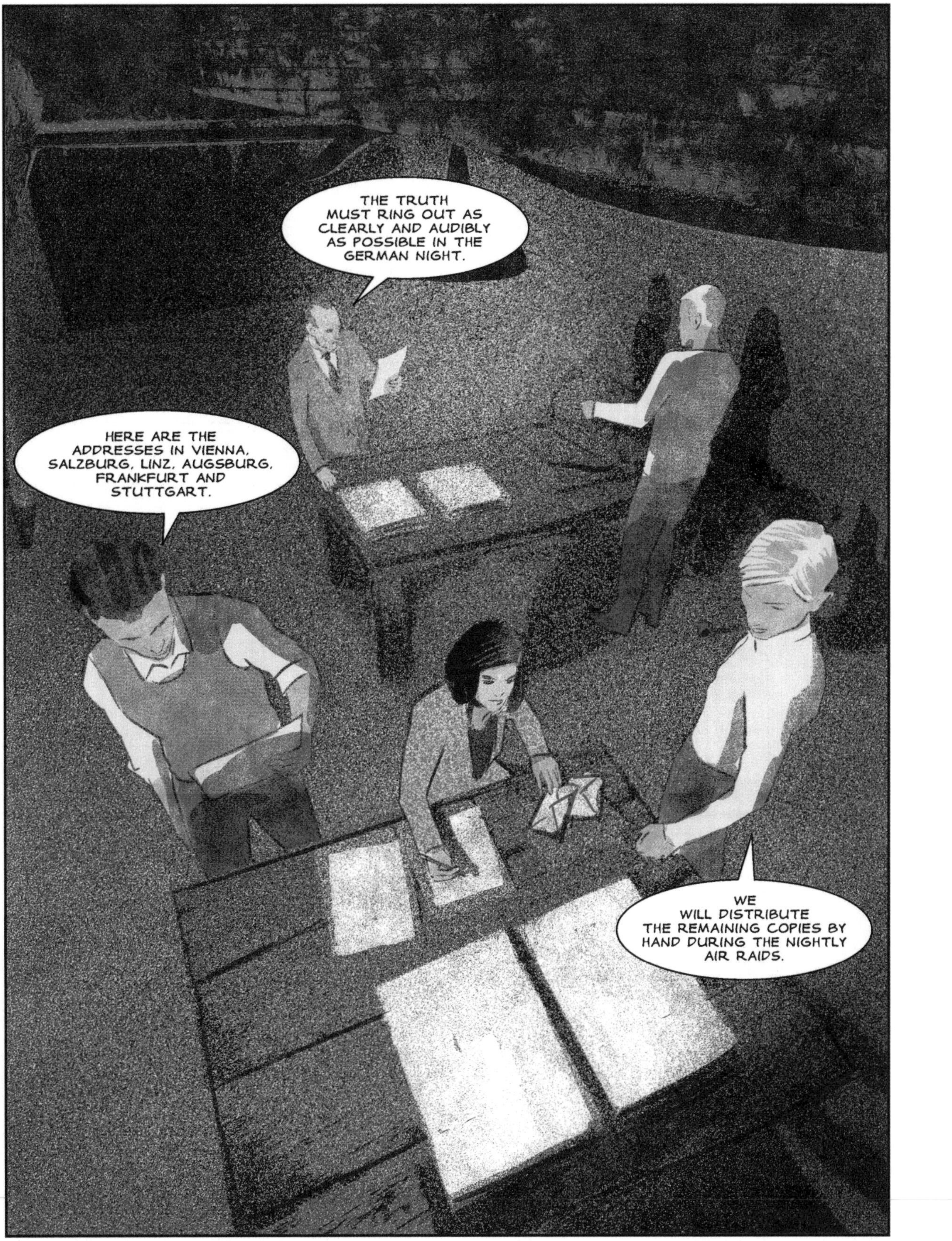
THE TRUTH MUST RING OUT AS CLEARLY AND AUDIBLY AS POSSIBLE IN THE GERMAN NIGHT.
HERE ARE THE ADDRESSES IN VIENNA, SALZBURG, LINZ, AUGSBURG, FRANKFURT AND STUTTGART.
WE WILL DISTRIBUTE THE REMAINING COPIES BY HAND DURING THE NIGHTLY AIR RAIDS.

ALONG LUDWIGSTRASSE, MUNICH, FEBRUARY 3, 1943

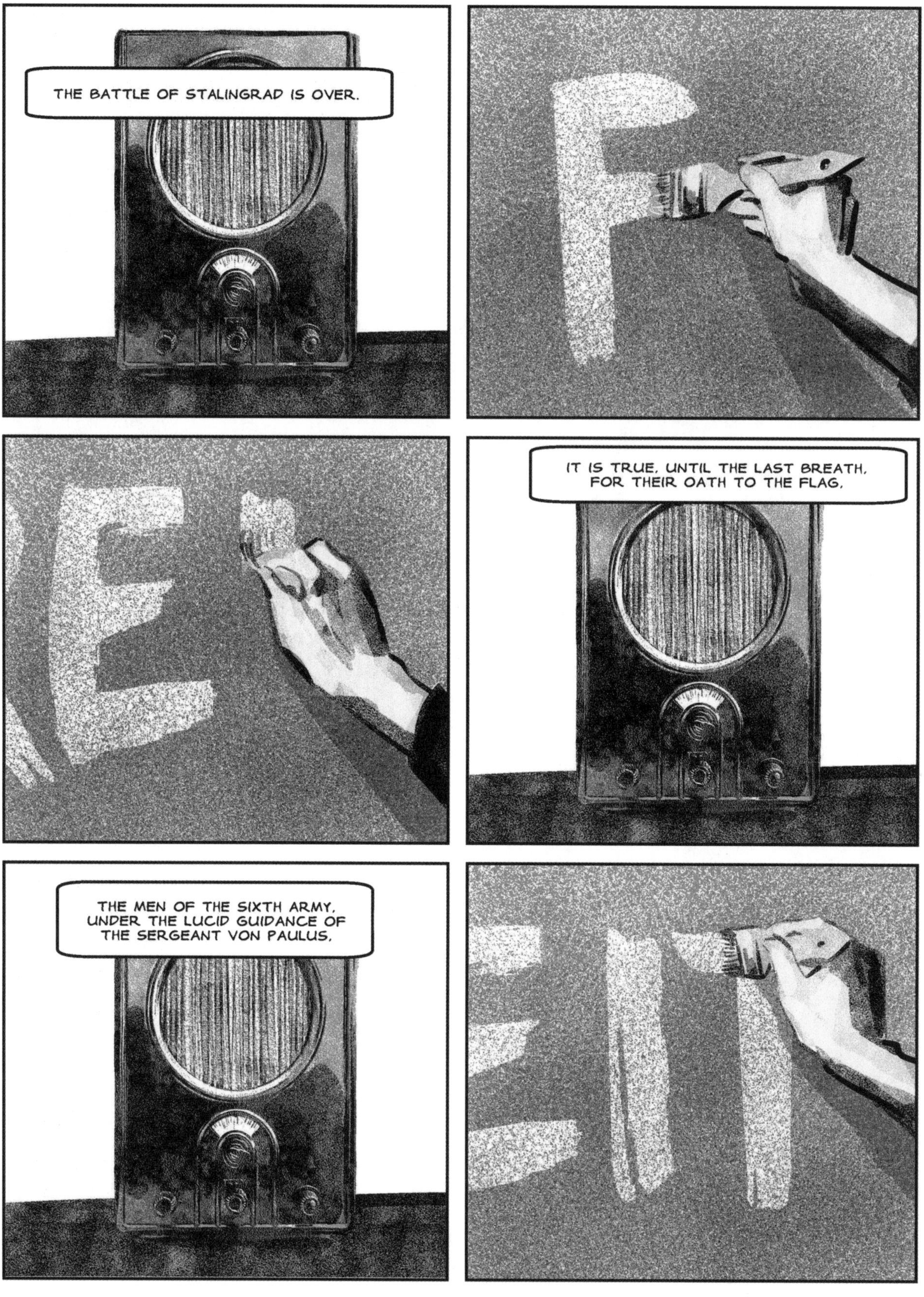

THE BATTLE OF STALINGRAD IS OVER.
IT IS TRUE, UNTIL THE LAST BREATH, FOR THEIR OATH TO THE FLAG,
THE MEN OF THE SIXTH ARMY, UNDER THE LUCID GUIDANCE OF THE SERGEANT VON PAULUS,

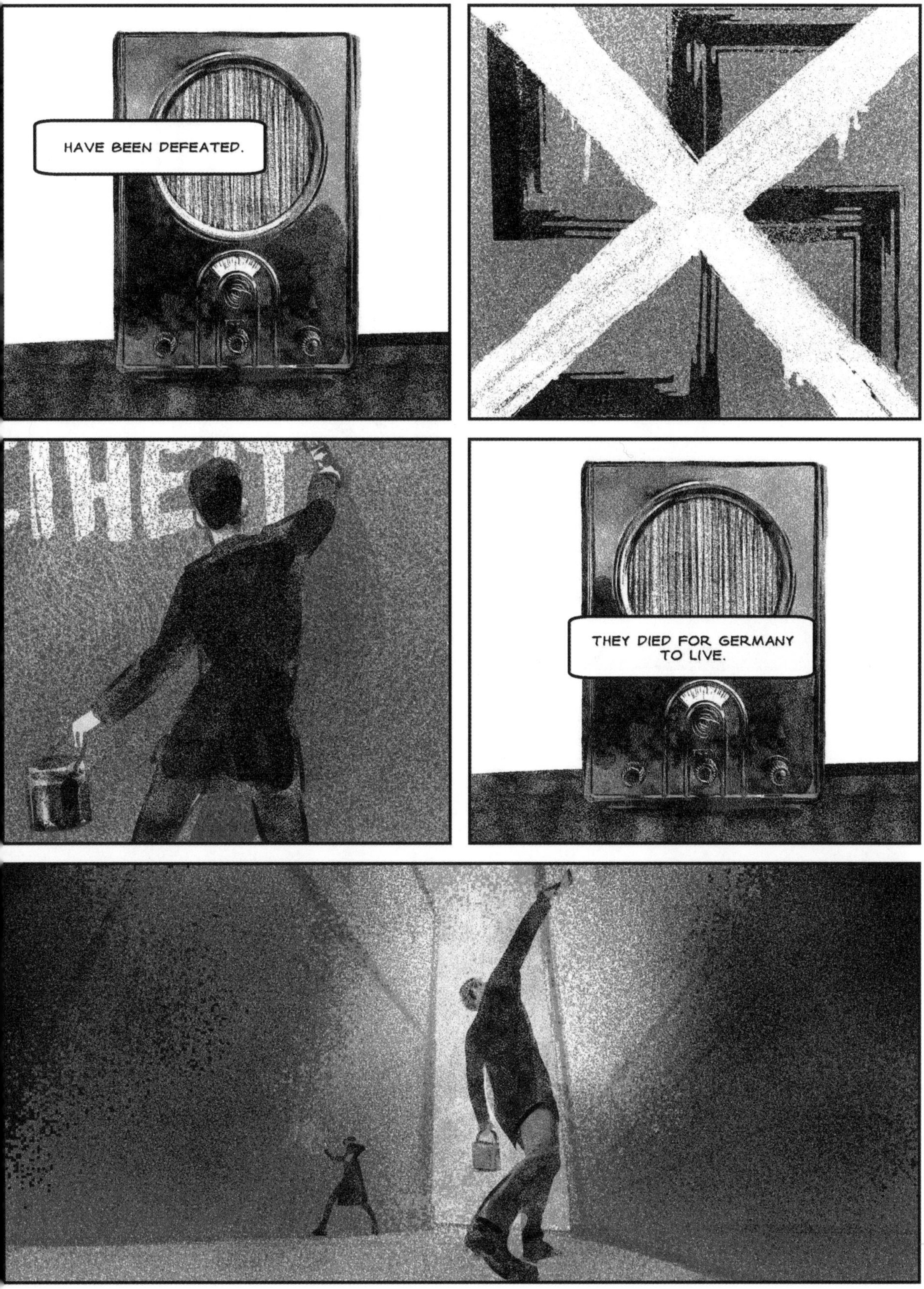
HAVE BEEN DEFEATED.
THEY DIED FOR GERMANY TO LIVE.

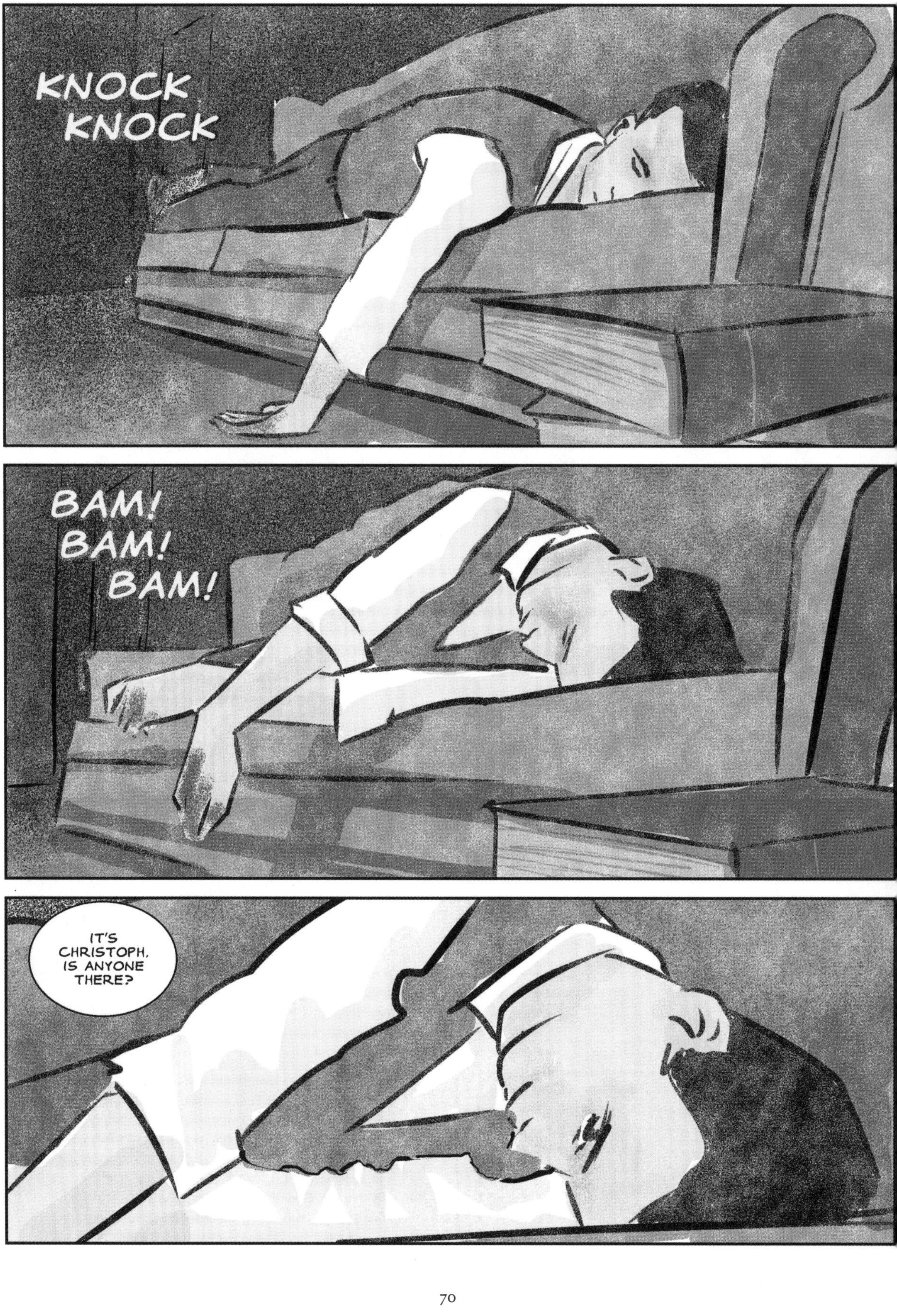
KNOCK
KNOCK
BAM!
BAM!
BAM!
IT'S CHRISTOPH. IS ANYONE THERE?

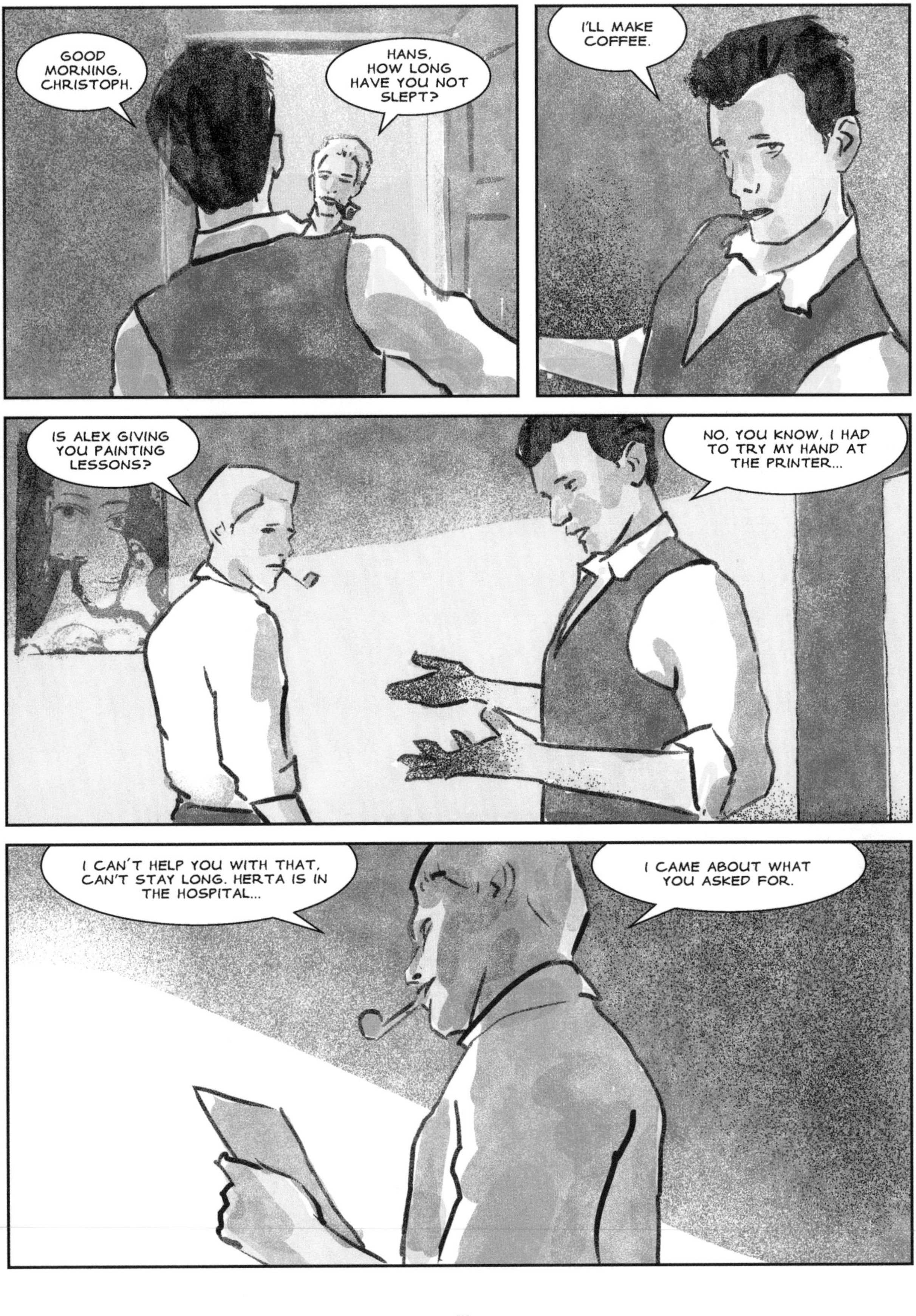
GOOD MORNING, CHRISTOPH.
HANS, HOW LONG HAVE YOU NOT SLEPT?
I'LL MAKE COFFEE.
IS ALEX GIVING YOU PAINTING LESSONS?
NO, YOU KNOW, I HAD TO TRY MY HAND AT THE PRINTER...
I CAN'T HELP YOU WITH THAT, CAN'T STAY LONG. HERTA IS IN THE HOSPITAL...
I CAME ABOUT WHAT YOU ASKED FOR.

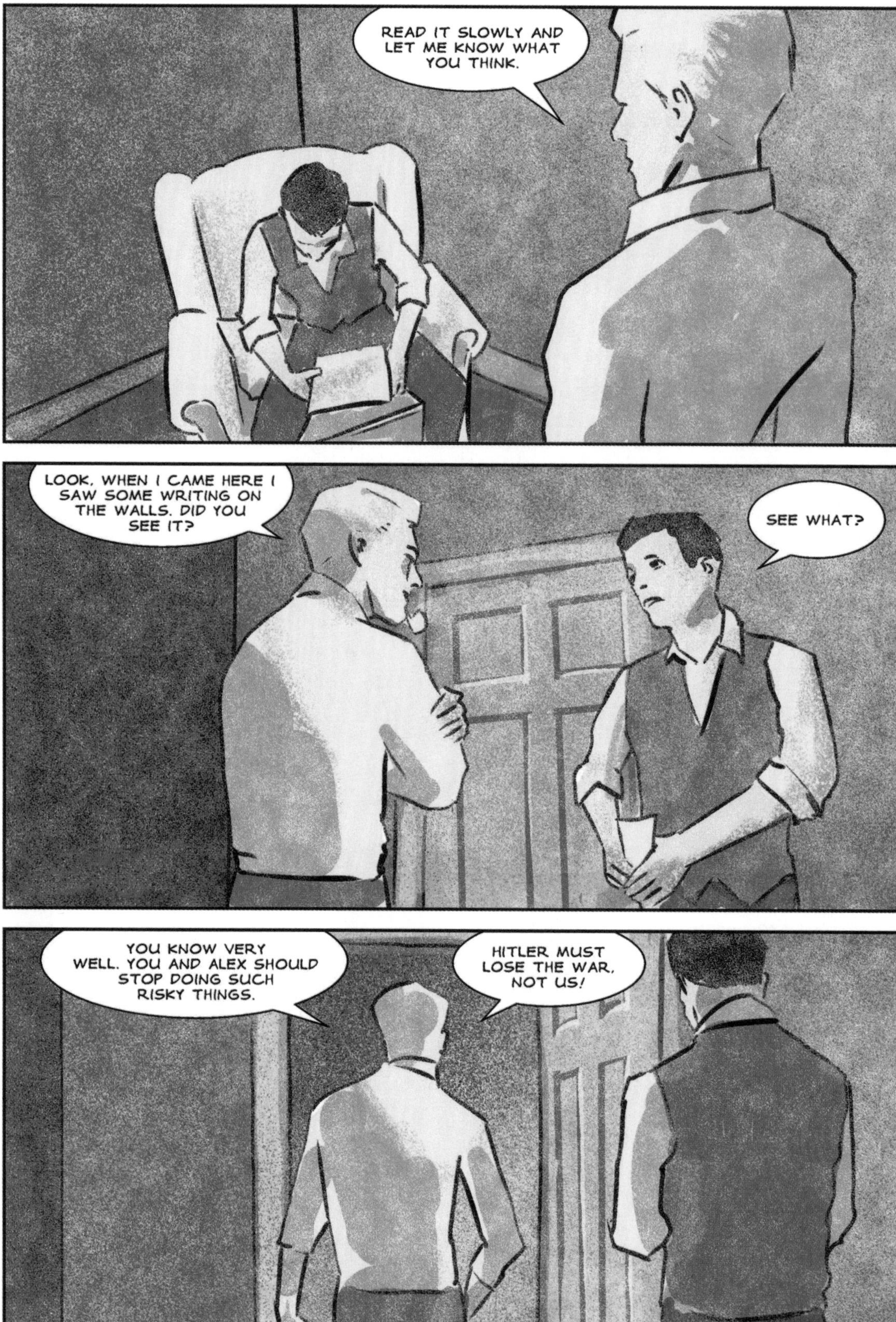
READ IT SLOWLY AND LET ME KNOW WHAT YOU THINK.
LOOK, WHEN I CAME HERE I SAW SOME WRITING ON THE WALLS. DID YOU SEE IT?
SEE WHAT?
YOU KNOW VERY WELL. YOU AND ALEX SHOULD STOP DOING SUCH RISKY THINGS.
HITLER MUST LOSE THE WAR, NOT US!

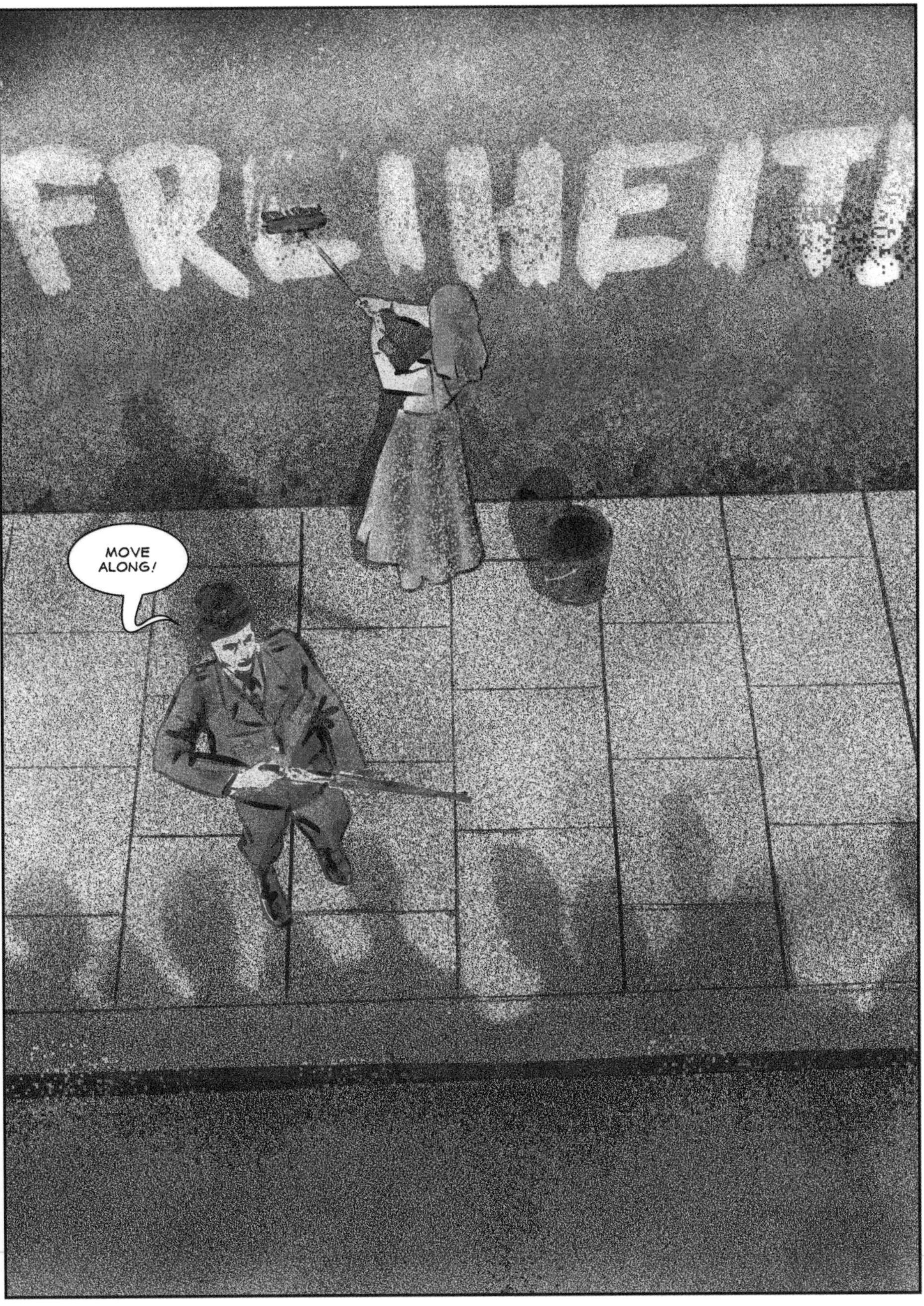
FREIHEIT!
MOVE ALONG!

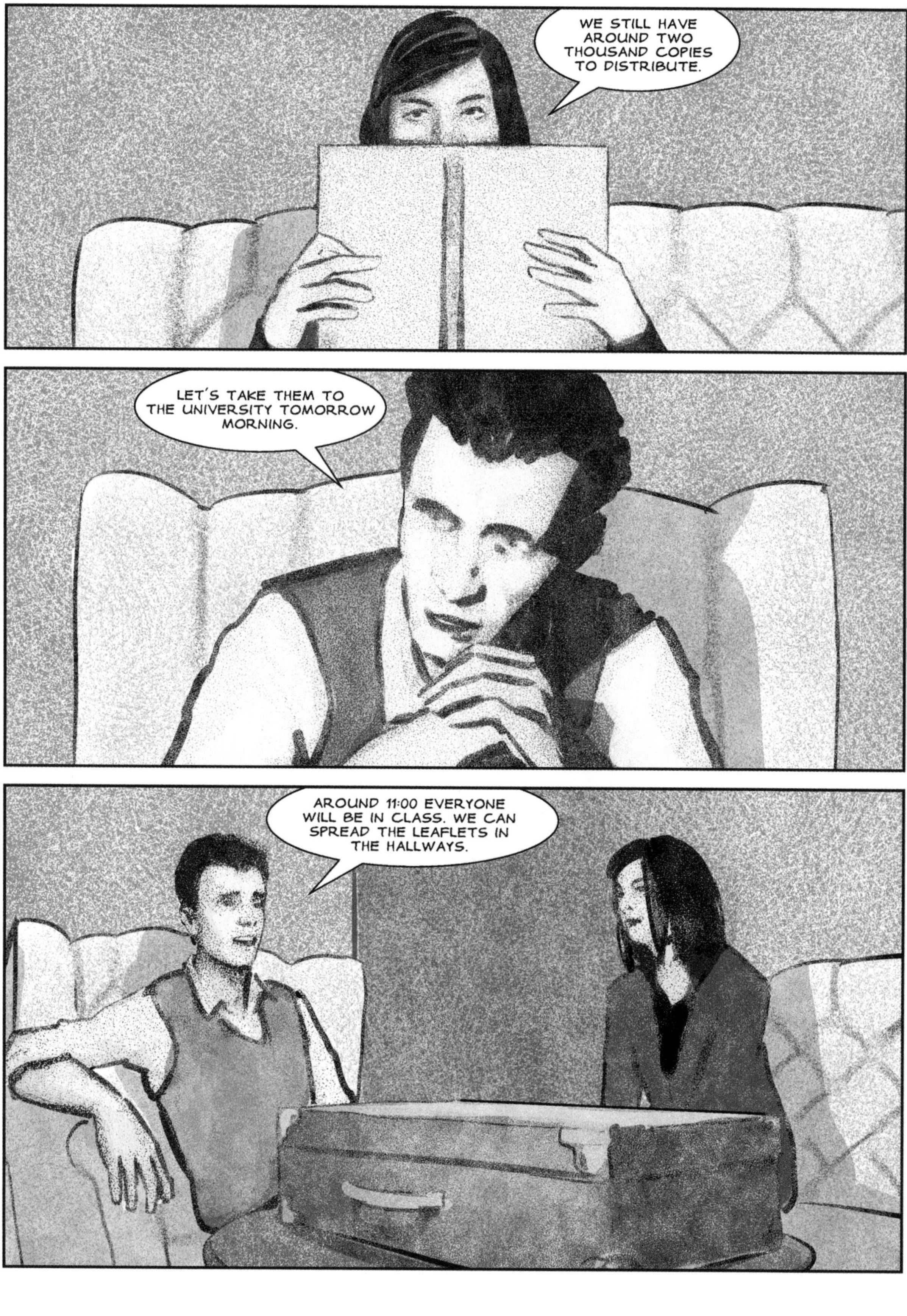
WE STILL HAVE AROUND TWO THOUSAND COPIES TO DISTRIBUTE.
LET'S TAKE THEM TO THE UNIVERSITY TOMORROW MORNING.
AROUND 11:00 EVERYONE WILL BE IN CLASS. WE CAN SPREAD THE LEAFLETS IN THE HALLWAYS.

UNIVERSITY OF MUNICH, FEBRUARY 18, 1943

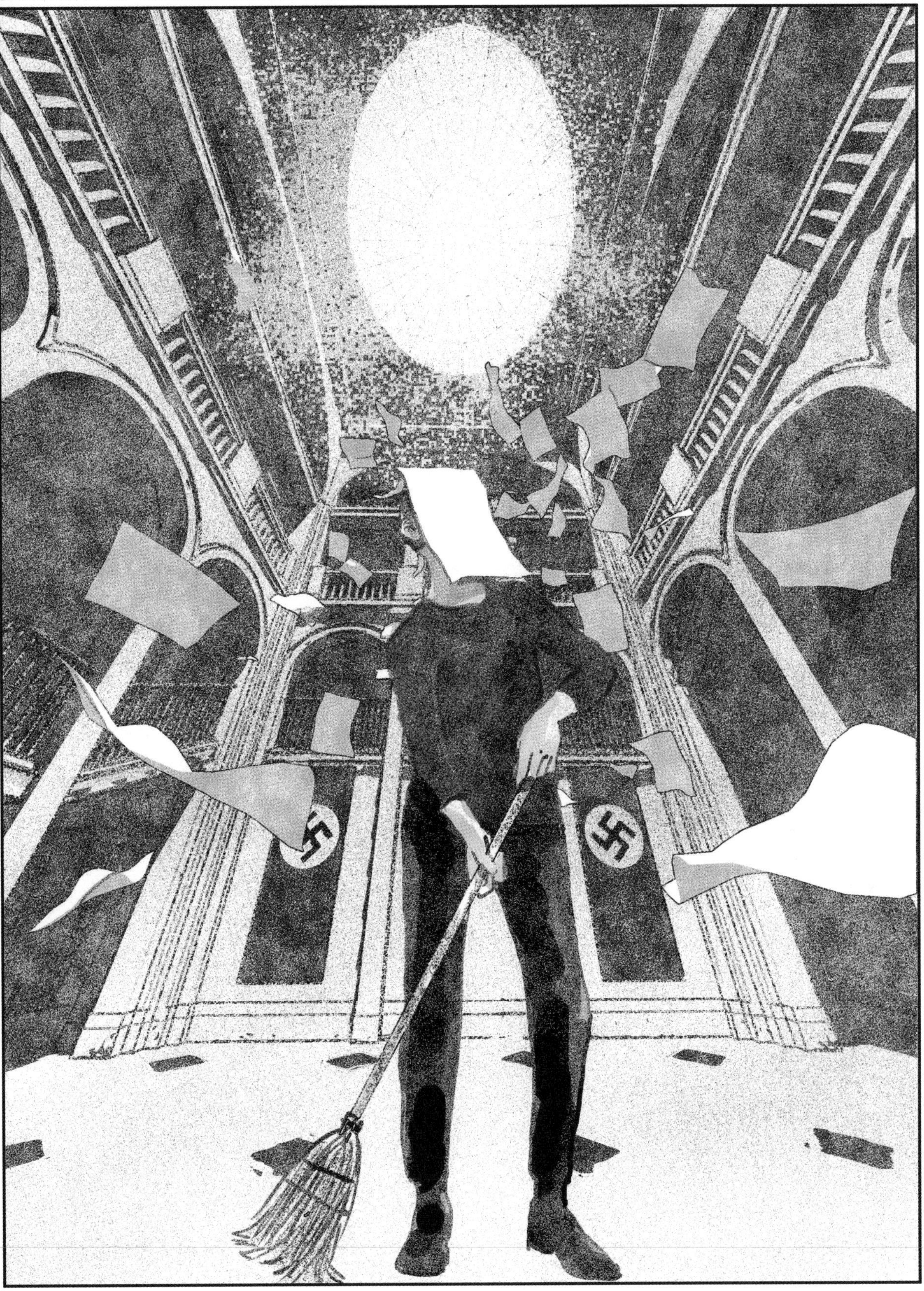

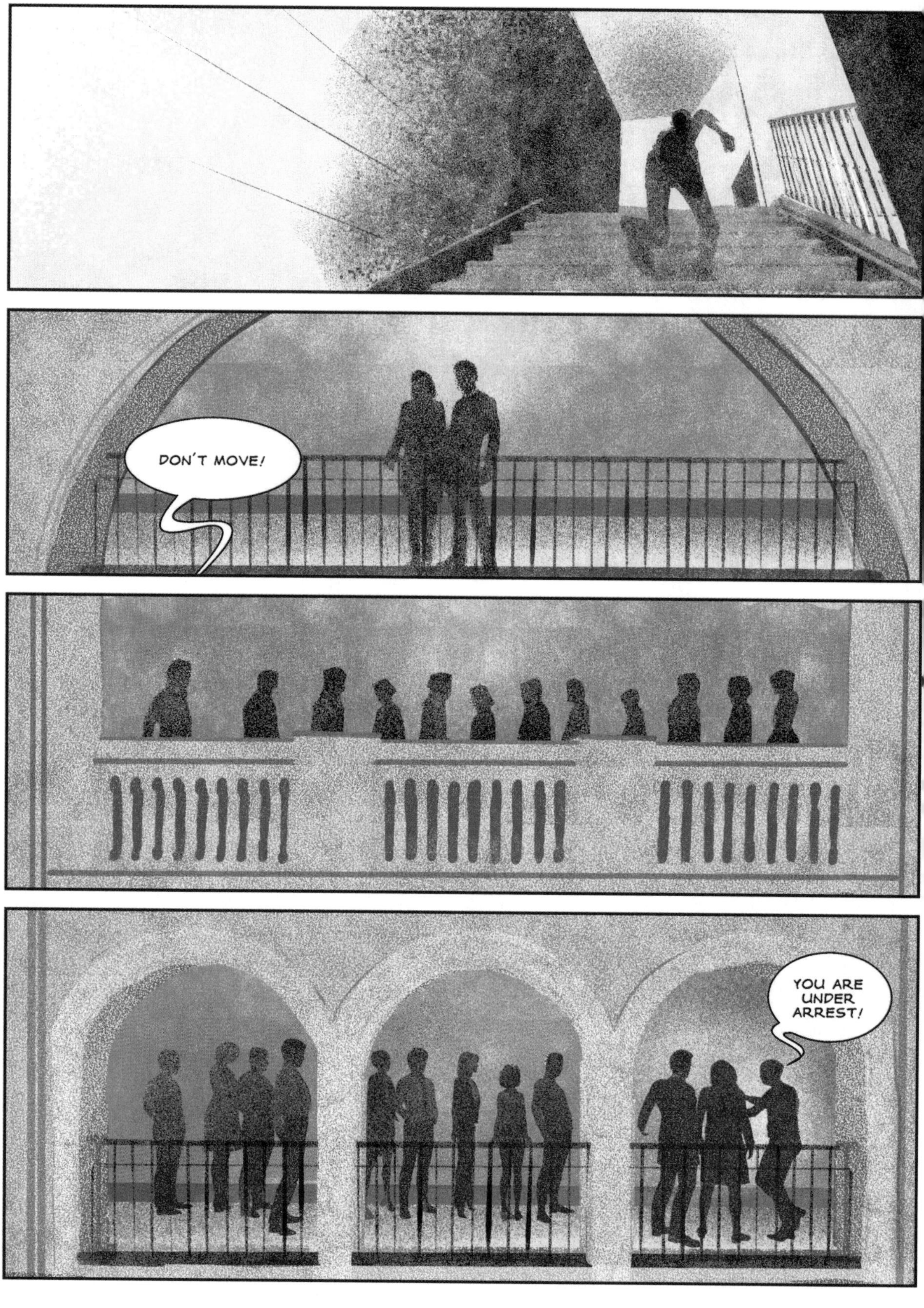
DON'T MOVE!
YOU ARE UNDER ARREST!

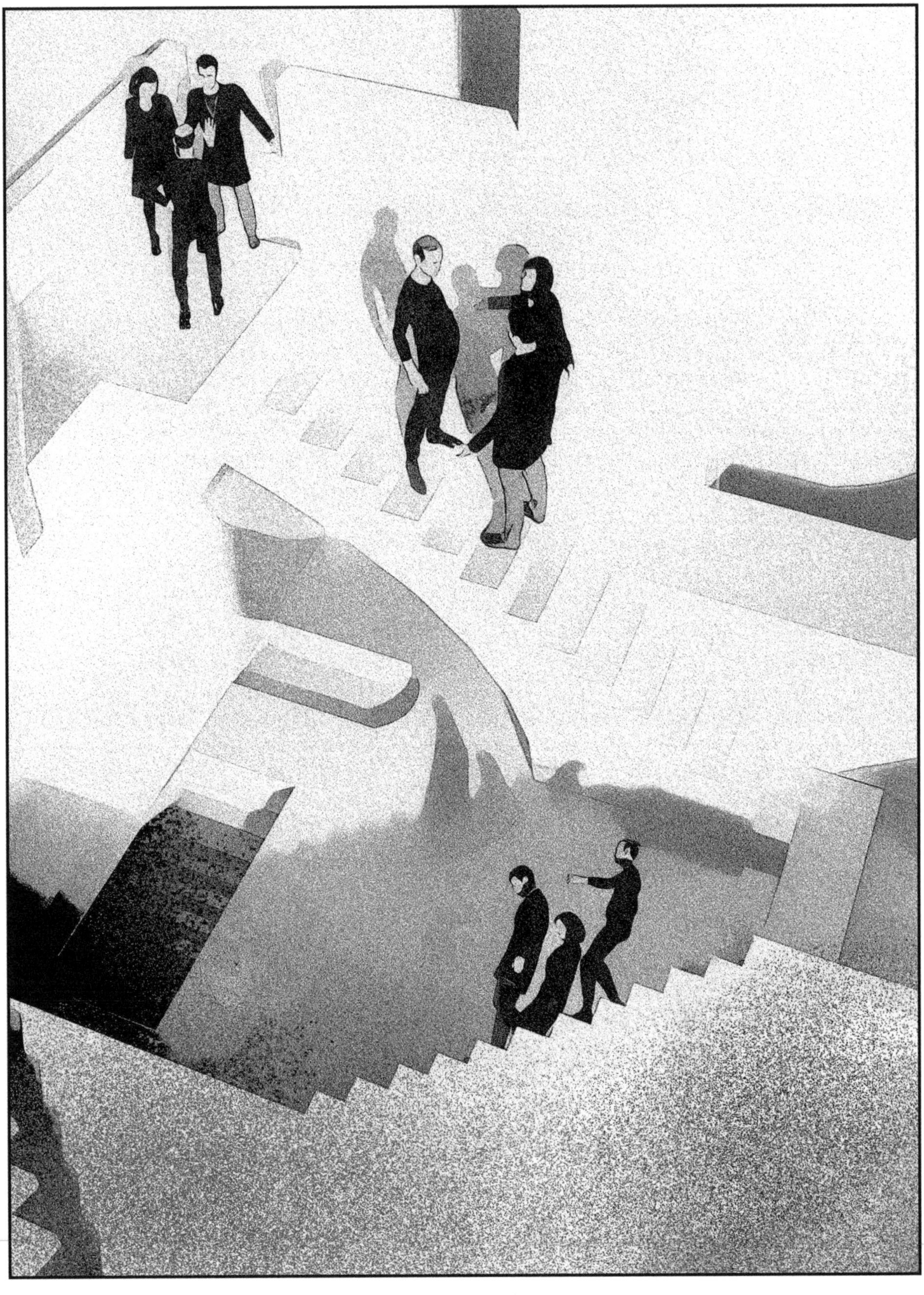

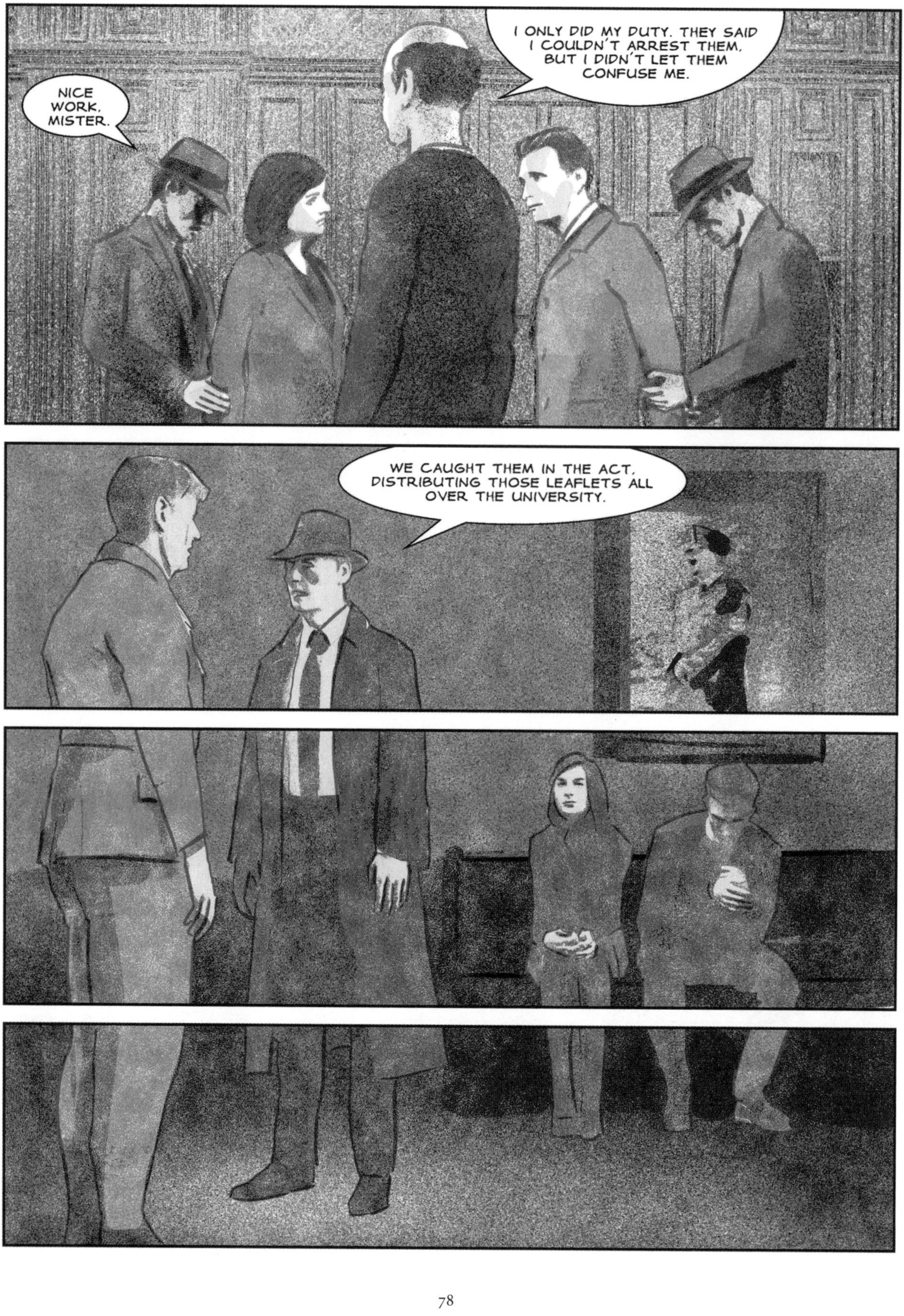
NICE WORK, MISTER.
I ONLY DID MY DUTY. THEY SAID I COULDN'T ARREST THEM, BUT I DIDN'T LET THEM CONFUSE ME.
WE CAUGHT THEM IN THE ACT, DISTRIBUTING THOSE LEAFLETS ALL OVER THE UNIVERSITY.

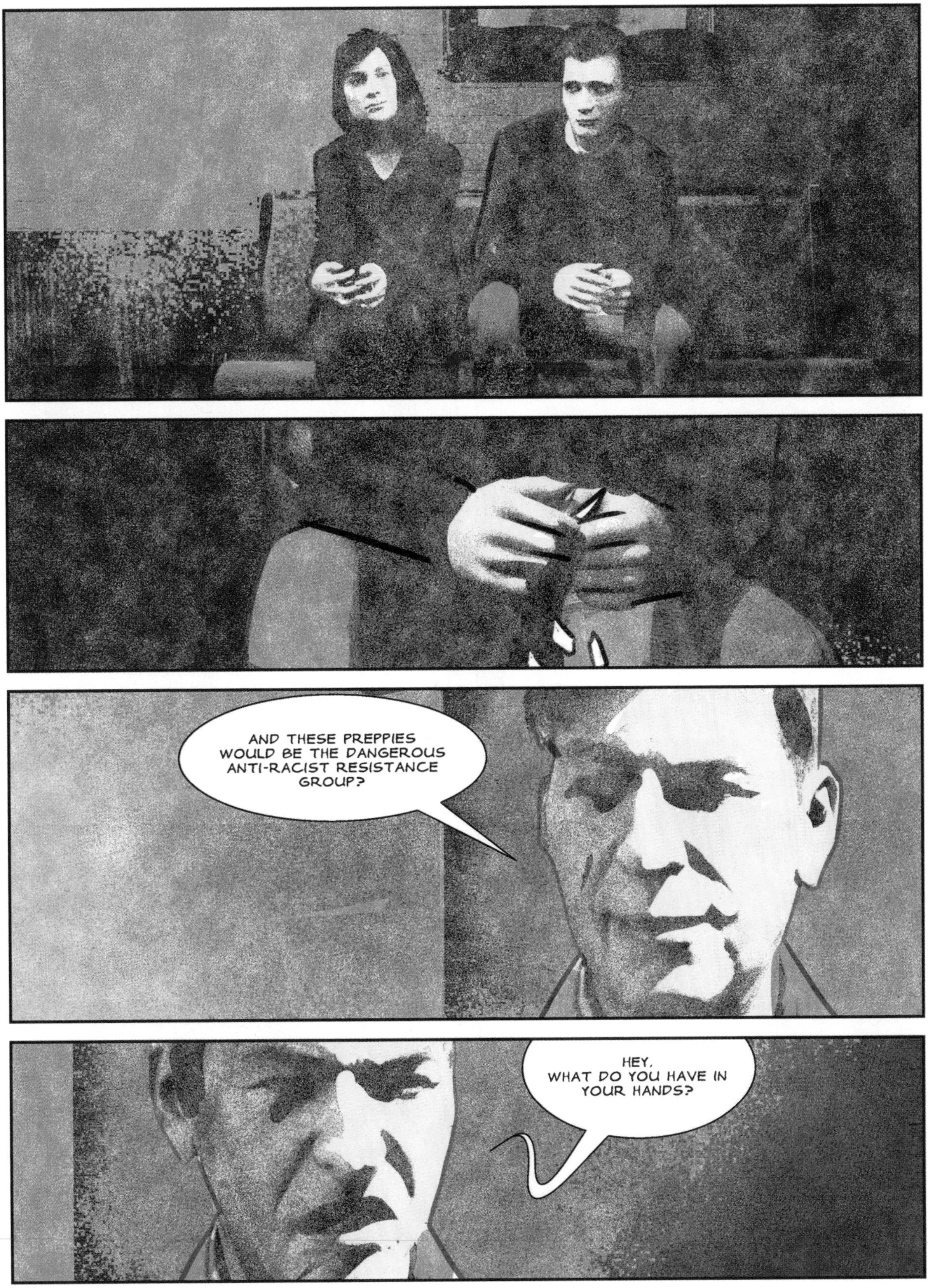
AND THESE PREPPIES WOULD BE THE DANGEROUS ANTI-RACIST RESISTANCE GROUP?
HEY, WHAT DO YOU HAVE IN YOUR HANDS?

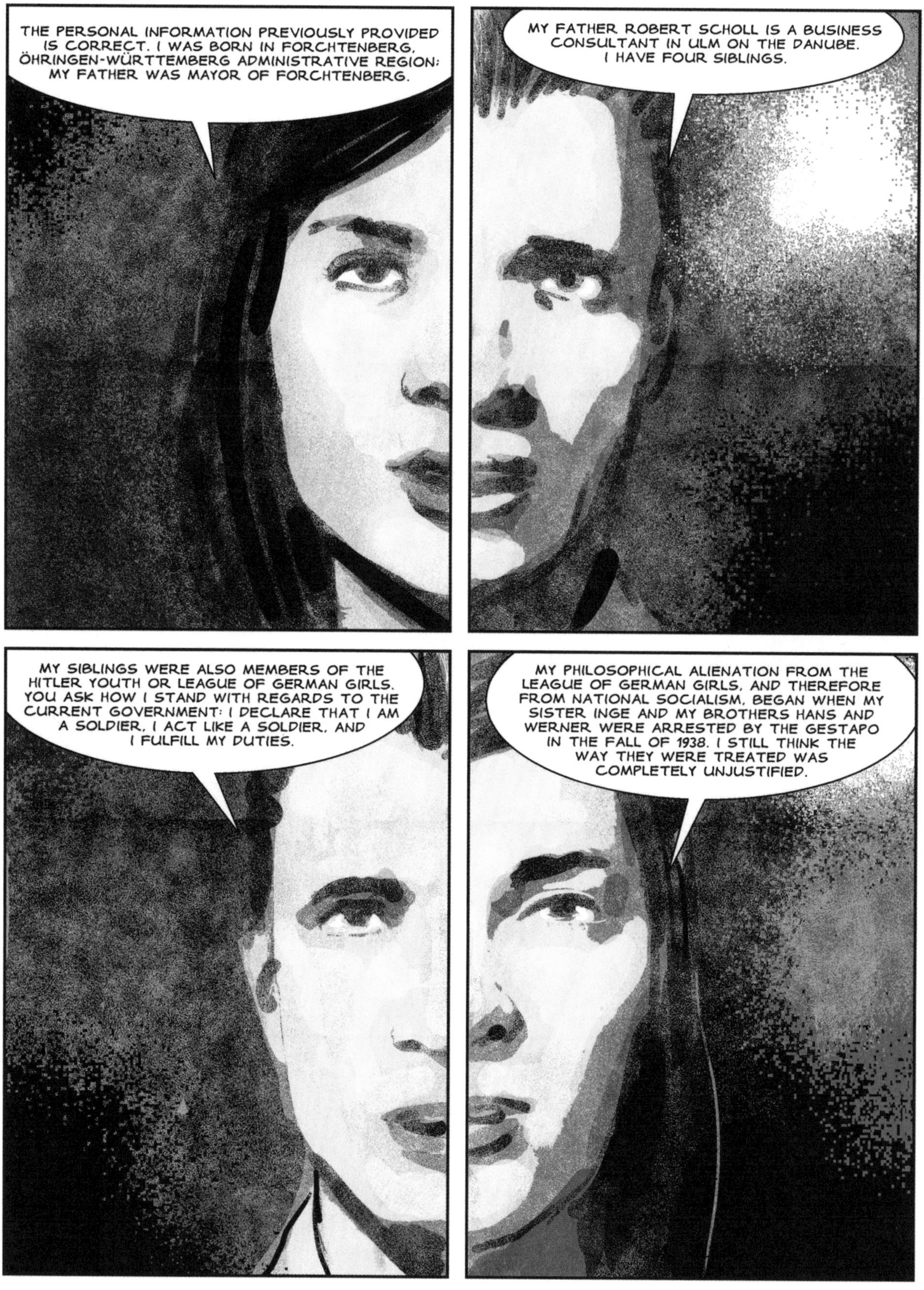
THE PERSONAL INFORMATION PREVIOUSLY PROVIDED IS CORRECT. I WAS BORN IN FORCHTENBERG, ÖHRINGEN-WÜRTTEMBERG ADMINISTRATIVE REGION; MY FATHER WAS MAYOR OF FORCHTENBERG.
MY FATHER ROBERT SCHOLL IS A BUSINESS CONSULTANT IN ULM ON THE DANUBE. I HAVE FOUR SIBLINGS.
MY SIBLINGS WERE ALSO MEMBERS OF THE HITLER YOUTH OR LEAGUE OF GERMAN GIRLS. YOU ASK HOW I STAND WITH REGARDS TO THE CURRENT GOVERNMENT: I DECLARE THAT I AM A SOLDIER, I ACT LIKE A SOLDIER, AND I FULFILL MY DUTIES.
MY PHILOSOPHICAL ALIENATION FROM THE LEAGUE OF GERMAN GIRLS, AND THEREFORE FROM NATIONAL SOCIALISM, BEGAN WHEN MY SISTER INGE AND MY BROTHERS HANS AND WERNER WERE ARRESTED BY THE GESTAPO IN THE FALL OF 1938. I STILL THINK THE WAY THEY WERE TREATED WAS COMPLETELY UNJUSTIFIED.

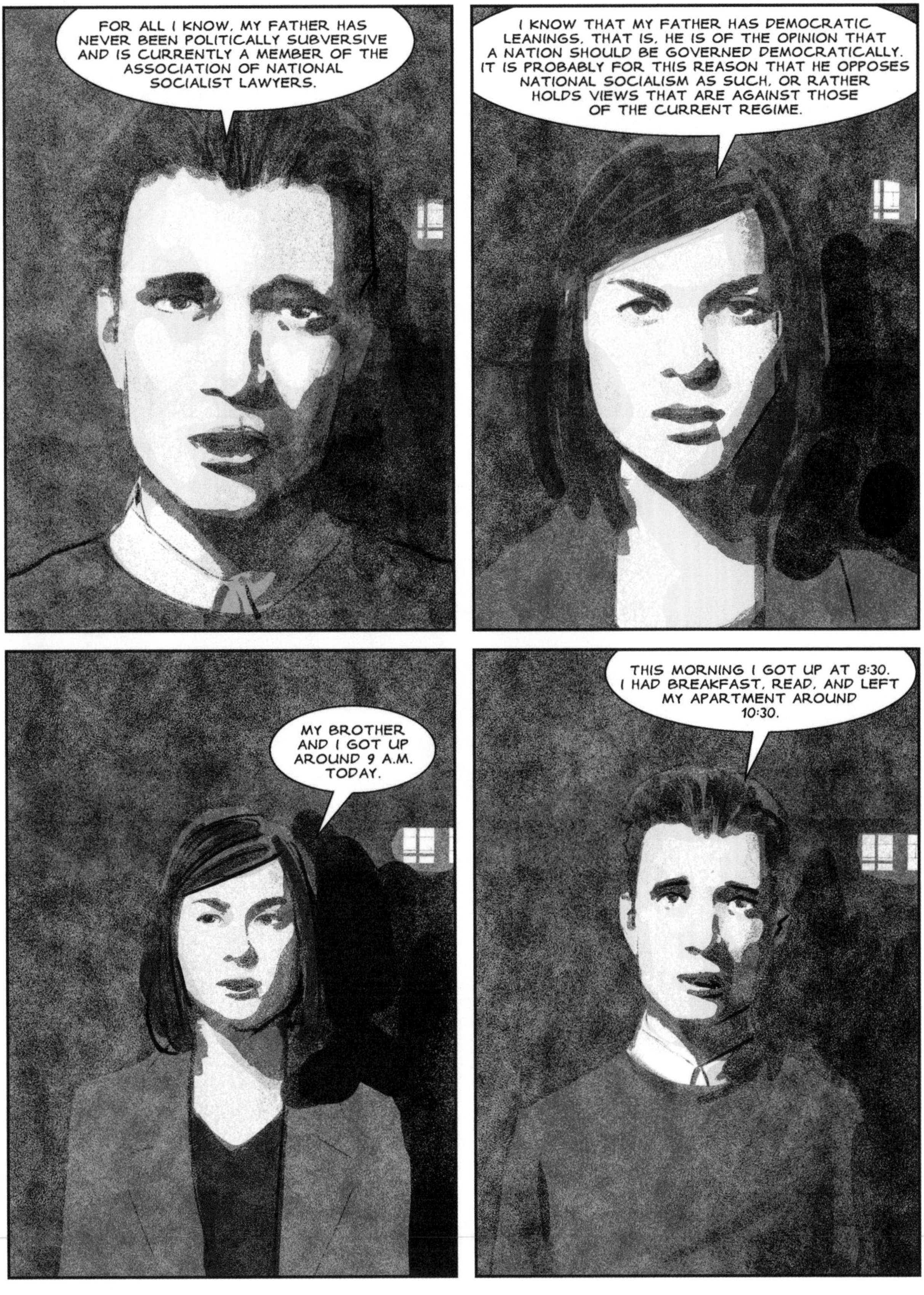
FOR ALL I KNOW, MY FATHER HAS NEVER BEEN POLITICALLY SUBVERSIVE AND IS CURRENTLY A MEMBER OF THE ASSOCIATION OF NATIONAL SOCIALIST LAWYERS.
I KNOW THAT MY FATHER HAS DEMOCRATIC LEANINGS, THAT IS, HE IS OF THE OPINION THAT A NATION SHOULD BE GOVERNED DEMOCRATICALLY. IT IS PROBABLY FOR THIS REASON THAT HE OPPOSES NATIONAL SOCIALISM AS SUCH, OR RATHER HOLDS VIEWS THAT ARE AGAINST THOSE OF THE CURRENT REGIME.
MY BROTHER AND I GOT UP AROUND 9 A.M. TODAY.
THIS MORNING I GOT UP AT 8:30. I HAD BREAKFAST, READ, AND LEFT MY APARTMENT AROUND 10:30.

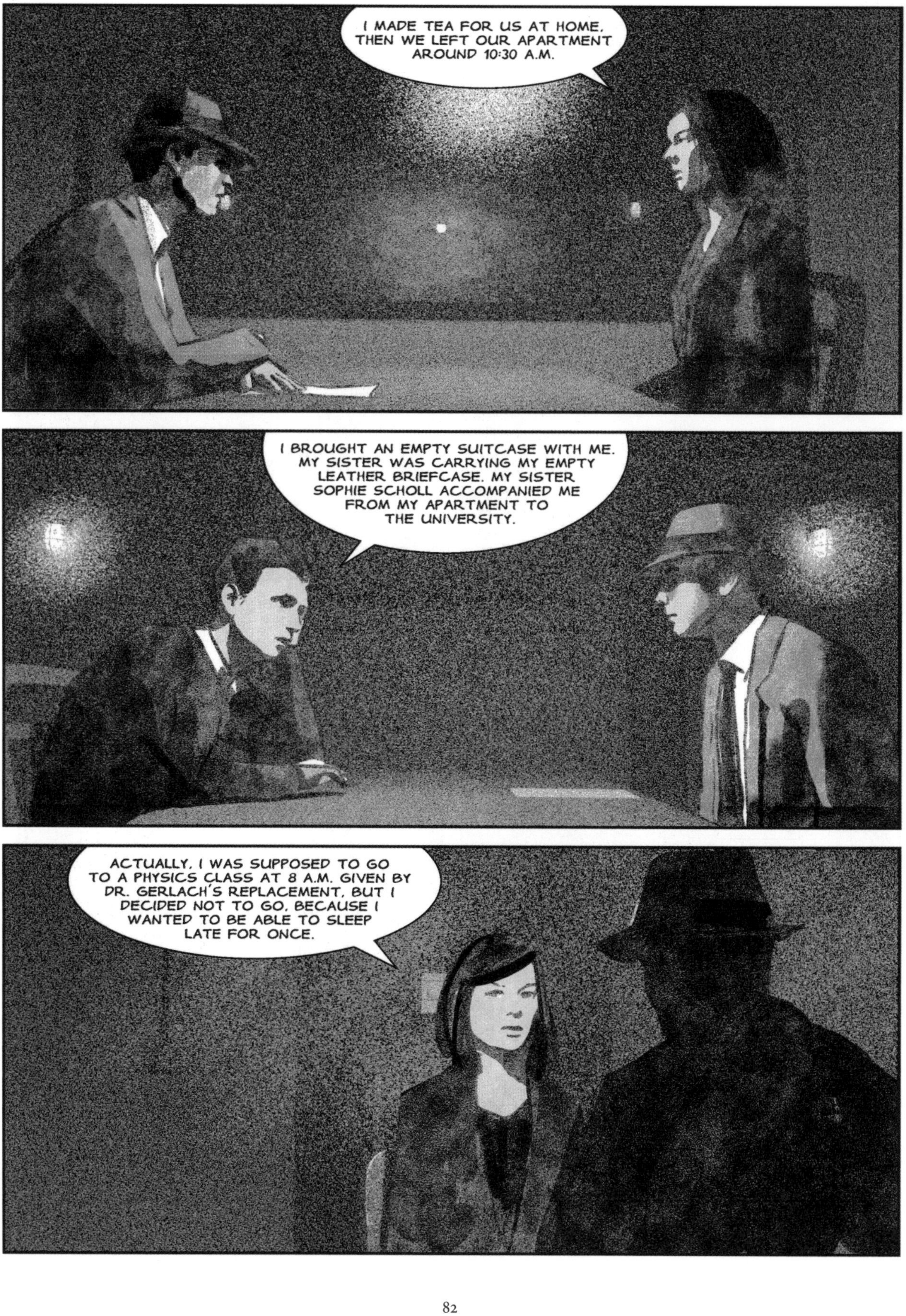
I MADE TEA FOR US AT HOME. THEN WE LEFT OUR APARTMENT AROUND 10:30 A.M.
I BROUGHT AN EMPTY SUITCASE WITH ME. MY SISTER WAS CARRYING MY EMPTY LEATHER BRIEFCASE. MY SISTER SOPHIE SCHOLL ACCOMPANIED ME FROM MY APARTMENT TO THE UNIVERSITY.
ACTUALLY, I WAS SUPPOSED TO GO TO A PHYSICS CLASS AT 8 A.M. GIVEN BY DR. GERLACH'S REPLACEMENT, BUT I DECIDED NOT TO GO, BECAUSE I WANTED TO BE ABLE TO SLEEP LATE FOR ONCE.

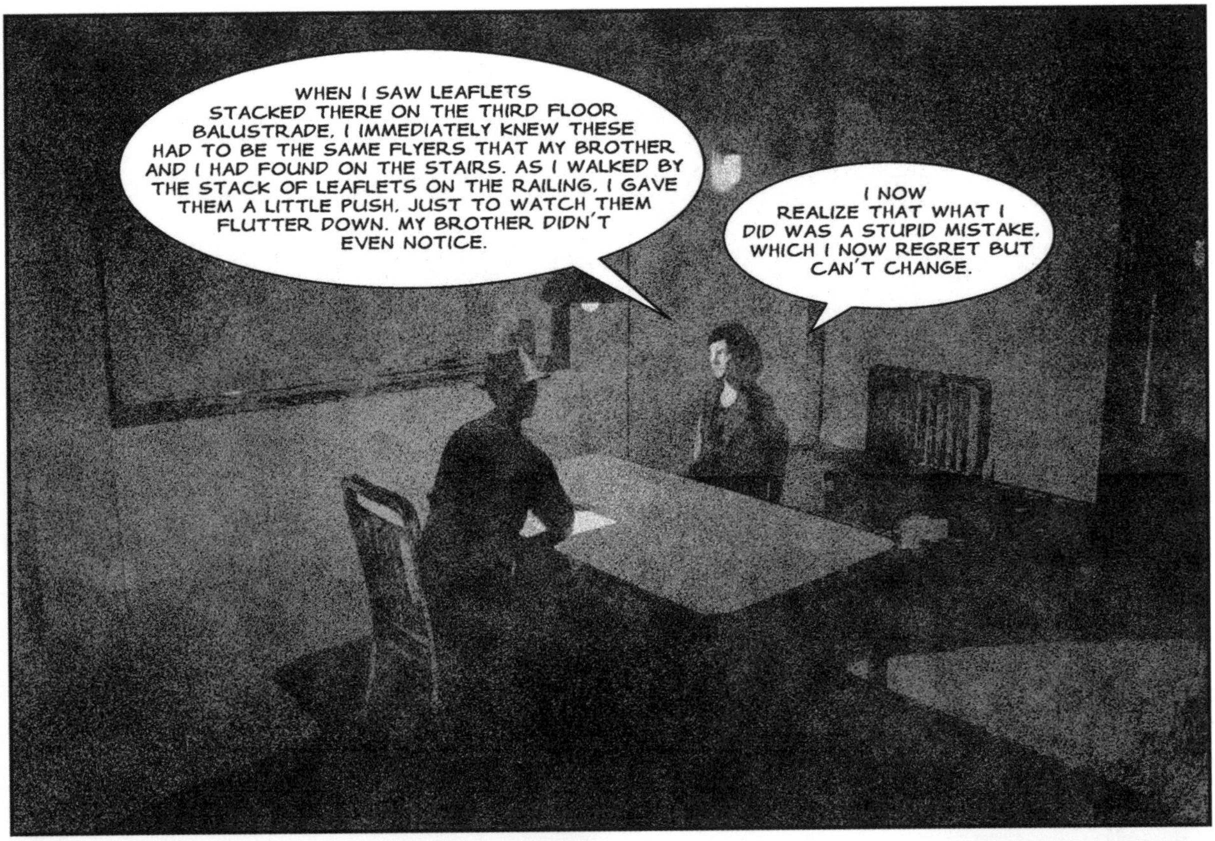
WHEN I SAW LEAFLETS STACKED THERE ON THE THIRD FLOOR BALUSTRADE, I IMMEDIATELY KNEW THESE HAD TO BE THE SAME FLYERS THAT MY BROTHER AND I HAD FOUND ON THE STAIRS. AS I WALKED BY THE STACK OF LEAFLETS ON THE RAILING, I GAVE THEM A LITTLE PUSH, JUST TO WATCH THEM FLUTTER DOWN. MY BROTHER DIDN'T EVEN NOTICE.
I NOW REALIZE THAT WHAT I DID WAS A STUPID MISTAKE, WHICH I NOW REGRET BUT CAN'T CHANGE.

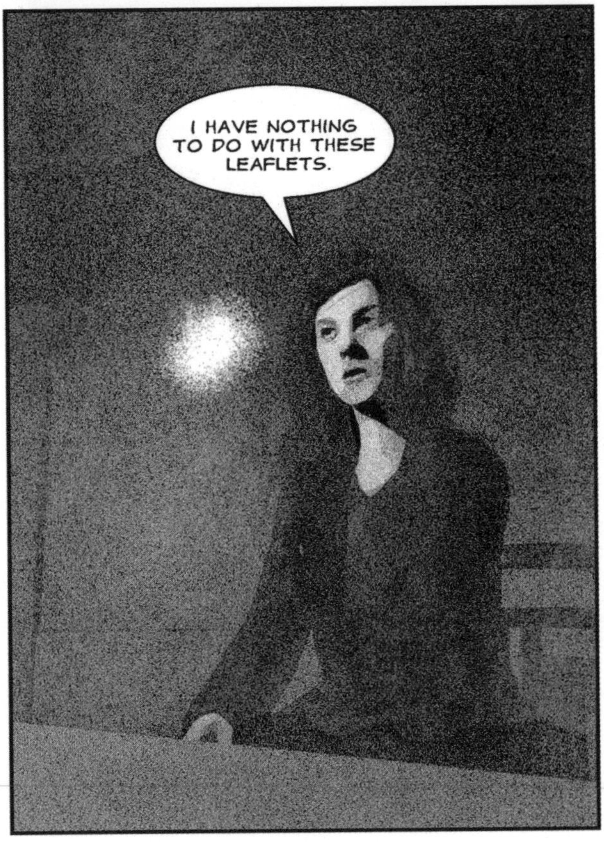
I HAVE NOTHING TO DO WITH THESE LEAFLETS.

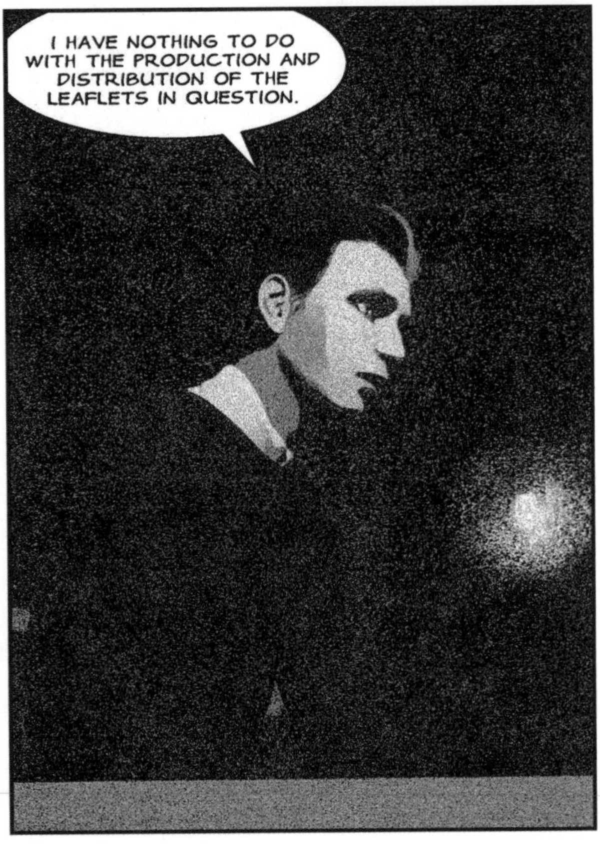
I HAVE NOTHING TO DO WITH THE PRODUCTION AND DISTRIBUTION OF THE LEAFLETS IN QUESTION.

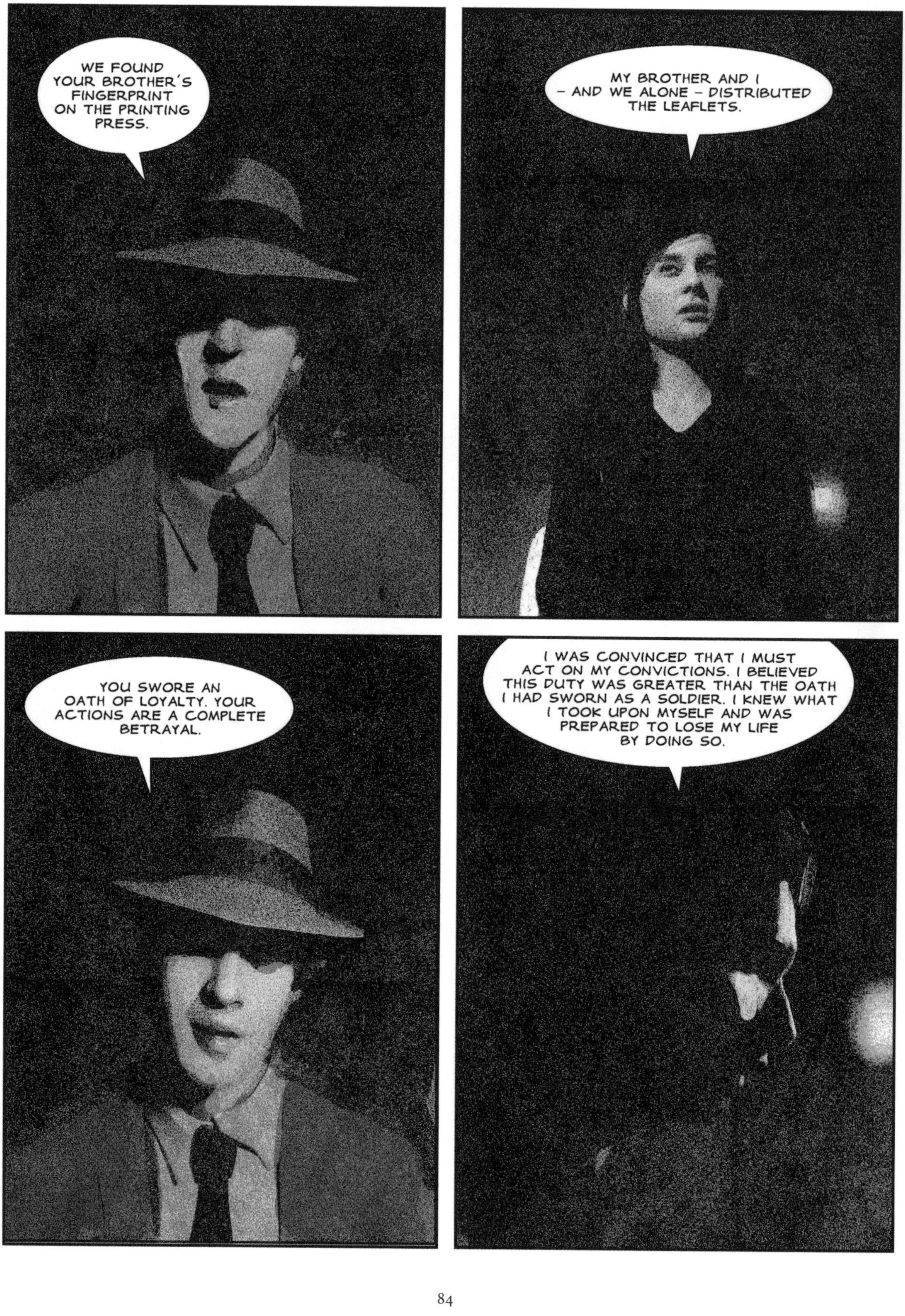
WE FOUND YOUR BROTHER'S FINGERPRINT ON THE PRINTING PRESS.
MY BROTHER AND I – AND WE ALONE – DISTRIBUTED THE LEAFLETS.
YOU SWORE AN OATH OF LOYALTY. YOUR ACTIONS ARE A COMPLETE BETRAYAL.
I WAS CONVINCED THAT I MUST ACT ON MY CONVICTIONS. I BELIEVED THIS DUTY WAS GREATER THAN THE OATH I HAD SWORN AS A SOLDIER. I KNEW WHAT I TOOK UPON MYSELF AND WAS PREPARED TO LOSE MY LIFE BY DOING SO.

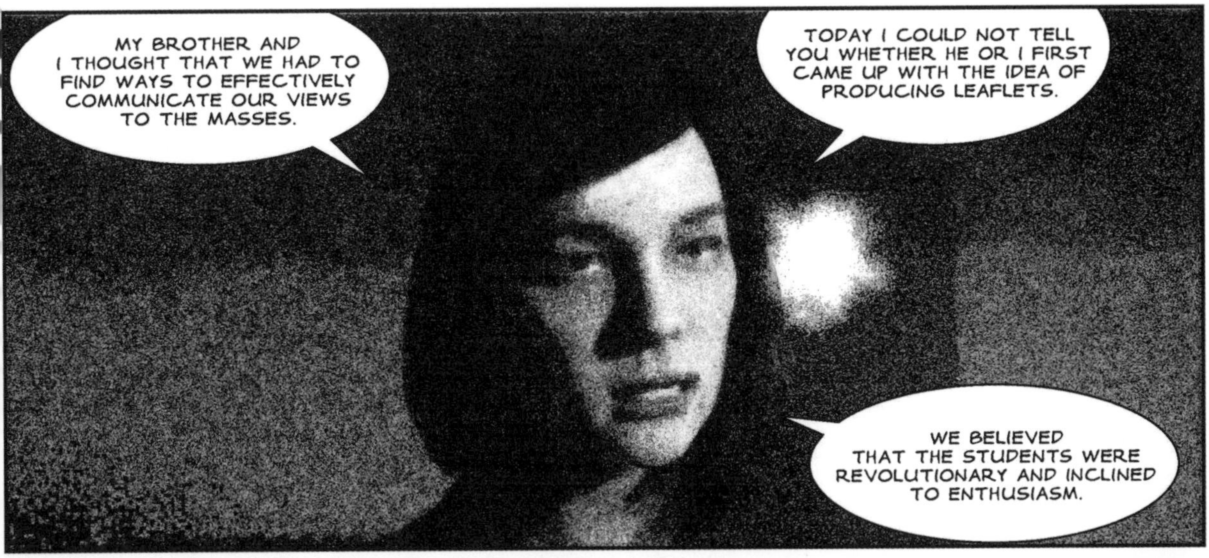
MY BROTHER AND I THOUGHT THAT WE HAD TO FIND WAYS TO EFFECTIVELY COMMUNICATE OUR VIEWS TO THE MASSES.
TODAY I COULD NOT TELL YOU WHETHER HE OR I FIRST CAME UP WITH THE IDEA OF PRODUCING LEAFLETS.
WE BELIEVED THAT THE STUDENTS WERE REVOLUTIONARY AND INCLINED TO ENTHUSIASM.

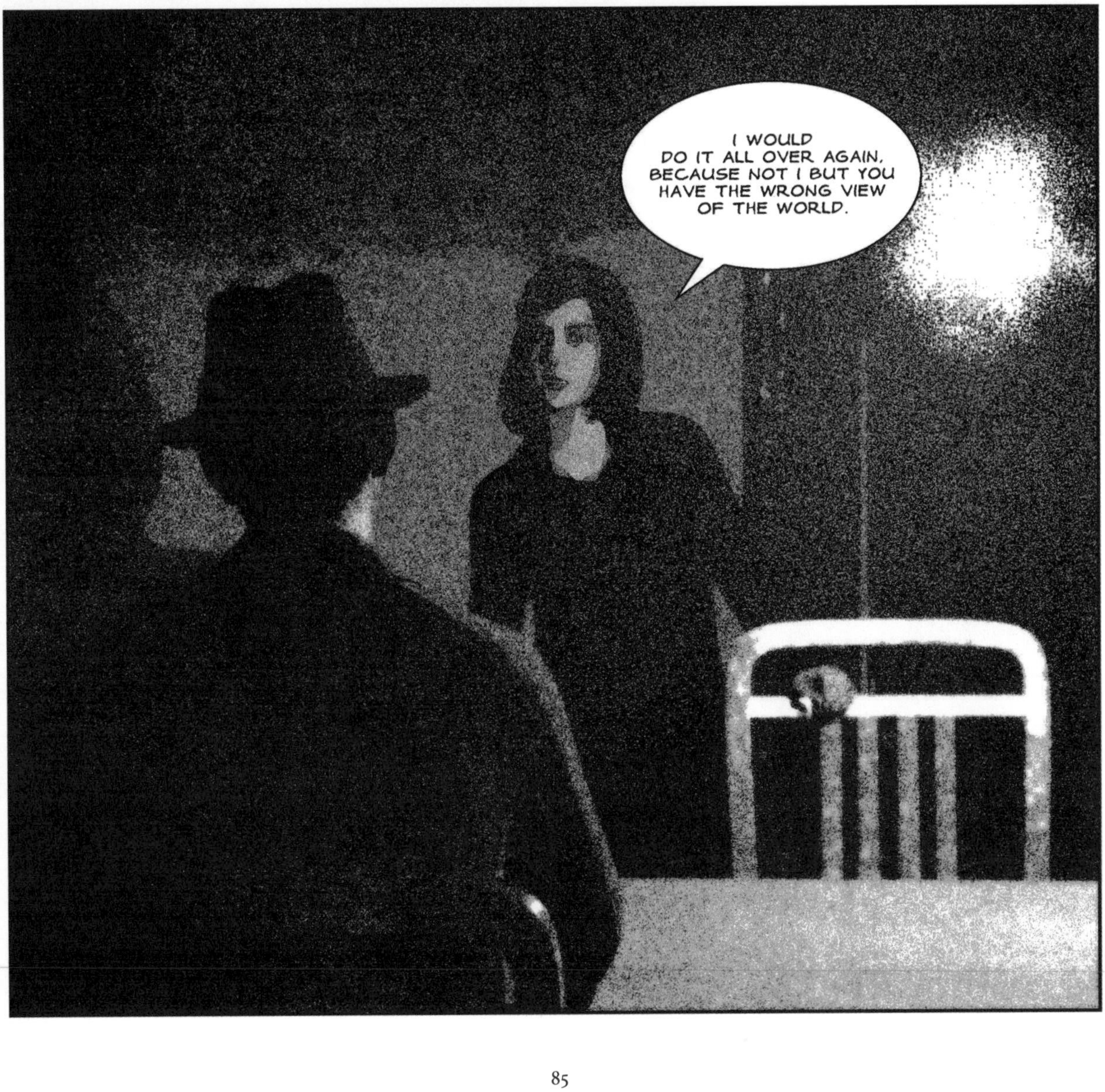
I WOULD DO IT ALL OVER AGAIN, BECAUSE NOT I BUT YOU HAVE THE WRONG VIEW OF THE WORLD.

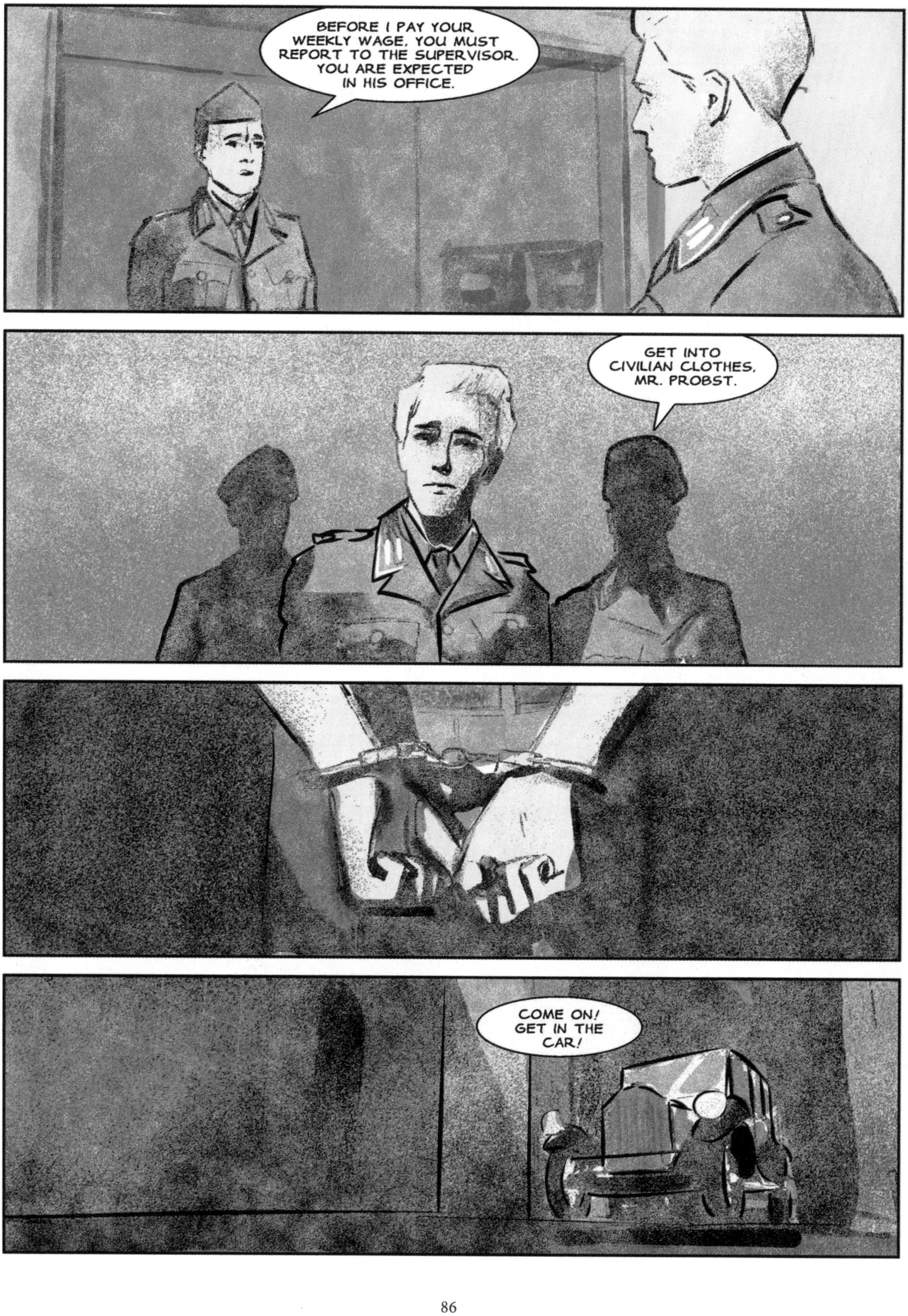
BEFORE I PAY YOUR WEEKLY WAGE, YOU MUST REPORT TO THE SUPERVISOR. YOU ARE EXPECTED IN HIS OFFICE.
GET INTO CIVILIAN CLOTHES, MR. PROBST.
COME ON! GET IN THE CAR!

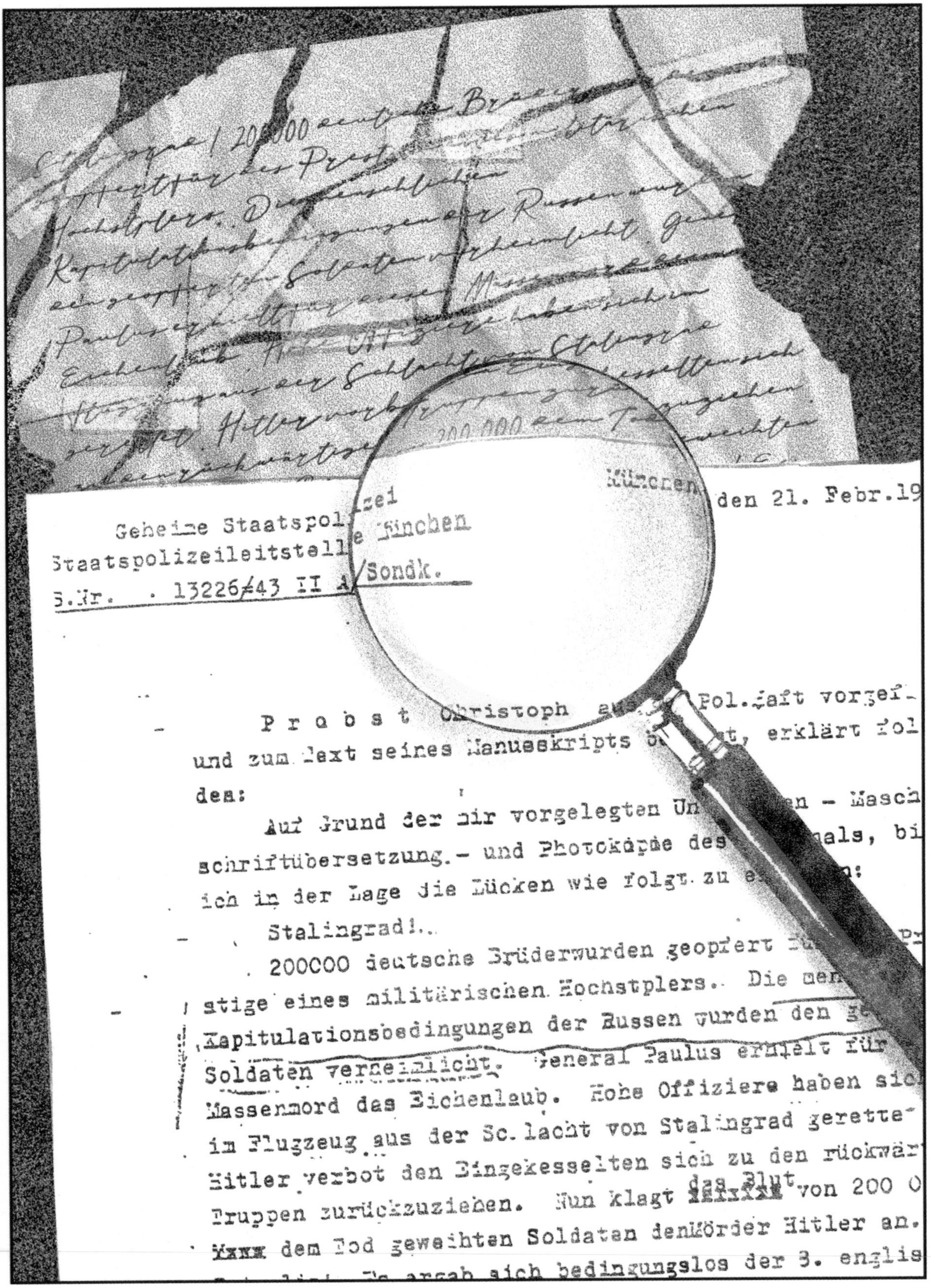

Geheime Staatspolizei
Staatspolizeileitstelle München
B.Nr. . 13226/43 II A /Sondk.

München, den 21. Febr.19

P r o b s t Christoph aus ... Pol.haft vorgef...
und zum Text seines Manuskripts b... t, erklärt fol-
dea:

    Auf Grund der mir vorgelegten Un... en - Masch...
schriftübersetzung.- und Photokopie des ... nals, bi...
ich in der Lage die Lücken wie folgt zu e... :

    Stalingrad!...

    200000 deutsche Brüder wurden geopfert ... Pr...
stige eines militärischen Hochstplers. Die men...
Kapitulationsbedingungen der Russen wurden den g...
Soldaten verheimlicht. General Paulus erhielt für...
Massenmord das Eichenlaub. Hohe Offiziere haben sic...
im Flugzeug aus der Schlacht von Stalingrad gerette...
Hitler verbot den Eingekesselten sich zu den rückwär...
Truppen zurückzuziehen. Nun klagt ...... von 200 0
xxxx dem Tod geweihten Soldaten den Mörder Hitler an.
... Es ergab sich bedingungslos der 8. englis...

87

FEBRUARY 22, 12:45 P.M.

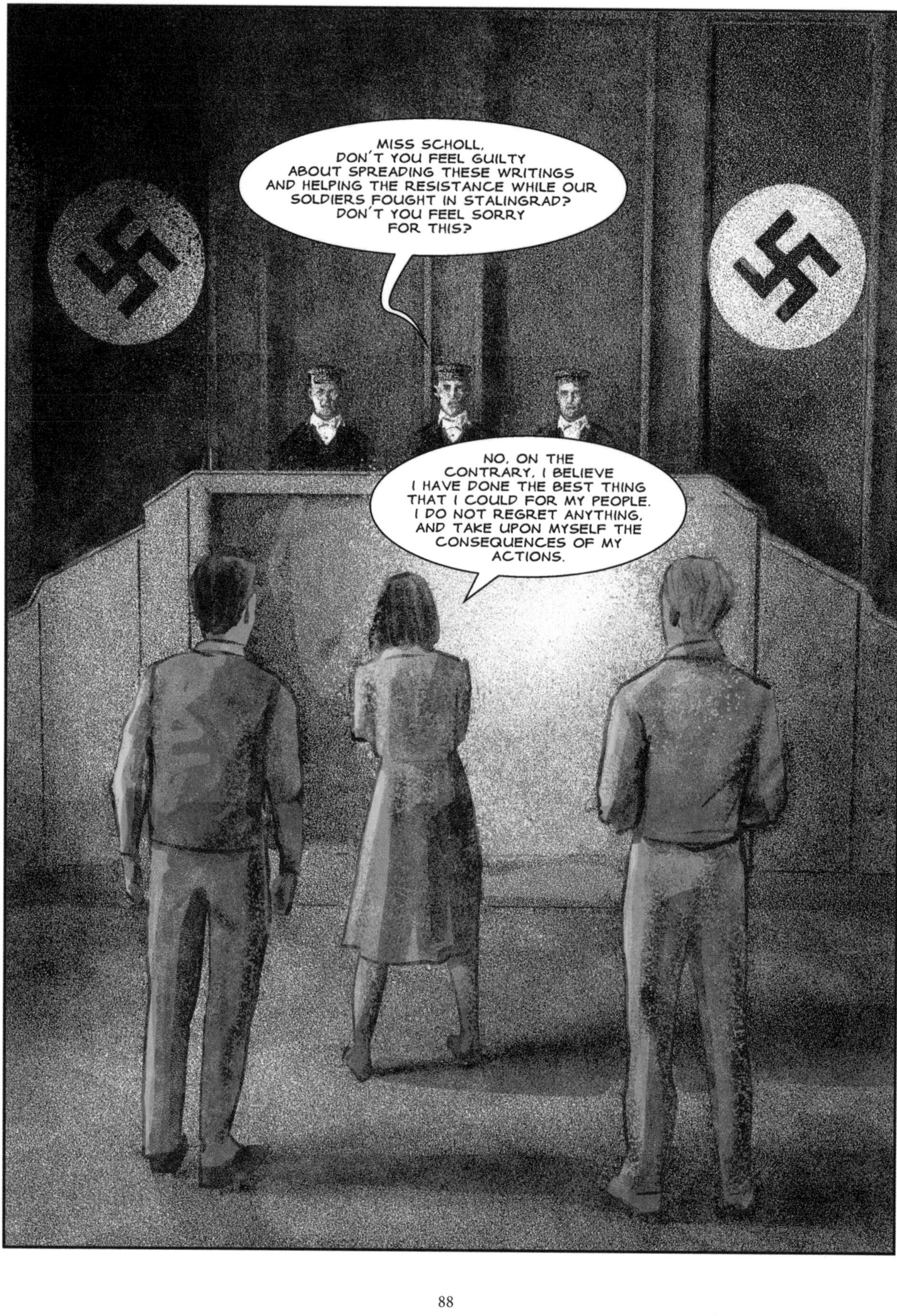
MISS SCHOLL, DON'T YOU FEEL GUILTY ABOUT SPREADING THESE WRITINGS AND HELPING THE RESISTANCE WHILE OUR SOLDIERS FOUGHT IN STALINGRAD? DON'T YOU FEEL SORRY FOR THIS?
NO, ON THE CONTRARY, I BELIEVE I HAVE DONE THE BEST THING THAT I COULD FOR MY PEOPLE. I DO NOT REGRET ANYTHING, AND TAKE UPON MYSELF THE CONSEQUENCES OF MY ACTIONS.

4:40 P.M.

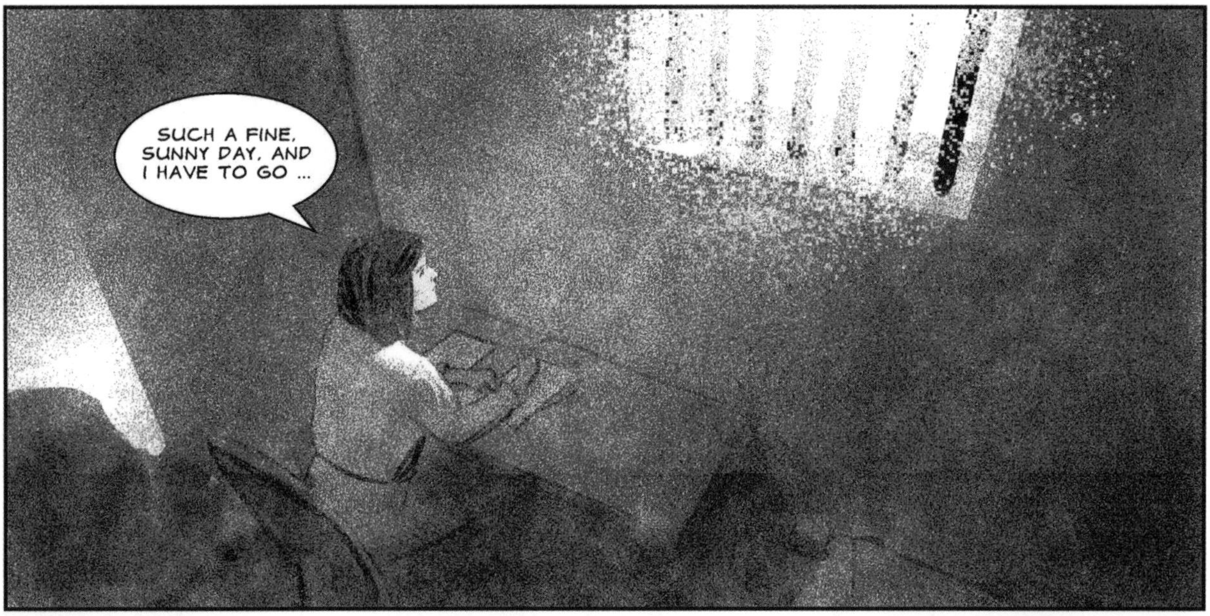
SUCH A FINE, SUNNY DAY, AND I HAVE TO GO ...

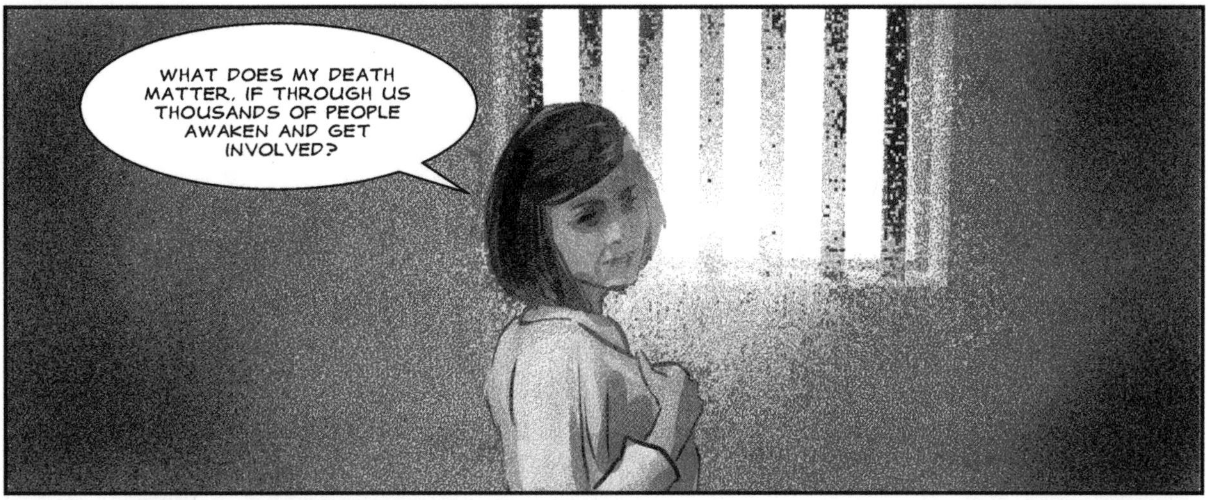
WHAT DOES MY DEATH MATTER, IF THROUGH US THOUSANDS OF PEOPLE AWAKEN AND GET INVOLVED?

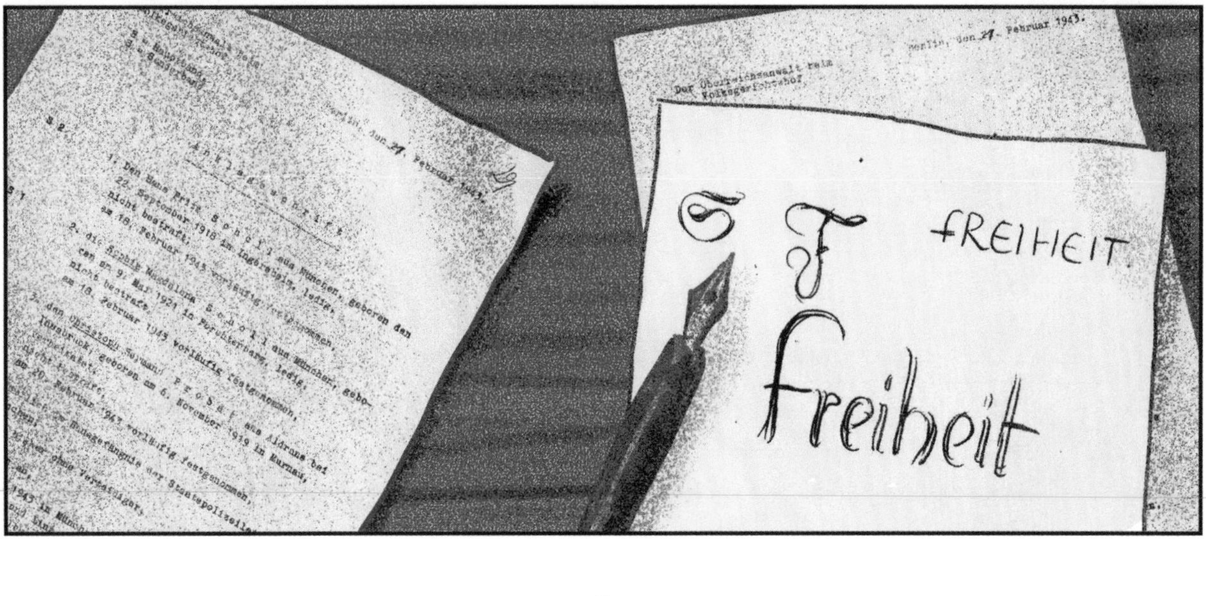
FREIHEIT.
freiheit

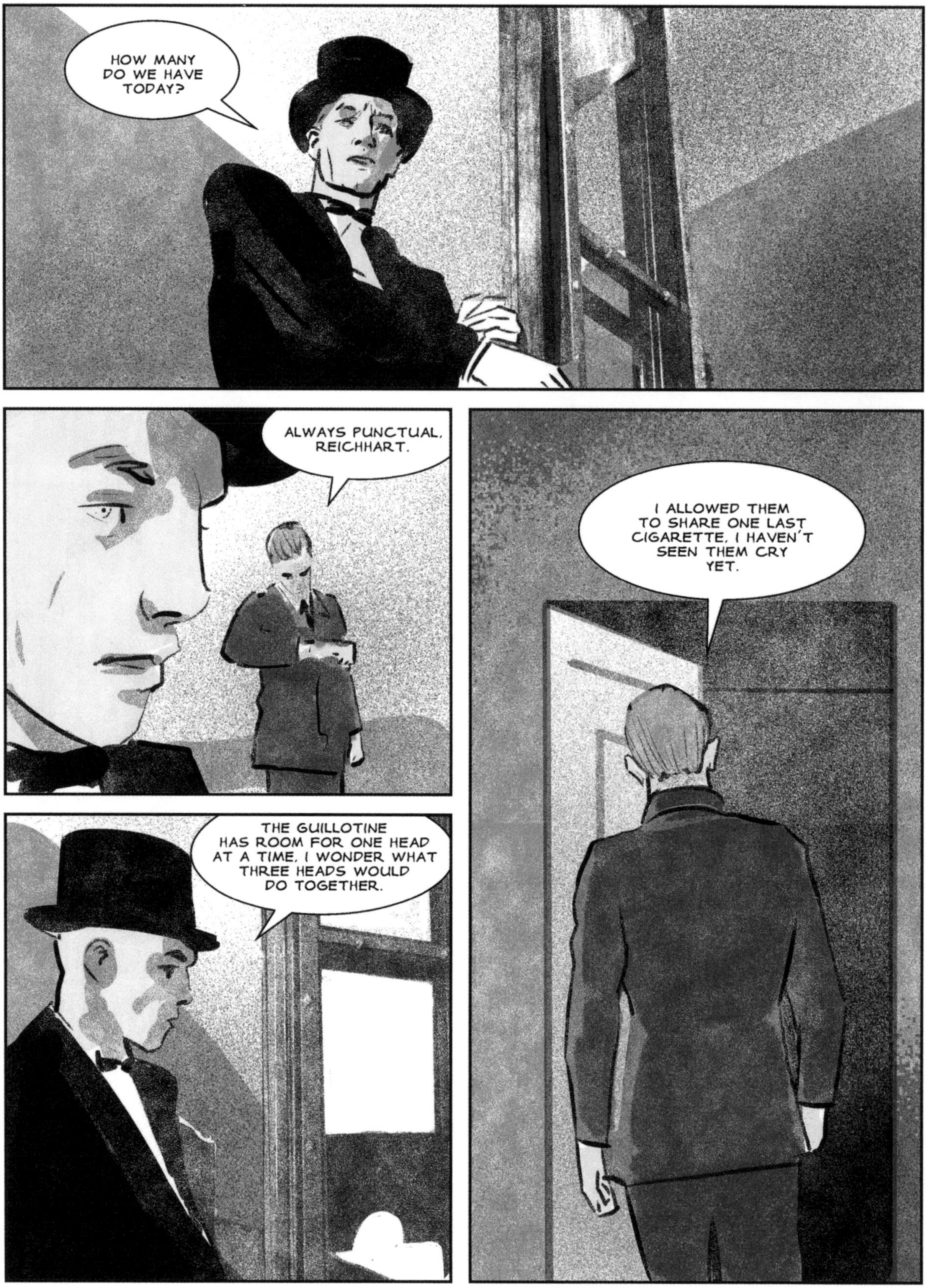
HOW MANY DO WE HAVE TODAY?
ALWAYS PUNCTUAL, REICHHART.
THE GUILLOTINE HAS ROOM FOR ONE HEAD AT A TIME, I WONDER WHAT THREE HEADS WOULD DO TOGETHER.
I ALLOWED THEM TO SHARE ONE LAST CIGARETTE, I HAVEN'T SEEN THEM CRY YET.

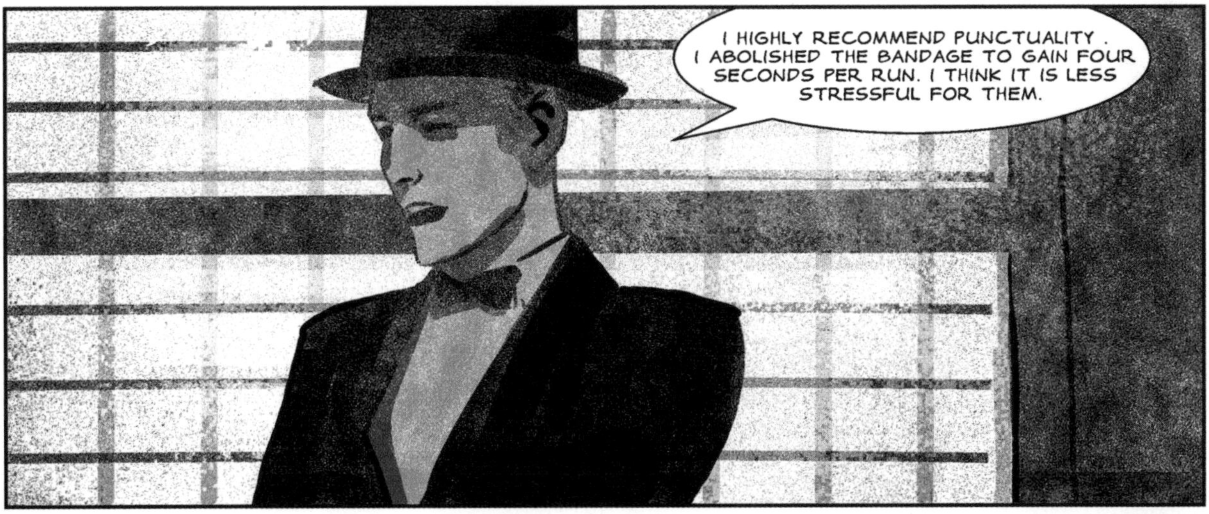
I HIGHLY RECOMMEND PUNCTUALITY . I ABOLISHED THE BANDAGE TO GAIN FOUR SECONDS PER RUN. I THINK IT IS LESS STRESSFUL FOR THEM.

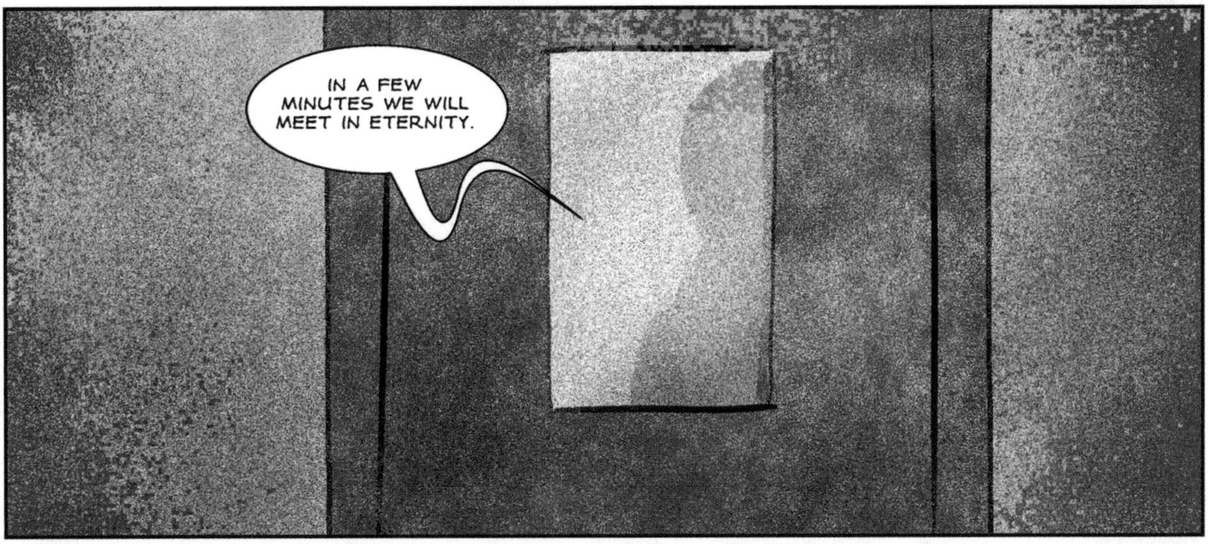
IN A FEW MINUTES WE WILL MEET IN ETERNITY.

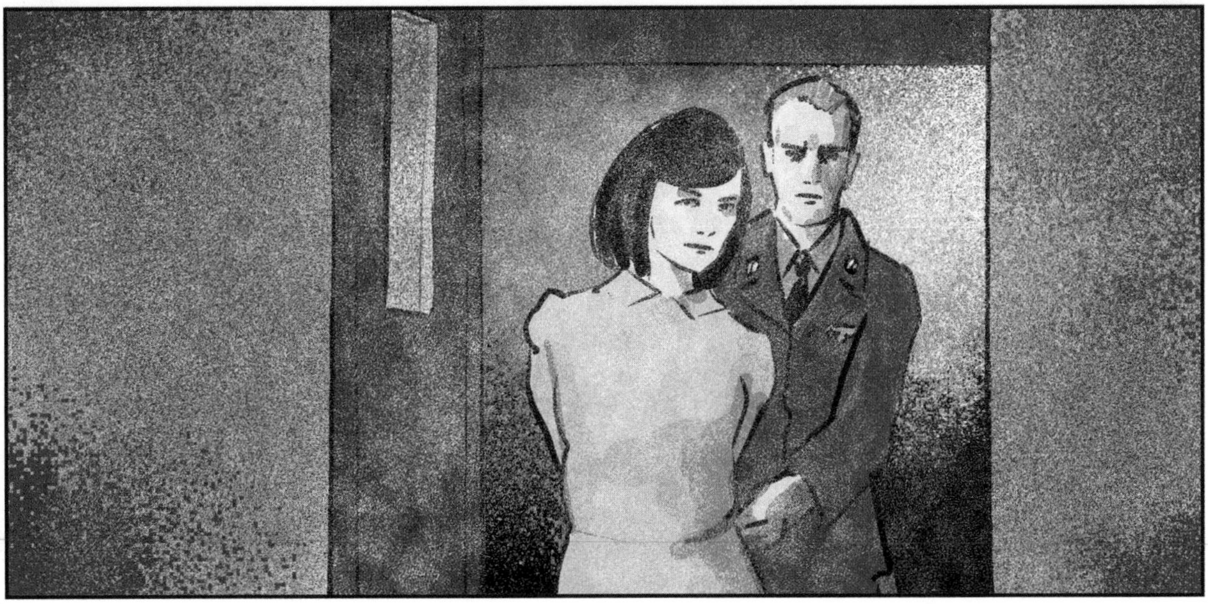

Sophie Scholl - Execution date February 22, 1943

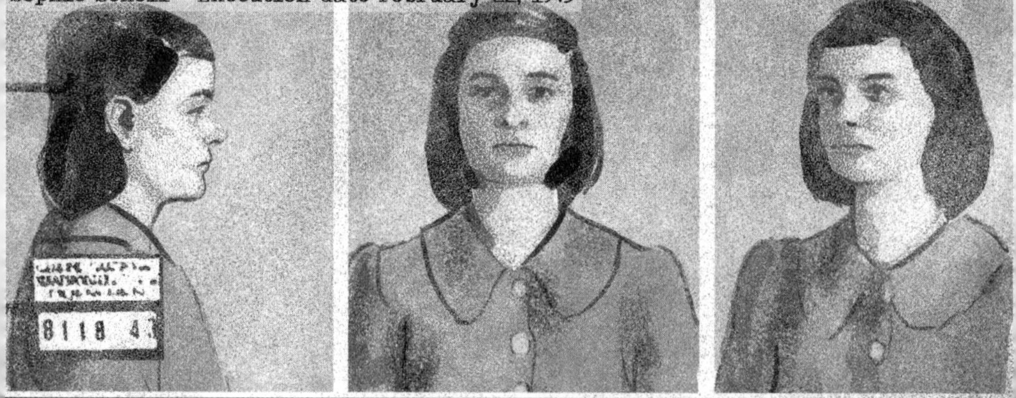
8118 4

Hans Scholl - Execution date February 22, 1943

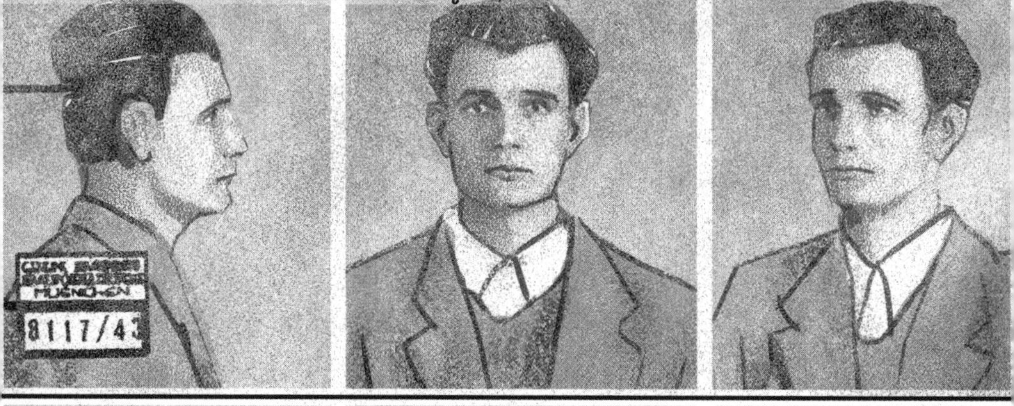
MUENCHEN
8117/43

Christoph Probst - Execution date February 22, 1943

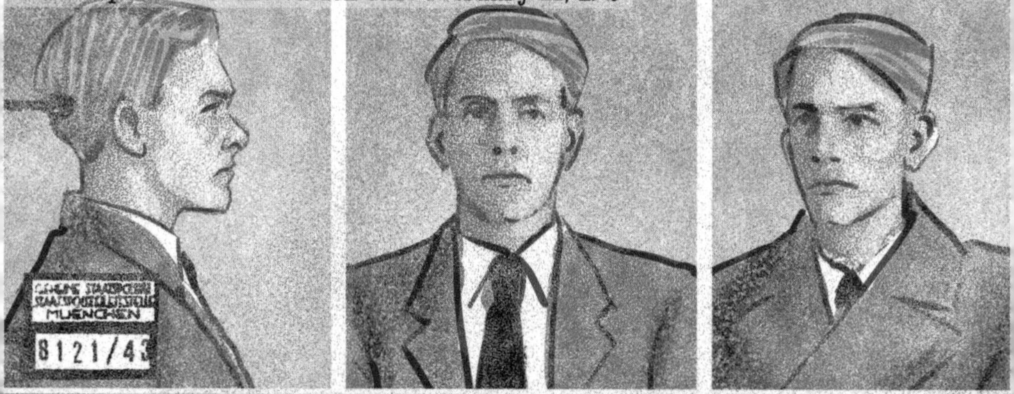
MUENCHEN
8121/43

ecution report Sophie Scholl:
17:00 the executioner Reichhart released the blade, which immediately severed the he the condemned from her trunk. The prison doctor confirmed that death had occurred. demned was calm and collected. Time elapsed between transfer to executioner and bla op: 6 seconds. The whole execution process, which took place without incident, lasted inutes, 48 seconds.

ecution report Hans Scholl:
17:02 p.m. the executioner Reichhart released the blade, which immediately severed the the condemned from the trunk. The prison doctor confirmed that death had taken plac e condemned was calm and collected. His last words were "Long live freedom." Time betw nsfer to executioner and blade drop: 7 seconds. The whole execution process, which to [illegible]

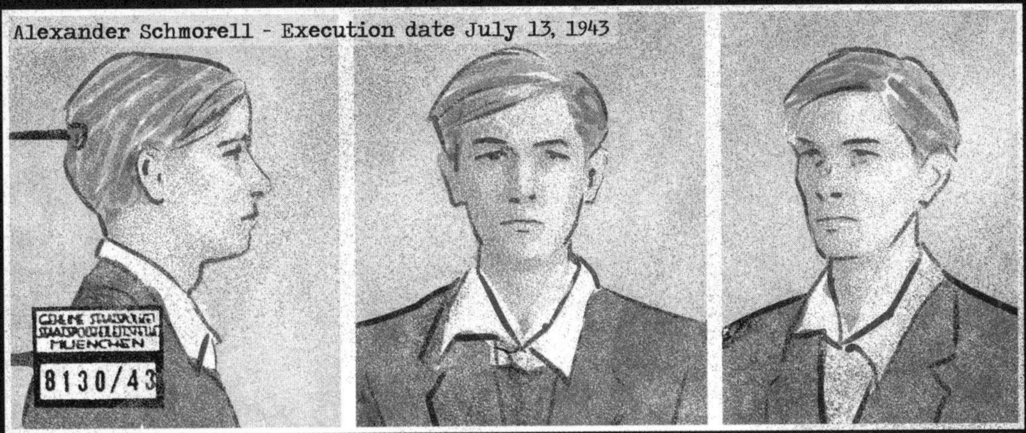
Alexander Schmorell - Execution date July 13, 1943
MUENCHEN
8130/43

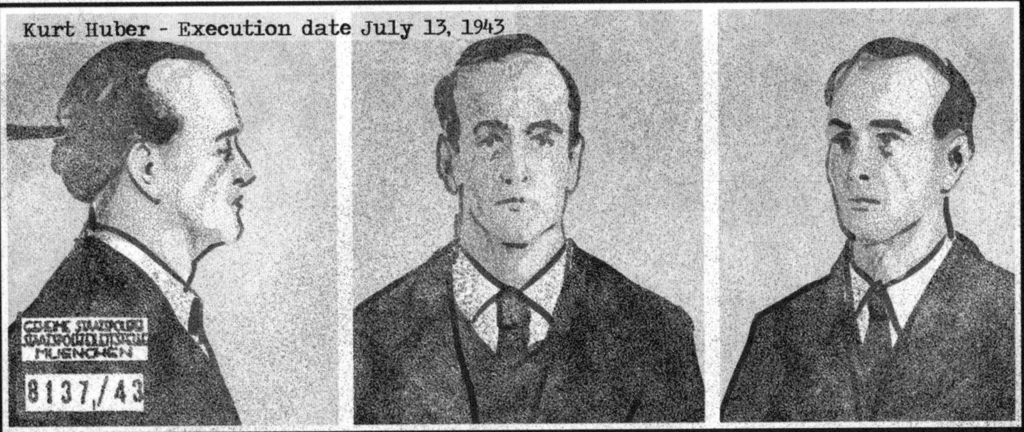
Kurt Huber - Execution date July 13, 1943
MUENCHEN
8137/43

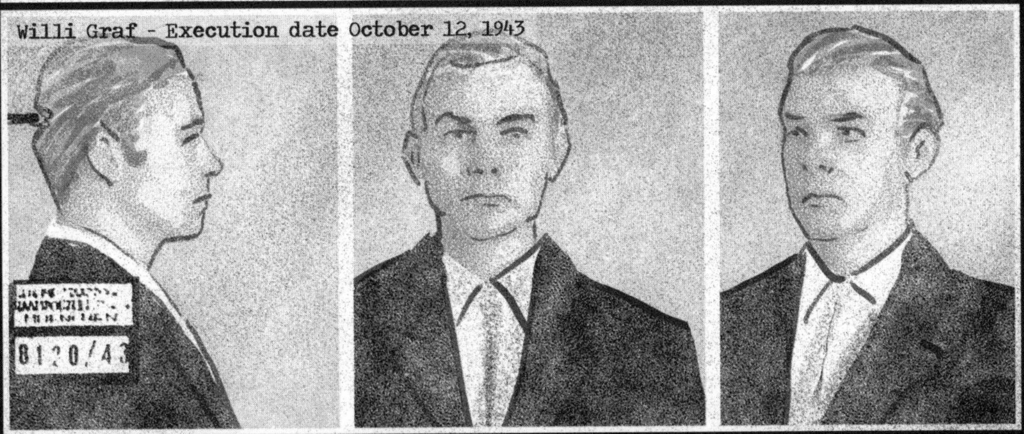
Willi Graf - Execution date October 12, 1943

Families are charged with an invoice of 600 marks for wear on the guillotine.

RAF AIRFIELD IN ENGLAND, JULY 1943

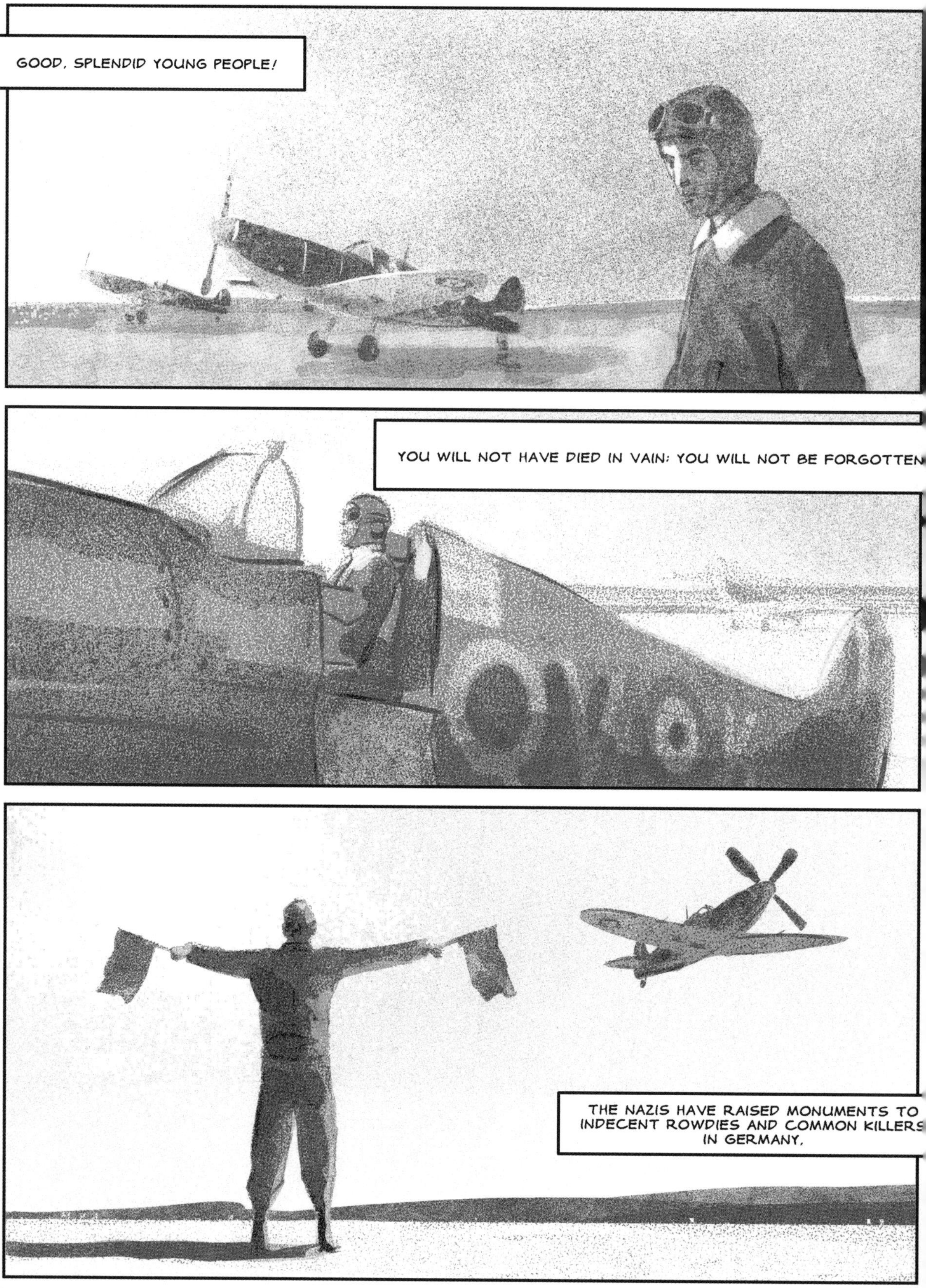
GOOD, SPLENDID YOUNG PEOPLE!
YOU WILL NOT HAVE DIED IN VAIN; YOU WILL NOT BE FORGOTTEN
THE NAZIS HAVE RAISED MONUMENTS TO INDECENT ROWDIES AND COMMON KILLERS IN GERMANY.

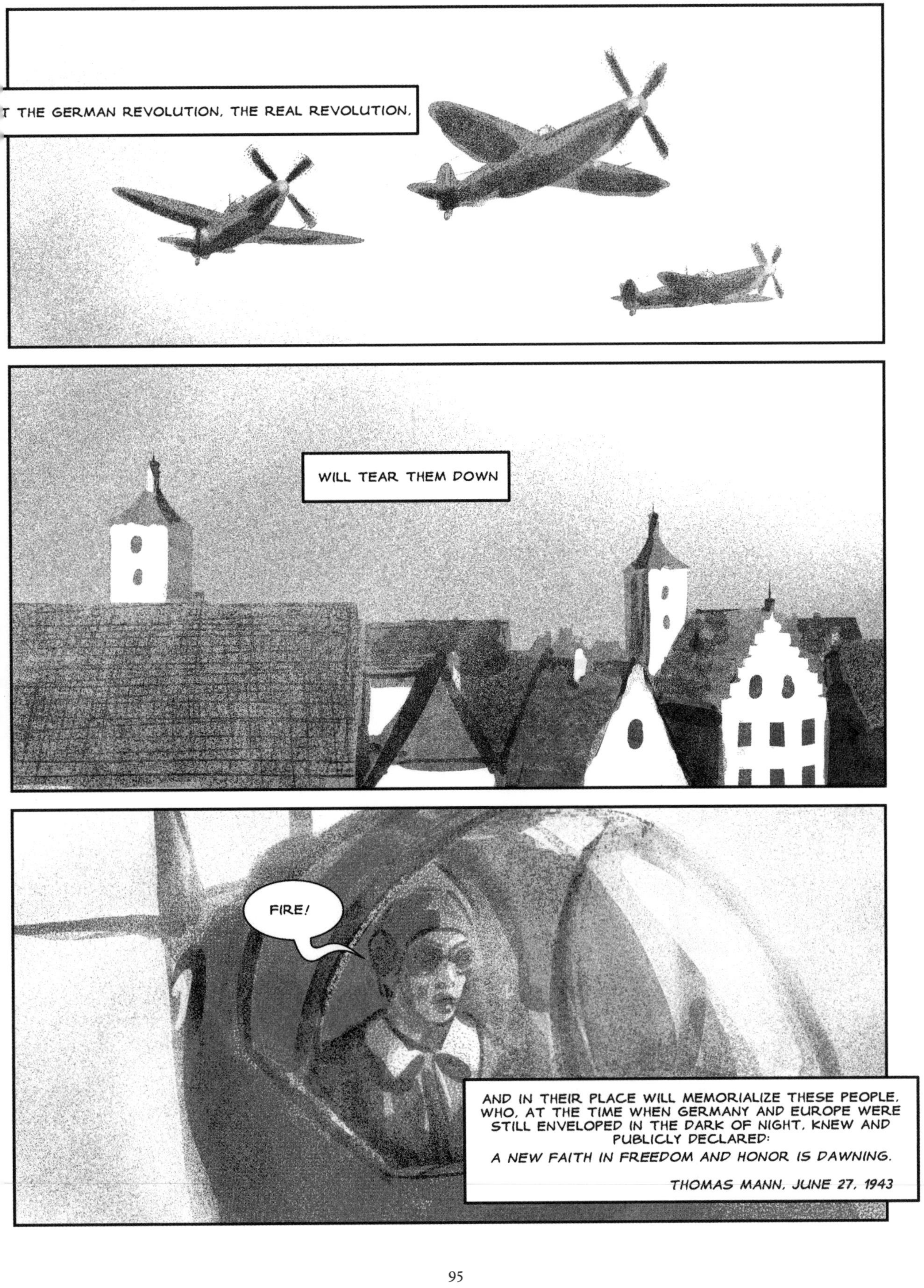
T THE GERMAN REVOLUTION, THE REAL REVOLUTION,
WILL TEAR THEM DOWN
FIRE!
AND IN THEIR PLACE WILL MEMORIALIZE THESE PEOPLE, WHO, AT THE TIME WHEN GERMANY AND EUROPE WERE STILL ENVELOPED IN THE DARK OF NIGHT, KNEW AND PUBLICLY DECLARED:
A NEW FAITH IN FREEDOM AND HONOR IS DAWNING.
THOMAS MANN, JUNE 27, 1943

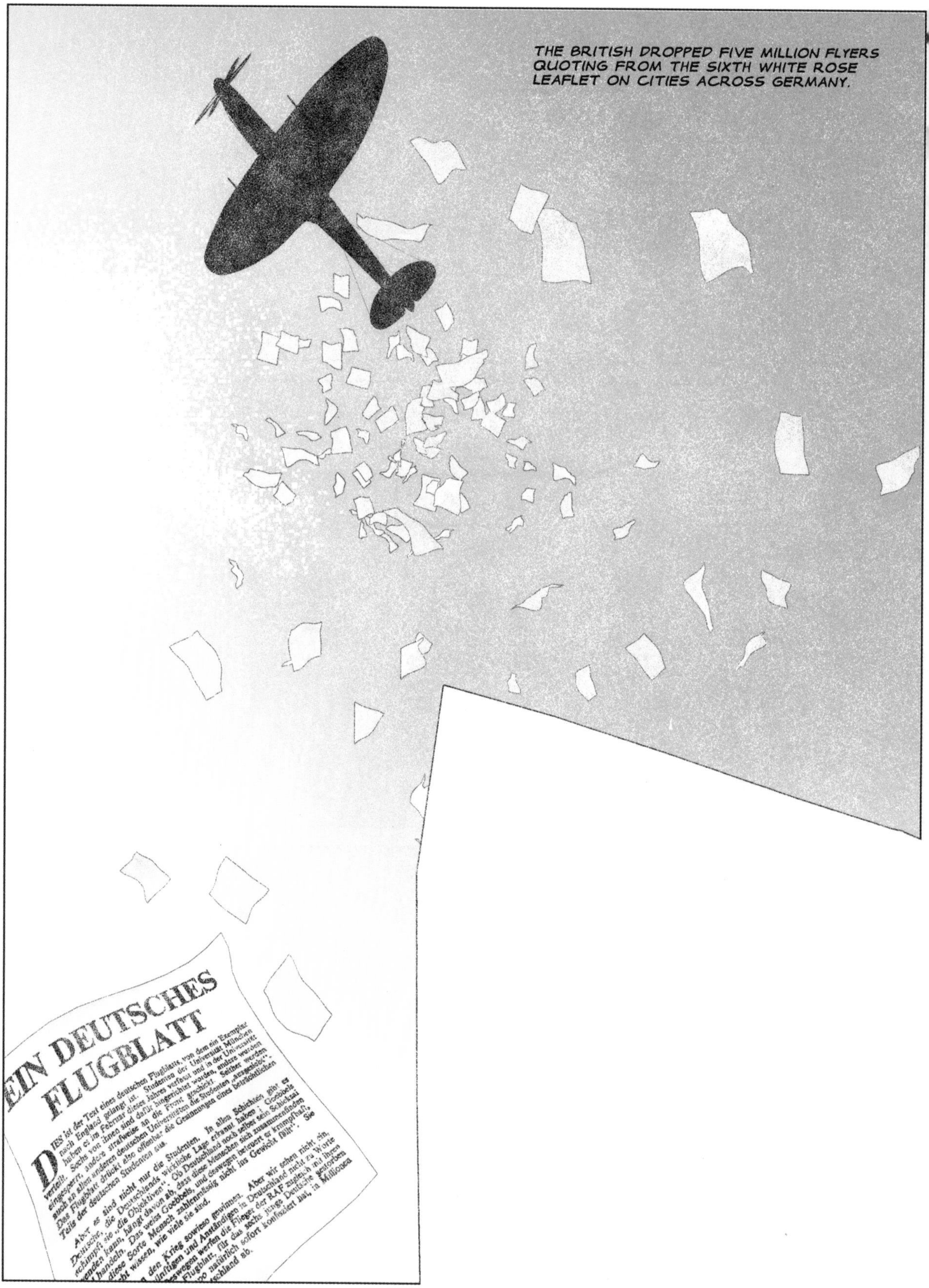

THE BRITISH DROPPED FIVE MILLION FLYERS QUOTING FROM THE SIXTH WHITE ROSE LEAFLET ON CITIES ACROSS GERMANY.
EIN DEUTSCHES FLUGBLATT

APPENDIX

Flugblätter der Weissen Rose.

I

Nichts ist eines Kulturvolkes unwürdiger, als sich ohne Widerstand von einer verantwortungslosen und dunklen Trieben ergebenen Herrscherclique "regieren" zu lassen. Ist es nicht so, dass sich jeder ehrliche Deutsche heute seiner Regierung schämt, und wer von uns ahnt das Ausmass der Schmach, die über uns und unsere Kinder kommen wird, wenn einst der Schleier von unseren Augen gefallen ist und die grauenvollsten und jegliches Mass unendlich überschreitenden Verbrechen ans Tageslicht treten? Wenn das deutsche Volk schon so in seinem tiefsten Wesen korrumpiert und zerfallen ist, dass es ohne eine Hand zu regen, im leichtsinnigen Vertrauen auf eine fragwürdige Gesetzmässigkeit der Geschichte, das Höchste, das ein Mensch besitzt, und das ihn über jede andere Kreatur erhöht, nämlich den freien Willen, preisgibt, die Freiheit des Menschen preisgibt, selbst mit einzugreifen in das Rad der Geschichte und es seiner vernünftigen Entscheidung unterzuordnen, wenn die Deutschen so jeder Individualität bar, schon so sehr zur geistlosen und feigen Masse geworden sind, dann, ja dann verdienen sie den Untergang.

Goethe spricht von den Deutschen als einem tragischen Volke, gleich dem der Juden und Griechen, aber heute hat es eher den Anschein, als sei es eine seichte, willenlose Herde von Mitläufern, denen das Mark aus dem Innersten gesogen und nun ihres Kernes beraubt, bereit sind sich in den Untergang hetzen zu lassen. Es scheint so - aber es ist nicht so; vielmehr hat man in langsamer, trügerischer, systematischer Vergewaltigung jeden einzelnen in ein geistiges Gefängnis gesteckt, und erst, als er ~~darin gefesselt lag, wurde er sich des Verhängnisses bewusst.~~ Wenige nur erkannten das drohende Verderben, und der Lohn für ihr heroisches Mahnen war der Tod. Ueber das Schicksal dieser Menschen wird noch zu reden sein.

Wenn jeder wartet, bis der Andere anfängt, werden die Boten der rächenden Nemesis unaufhaltsam näher und näher rücken, dann wird auch das letze Opfer sinnlos in den Rachen des unersättlichen Dämons geworfen sein. Daher muss jeder Einzelne seiner Verantwortung als Mitglied der christlichen und abendländischen Kultur bewusst in dieser letzten Stunde sich wehren so viel er kann, arbeiten wider die Geisel der Menschheit, wider den Faschismus und jedes ihm ähnliche System des absoluten Staates. Leistet passiven Widerstand - W i d e r s t a n d - wo immer Ihr auch seid, verhindert das Weiterlaufen dieser ateistischen Kriegsmaschine, ehe es zu spät ist, ehe die letzten Städte ein Trümmerhaufen sind, gleich Köln, und ehe die letzte Jugend des Volkes irgendwo für die Hybris eines Untermenschen verblutet ist. Vergesst nicht, dass ein jedes Volk diejenige Regierung verdient, die es erträgt!

Aus Friedrich Schiller, "Die Gesetzgebung des Lykurgus und Solon":

"....Gegen seinen eigenen Zweck gehalten, ist die Gestzgebung des Lykurgus ein Meisterstück der Staats- und Menschenkunde. Er wollte einen mächtigen, in sich selbst gegründeten, unzerstörbaren Staat; politische Stärke und Dauerhaftigkeit waren das Ziel, wonach er strebte, und dieses Ziel hat er so weit erreicht, als unter seinen Umständen möglich war. Aber hält man den Zweck, welchen Lykurgus sich vorsetzte, gegen den Zweck der Menschheit, so muss eine tiefe Missbilligung an die Stelle der Bewunderung treten, die uns der erste, flüchtige Blick abgewonnen hat. Alles darf dem Besten des Staates zum Opfer gebracht werden, nur dasjenige nicht, dem der Staat selbst nur als ein Mittel dient. Der Staat selbst ist niemals Zweck, er ist nur wichtig als eine Bedingung, unter welcher der Zweck der Menschheit erfülltwerden kann, und dieser Zweck der Menschheit ist kein anderer, als Ausbildung aller Kräfte des Menschen, Fort-

Front page of the first leaflet

Nothing is so unworthy of a civilized nation as allowing itself to be governed without opposition by an irresponsible clique that has yielded to base instinct. It is certain that today every honest German is ashamed of the government. Who among us has any conception of the dimensions of shame that will befall us and our children when one day the veil has fallen from our eyes and the most horrible of crimes – crimes that infinitely outdistance every human measure – reach the light of day? If the German people are already so corrupted and spiritually crushed that they do not raise a hand, frivolously trusting in a questionable faith in lawful order of history; if they surrender man's highest principle, that which raises him above all God's other creatures, his free will; if they abandon the will to take decisive action and turn the wheel of history and thus subject it to their own rational decision; if they are so devoid of all individuality, having already gone so far along the road toward turning into a spiritless and cowardly mass – then, yes, they deserve their downfall.

Goethe speaks of the Germans as a tragic people, like the Jews and the Greeks, but today it would appear rather that they are a spineless, will-less herd of hangers-on, who now – the marrow sucked out of their bones, robbed of their center of stability – are waiting to be hounded to their destruction. So it seems – but it is not so. Rather, by means of gradual, treacherous, systematic abuse, the system has put every individual into a spiritual prison. Only now, finding themselves lying in fetters, have they become aware of their fate. Only a few recognized the threat of ruin, and the reward for their heroic warning was death. We will have more to say about the fate of these persons.

If everyone waits until someone else makes a start, the messengers of avenging Nemesis will come steadily closer; then even the last victim will have been cast senselessly into the maw of the insatiable demon. Therefore every individual, conscious of his responsibility as a member of Christian and Western civilization, must defend himself as best he can at this late hour, he must work against the scourges of mankind, against fascism and any similar system of totalitarianism.

Offer passive resistance – *resistance* – wherever you may be, forestall the spread of this atheistic war machine before it is too late, before the last cities have been reduced to rubble like Cologne, and before the nation's last young man has given his blood on some battlefield for the hubris of a subhuman. Do not forget that every people deserves the regime it is willing to endure!

Leaflet translations by Arthur R. Schultz

From Freidrich Schiller's "The Lawgiving of Lycurgus and Solon":

Viewed in relation to its purposes, the law code of Lycurgus is a masterpiece of political science and knowledge of human nature. He desired a powerful, unassailable state, firmly established on its own principles. Political effectiveness and permanence were the goal toward which he strove, and he attained this goal to the full extent possible under the circumstances. But if one compares the purpose Lycurgus had in view with the purposes of humankind, then a deep abhorrence takes the place of the approbation which we felt at first glance. Anything may be sacrificed to the good of the state except that end for which the state serves as a means. The state is never an end in itself; it is important only as a condition under which the purpose of humankind can be attained, and this purpose is none other than the development of all man's power, his progress and improvement. If a state prevents the development of the capacities which reside in man, if it interferes with the progress of the human spirit, then it is reprehensible and injurious, no matter how excellently devised, how perfect in its own way. Its very permanence in that case amounts more to a reproach than to a basis for fame; it becomes a prolonged evil, and the longer it endures, the more harmful it is. . . .

At the price of all moral feeling a political system was set up, and the resources of the state were mobilized to that end. In Sparta there was no conjugal love, no mother love, no filial devotion, no friendship; people were citizens only, and all virtue was civic virtue.

A law of the state made it the duty of Spartans to be inhumane to their slaves; in these unhappy victims of war humanity itself was insulted and mistreated. In the Spartan code of law the dangerous principle was promulgated that people are to be looked upon as means and not as ends – and the foundation of natural law and of morality were destroyed by that law. . . .

What an admirable sight is afforded, by contrast, by the rough soldier Gaius Marcius in his camp before Rome, when he renounced vengeance and victory because he could not endure to see a mother's tears! . . .

The state [of Lycurgus] could endure only under the one condition: that the spirit of the people remained quiescent. Hence it could be maintained only if it failed to achieve the highest, the sole purpose of a state.

From Goethe's *The Awakening of Epimenides*, Act II, Scene 4:

SPIRITS:
Though he who has boldly risen from the abyss
Through an iron will and cunning
May conquer half the world,
Yet to the abyss he must return.
Already a terrible fear has seized him;
In vain he will resist!
And all who still stand with him
Must perish in his fall.

HOPE:
Now I find my good men
Are gathered in the night,
To wait in silence, not to sleep.
And the glorious word of liberty
They whisper and murmur,
Till in unaccustomed strangeness,
On the steps of our temple
Once again in delight they cry:

Freedom! Freedom! Freedom!

Please make as many copies of this leaflet as you can and distribute them.

It is impossible to engage in intellectual discourse with National Socialism because it is not an intellectually defensible program. It is false to speak of a National Socialist philosophy, for if there were such an entity, one would have to try by means of analysis and discussion either to prove its validity or to combat it. In actuality, however, we face a totally different situation. At its very inception this movement depended on the deception and betrayal of one's fellow man; even at that time it was inwardly corrupt and could support itself only by constant lies. After all, Hitler states in an early edition of "his" book (a book written in the worst German I have ever read, in spite of the fact that it has been elevated to the position of the Bible in this nation of poets and thinkers): "It is unbelievable, to what extent one must betray a people in order to rule it." If at the start this cancerous growth in the nation was not particularly noticeable, it was only because there were still enough forces at work that operated for the good, so that it was kept under control. As it grew larger, however, and finally in an ultimate spurt of growth attained ruling power, the tumor broke open, as it were, and infected the whole body. The greater part of its former opponents went into hiding. The German intellectuals fled to their cellars, there, like plants struggling in the dark, away from light and sun, gradually to choke to death. Now the end is at hand. Now it is our task to find one another again, to spread information from person to person, to keep a steady purpose, and to allow ourselves no rest until the last man is persuaded of the urgent need of his struggle against this system. When thus a wave of unrest goes through the land, when "it is in the air," when many join the cause, then in a great final effort this system can be shaken off. After all, an end in terror is preferable to terror without end.

We are not in a position to draw up a final judgment about the meaning of our history. But if this catastrophe can be used to further the public welfare, it will be only by virtue of the fact that we are cleansed by suffering; that we yearn for the light in the midst of deepest night, summon our strength, and finally help in shaking off the yoke which weighs on our world.

We do not want to discuss here the question of the Jews, nor do we want in this leaflet to compose a defense or apology. No, only by way of example do we want to cite the fact that since the conquest of Poland *three hundred thousand* Jews have been murdered in this country in the most bestial way. Here we see the most frightful crime against human dignity, a crime that is unparalleled in the whole of history. For Jews, too, are human beings – no matter what position we take with respect to the Jewish question – and a crime of this dimension has been perpetrated against human beings. Someone may say that the Jews deserve their fate. This assertion would be a monstrous impertinence; but let us assume that someone said this – what position has he then taken toward the fact that the entire Polish aristocratic youth is being annihilated? (May God grant that this program has not yet fully achieved its aim as yet!) All male offspring of the houses of the nobility between the ages of fifteen and twenty were transported to concentration camps in Germany and sentenced to forced labor, and all the girls of this age group were sent to Norway, into the bordellos of the SS! Why tell you these things, since you are fully aware of them – or if not of these, then of other equally grave crimes committed by this frightful subhumanity? Because here we touch on a problem which involves us deeply and forces us all to take thought. Why do the German people behave so apathetically in the face of all these abominable crimes, crimes so unworthy of the human race? Hardly anyone thinks about that. It is accepted as fact and put out of mind. The German people slumber on in their dull, stupid sleep and encourage these fascist criminals; they give them the opportunity to carry on their depredations; and of course they do so. Is this a sign that the Germans are brutalized in their simplest human feelings, that no chord within them cries out at the sight of such deeds, that they have sunk into a fatal consciencelessness from which they will never, never awake? It seems to be so, and will certainly be so, if the German does not at last start up out of his stupor, if he does not protest wherever and whenever he can against this clique of criminals, if he shows no sympathy for these hundreds of thousands of victims. He must evidence not only sympathy; no, much more: a sense of *complicity* in guilt. For through his apathetic behavior he gives these evil men the opportunity to act as they do; he tolerates this "government" which has taken upon itself such an infinitely great burden of guilt; indeed, he himself is to blame for the fact that it came about at all! Each man wants to be exonerated of a guilt of this kind, each one continues on his way with the most placid, the calmest conscience. But he cannot be exonerated; he is *guilty, guilty, guilty*! It is not too late, however, to do away with this most reprehensible of all miscarriages of government, so as to avoid being burdened with even greater guilt. Now, when in recent years our eyes have been opened, when we know exactly who our adversary is, it is high time to root out this brown horde. Up until the outbreak of the war the larger part of the German people was blinded; the Nazis did not show themselves in their true aspect. But now, now that we have recognized them for what they are, it must be the sole and first duty, the holiest duty of every German to destroy these beasts.

If the people are barely aware that the government exists, they are happy. When the government is felt to be oppressive, they are broken.

Good fortune, alas! builds itself upon misery. Good fortune, alas! is the mask of misery. What will come of this? We cannot foresee the end. Order is upset and turns to disorder, good becomes evil. The people are confused. Is it not so, day in, day out, from the beginning?

The wise man is therefore angular, though he does not injure others; he has sharp corners, though he does not harm; he is upright but not gruff. He is clearminded, but he does not try to be brilliant.

LAO-TZU

Whoever undertakes to rule the kingdom and to shape it according to his whim – I foresee that he will fail to reach his goal. That is all.

The kingdom is a living being. It cannot be constructed, in truth! He who tries to manipulate it will spoil it, he who tries to put it under his power will lose it.

Therefore: Some creatures go out in front, others follow, some have warm breath, others cold, some are strong, some weak, some attain abundance, others succumb.

The wise man will accordingly forswear excess, he will avoid arrogance and not overreach.

LAO-TZU

Please make as many copies as possible of this leaflet and distribute them.

Salus publica suprema lex

All ideal forms of government are utopias. A state cannot be constructed on a purely theoretical basis; rather, it must grow and ripen in the way an individual human being matures. But we must not forget that at the starting point of every civilization the state was already there in rudimentary form. The family is as old as humanity, and out of this initial bond humans, endowed with reason, created for themselves a state founded on justice, whose highest law was the common good. The state should exist as a parallel to the divine order, and the highest of all utopias, the *civitas dei*, is the model which in the end it should approximate. Here we will not pass judgment on the many possible forms of the state – democracy, constitutional monarchy, and so on. But one matter needs to be brought out clearly and unambiguously. Every individual human being has a claim to a useful and just state, a state which secures freedom of the individual as well as the good of the whole. For, according to God's will, people are intended to pursue their natural goal, their earthly happiness, in self-reliance and self-chosen activity, freely and independently within the community of life and work of the nation.

But our present "state" is the dictatorship of evil. "Oh, we've known that for a long time," I hear you object, "and it isn't necessary to bring that to our attention again." But, I ask you, if you know that, why do you not bestir yourselves, why do you allow these men who are in power to rob you step by step, openly and in secret, of one domain of your rights after another, until one day nothing, nothing at all will be left but a mechanized state system presided over by criminals and drunks? Is your spirit already so crushed by abuse that you forget it is your right – or rather, your *moral duty* – to eliminate this system? But if a man no longer can summon the strength to demand his right, then it is absolutely certain that he will perish. We would deserve to be dispersed through the earth like dust before the wind if we do not muster our powers at this late hour and finally find the courage which up to now we have lacked. Do not hide your cowardice behind a cloak of expediency, for with every new day that you hesitate, failing to oppose this offspring of hell, your guilt, as in a parabolic curve, grows higher and higher.

Many, perhaps most, of the readers of these leaflets do not see clearly how they can practice an effective opposition. They do not see any avenues open to them. We want to try to show them that everyone is in a position to contribute to the overthrow of this system. It is not possible through solitary withdrawal, in the manner of embittered hermits, to prepare the ground for the overturn of this "government" or bring about the revolution at the earliest possible moment. No, it can be done only by the cooperation of many convinced, energetic people – people who are agreed as to the means they must use to attain their goal. We have no great number of choices as to these means. The only one available is *passive resistance*.

The meaning and the goal of passive resistance is to topple National Socialism, and in this struggle we must not recoil from any course, any action, whatever its nature. At *all* points we must oppose National Socialism, wherever it is open to attack. We must soon bring this monster of a state to an end. A victory of fascist Germany in this war would have immeasurable, frightful consequences. The military victory over Bolshevism dare not become the primary concern of the Germans. The defeat of the Nazis must *unconditionally* be the first order of business. The greater necessity of this latter requirement will be discussed in one of our forthcoming leaflets.

And now every convinced opponent of National Socialism must ask himself how he can fight against the present "state" in the most effective way, how he can strike it the most telling blows. Through passive resistance, without a doubt. We cannot provide each man with the blueprint for his acts, we can only suggest them in general terms, and he alone will find the way of achieving this end:

Sabotage in armament plants and war industries, sabotage at all gatherings, rallies, public ceremonies, and organizations of the National Socialist Party. Obstruction of the smooth functioning of the war machine (a machine for war that goes on solely to shore up and perpetuate the National Socialist Party and its dictatorship). *Sabotage* in all the areas of science and scholarship which further the continuation of the war – whether in universities, technical schools, laboratories, research institutes, or technical bureaus. *Sabotage* in all cultural institutions which could potentially enhance the "prestige" of the fascists among the people. *Sabotage* in all branches of the arts which have even the slightest dependence on National Socialism or render it service. *Sabotage* in all publications, all newspapers, that are in the pay of the "government" and that defend its ideology and aid in disseminating the brown lie. Do not give a penny to public drives (even when they are conducted under the pretense of charity). For this is only a disguise. In reality the proceeds aid neither the Red Cross nor the needy. The government does not need this money; it is not financially interested in these money drives. After all, the presses run continuously to manufacture any desired amount of paper currency. But the populace must be kept constantly under tension, the pressure of the bit must not be allowed to slacken! Do not contribute to the collections of metal, textiles, and the like. Try to convince all your acquaintances, including those in the lower social classes, of the senselessness of continuing, of the hopelessness of this war; of our spiritual and economic enslavement at the hands of the National Socialists; of the destruction of all moral and religious values; and urge them to *passive resistance*!

Aristotle, *Politics*: ". . . and further, it is part [of the nature of tyranny] to strive to see to it that nothing is kept hidden of that which any subject says or does, but that everywhere he will be spied upon, . . . and further, to set man against man and friend against friend, and the common people against the privileged and the wealthy. Also it is part of these tyrannical measures, to keep the subjects poor, in order to pay the guards and soldiers, and so that they will be occupied with earning their livelihood and will have neither leisure nor opportunity to engage in conspiratorial acts. . . . Further, [to levy] such taxes on income as were imposed in Syracuse, for under Dionysius the citizens gladly paid out their whole fortunes in taxes within five years. Also, the tyrant is inclined constantly to ferment wars."

Please duplicate and distribute!

There is an ancient maxim that we repeat to our children: "He who won't listen will have to feel." But a wise child will not burn his fingers the second time on a hot stove. In the past weeks Hitler has chalked up successes in Africa and in Russia. In consequence, optimism on the one hand and distress and pessimism on the other have grown within the German people with a rapidity quite inconsistent with traditional German apathy. On all sides one hears among Hitler's opponents – the better segments of the population – exclamations of despair, words of disappointment and discouragement, often ending with the question: "Will Hitler now, after all . . . ?"

Meanwhile the German offensive against Egypt has ground to a halt. Rommel has to bide his time in a dangerously exposed position. But the push into the East proceeds. This apparent success has been purchased at the most horrible expense of human life, and so it can no longer be counted an advantage. Therefore we must warn against *all* optimism.

Neither Hitler nor Goebbels can have counted the dead. In Russia thousands are lost daily. It is the time of the harvest, and the reaper cuts into the ripe grain with wide strokes. Mourning takes up her abode in the country cottages, and there is no one to dry the tears of the mothers. Yet Hitler feeds with lies those people whose most precious belongings he has stolen and whom he has driven to a meaningless death.

Every word that comes from Hitler's mouth is a lie. When he says peace, he means war, and when he blasphemously uses the name of the Almighty, he means the power of evil, the fallen angel, Satan. His mouth is the foul-smelling maw of hell, and his might is at bottom accursed. True, we must conduct a struggle against the National Socialist terrorist state with rational means; but whoever today still doubts the reality of the existence of demonic powers has failed by a wide margin to understand the metaphysical background of this war. Behind the concrete, the visible events, behind all objective, logical considerations, we find the irrational element: the struggle against the demon, against the servants of the Antichrist. Everywhere and at all times demons have been lurking in the dark, waiting for the moment when man is weak; when of his own volition he leaves his place in the order of creation as founded for him by God in freedom; when he yields to the force of evil, separates himself from the powers of a higher order; and after voluntarily taking the first step, he is driven on to the next and the next at a furiously accelerating rate. Everywhere and at all times of greatest trial men have appeared, prophets and saints who cherished their freedom, who preached the One God and who with his help brought the people to a reversal of their downward course. Man is free, to be sure, but without the true God he is defenseless against the principle of evil. He is like a rudderless ship, at the mercy of the storm, an infant without his mother, a cloud dissolving into thin air.

I ask you, you as a Christian wrestling for the preservation of your greatest treasure, whether you hesitate, whether you incline toward intrigue, calculation, or procrastination in the hope that someone else will raise his arm in your defense? Has God not given you the strength, the will to fight? We *must* attack evil where it is strongest, and it is strongest in the power of Hitler.

> So I returned, and considered all the oppressions that are done under the sun: and behold the tears of such as were oppressed, and they had no comforter; and on the side of their oppressors there was power; but they had no comforter. Wherefore I praised the dead which are already dead more than the living which are yet alive.
>
> ECCLESIASTES 4

> True anarchy is the generative element of religion. Out of the annihilation of every positive element she lifts her gloriously radiant countenance as the founder of a new world. . . . If Europe were about to awaken again, if a state of states, a teaching of political science were at hand! Should hierarchy then . . . be the principle of the union of states? Blood will stream over Europe until the nations become aware of the frightful madness which drives them in circles. And then, struck by celestial music and made gentle, they approach their former altars all together, hear about the works of peace, and hold a great celebration of peace with fervent tears before the smoking altars. Only religion can reawaken Europe, establish the rights of the peoples, and install Christianity in new splendor visibly on earth in its office as guarantor of peace.
>
> NOVALIS

We wish expressly to point out that the White Rose is not in the pay of any foreign power. Though we know that National Socialist power must be broken by military means, we are trying to achieve a renewal from within of the severely wounded German spirit. This rebirth must be preceded, however, by the clear recognition of all the guilt with which the German people have burdened themselves, and by an uncompromising battle against Hitler and his all too many minions, party members, Quislings, and the like. With total brutality the chasm that separates the better portion of the nation from everything that is identified with National Socialism must be opened wide. For Hitler and his followers there is no punishment on this earth commensurate with their crimes. But out of love for coming generations we must make an example after the conclusion of the war, so that no one will ever again have the slightest urge to try a similar action. And do not forget the petty scoundrels in this regime; note their names, so that none will go free! They should not find it possible, having had their part in these abominable crimes, at the last minute to rally to another flag and then act as if nothing had happened!

To set you at rest, we add that the addresses of the readers of the White Rose are not recorded in writing. They were picked at random from directories.

We will not be silent. We are your bad conscience. The White Rose will not leave you in peace!

A Call to All Germans!

The war is approaching its destined end. As in the year 1918, the German government is trying to focus attention exclusively on the growing threat of submarine warfare, while in the East the armies are constantly in retreat and invasion is imminent in the West. Mobilization in the United States has not yet reached its climax, but already it exceeds anything that the world has ever seen. It has become a mathematical certainty that Hitler is leading the German people into the abyss. *Hitler cannot win the war; he can only prolong it.* The guilt of Hitler and his minions goes beyond all measure. Retribution comes closer and closer.

But what are the German people doing? They will not see and will not listen. Blindly they follow their seducers into ruin. *Victory at any price!* is inscribed on their banner. "I will fight to the last man," says Hitler – but in the meantime the war has already been lost.

Germans! Do you and your children want to suffer the same fate that befell the Jews? Do you want to be judged by the same standards as your traducers? Are we to be forever a nation which is hated and rejected by all humankind? No. Dissociate yourselves from National Socialist gangsters. Prove by your deeds that you think otherwise. A new war of liberation is about to begin. The better part of the nation will fight on our side. Cast off the cloak of indifference you have wrapped around you. Make the decision *before it is too late.* Do not believe the National Socialist propaganda which has driven the fear of Bolshevism into your bones. Do not believe that Germany's welfare is linked to the victory of National Socialism for good or ill. A criminal regime cannot achieve a German victory. Separate yourselves *in time* from everything connected with National Socialism. In the aftermath a terrible but just judgment will be meted out to those who stayed in hiding, who were cowardly and hesitant.

What can we learn from the outcome of this war – this war that never was a national war?

The imperialist ideology of force, from whatever side it comes, must be shattered for all time. A one-sided Prussian militarism must never again be allowed to assume power. Only in large-scale cooperation among the nations of Europe can the ground be prepared for reconstruction. Centralized hegemony, such as the Prussian state has tried to exercise in Germany and in Europe, must be cut down at its inception. The Germany of the future must be a federal state. At this juncture only a sound federal system can imbue a weakened Europe with a new life. The workers must be liberated from their condition of downtrodden slavery under National Socialism. The illusory structure of autonomous national industry must disappear. Every nation and each person have a right to the goods of the whole world!

Freedom of speech, freedom of religion, the protection of individual citizens from the arbitrary will of criminal regimes of violence – these will be the bases of the New Europe.

Support the resistance. Distribute the leaflets!

Fellow Fighters in the Resistance!

Shaken and broken, our people behold the loss of the men of Stalingrad. Three hundred and thirty thousand German men have been senselessly and irresponsibly driven to death and destruction by the inspired strategy of our World War I Private First Class. Führer, we thank you!

The German people are in ferment. Will we continue to entrust the fate of our armies to a dilettante? Do we want to sacrifice the rest of German youth to the base ambitions of a Party clique? No, never! The day of reckoning has come – the reckoning of German youth with the most abominable tyrant our people have ever been forced to endure. In the name of German youth we demand restitution by Adolf Hitler's state of our personal freedom, the most precious treasure we have, out of which he has swindled us in the most miserable way.

We grew up in a state in which all free expression of opinion is unscrupulously suppressed. The Hitler Youth, the SA, the SS have tried to drug us, to revolutionize us, to regiment us in the most promising young years of our lives. "Philosophical training" is the name given to the despicable method by which our budding intellectual development is muffled in a fog of empty phrases. A system of selection of leaders at once unimaginably devilish and narrow-minded trains up its future party bigwigs in the "Castles of the Knightly Order" to become godless, impudent, and conscienceless exploiters and execu-tioners – blind, stupid hangers-on of the Führer. We "intellectual workers" are the ones who should put obstacles in the path of this caste of overlords. Soldiers at the front are regimented like schoolboys by student leaders and trainees for the post of Gauleiter, and the lewd jokes of the Gauleiters insult the honor of the women students. German women students at the university in Munich have given a dignified reply to the besmirching of their honor, and German students have defended the women in the universities and have stood firm. . . . That is a beginning of the struggle for our free self-determination – without which intellectual and spiritual values cannot be created. We thank the brave comrades, both men and women, who have set us a brilliant example.

For us there is but one slogan: fight against the party! Get out of the party organizations, which are used to keep our mouths sealed and hold us in political bondage! Get out of the lecture rooms of the SS corporals and sergeants and the party bootlickers! We want genuine learning and real freedom of opinion. No threat can terrorize us, not even the shutting down of the institutions of higher learning. This is the struggle of each and every one of us for our future, our freedom, and our honor under a regime conscious of its moral responsibility.

Freedom and honor! For ten long years Hitler and his coadjutors have manhandled, squeezed, twisted, and debased these two splendid German words to the point of nausea, as only dilettantes can, casting the highest values of a nation before swine. They have sufficiently demonstrated in the ten years of destruction of all material and intellectual freedom, of all moral substance among the German people, what they understand by freedom and honor. The frightful bloodbath has opened the eyes of even the stupidest German – it is a slaughter which they arranged in the name of "freedom and honor of the German nation" throughout Europe, and which they daily start anew.

The name of Germany is dishonored for all time if German youth does not finally rise, take revenge, and atone, smash its tormentors, and set up a new Europe of the spirit. Students! The German people look to us. As in 1813 the people expected us to shake off the Napoleonic yoke, so in 1943 they look to us to break the National Socialist terror through the power of the spirit. Beresina and Stalingrad are burning in the East. The dead of Stalingrad implore us to take action.

"Up, up, my people, let smoke and flame be our sign!"

Our people stand ready to rebel against the National Socialist enslavement of Europe in a fervent new breakthrough of freedom and honor.

Other Titles from Plough

WHITE ROSE
Letters and Diaries of
Hans and Sophie Scholl

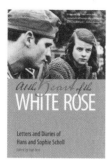

At the Heart of the White Rose

Letters and Diaries of Hans and Sophie Scholl

Edited by Inge Jens, translated by J. Maxwell Brownjohn

What made them risk their lives? Personal letters and diaries provide an intimate view into the Scholls' hearts and minds, revealing that they were not primarily motivated by political beliefs but rather came to their convictions through personal spiritual search.

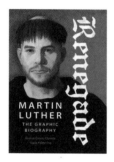

Renegade
MARTIN
LUTHER
THE GRAPHIC
BIOGRAPHY

Renegade

Martin Luther, the Graphic Biography

Dacia Palmerino and Andrea Grosso Ciponte

Five hundred years ago a brash young monk single-handedly confronted the most powerful institutions of his day. His bold stand sparked the Protestant Reformation and marked one of the great turning points in history.

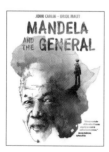

MANDELA
AND THE GENERAL

Mandela and the General

John Carlin and Oriol Malet

Nelson Mandela, the anti-apartheid hero, knew he couldn't avert a bloodbath on his own. He would have to win the trust of his arch-enemy, the white nationalist militia leader Constand Viljoen.

Plough Publishing House

151 Bowne Drive, PO Box 398, Walden, NY 12586, USA

Brightling Road, Robertsbridge, East Sussex TN32 5DR, UK

4188 Gwydir Highway, Elsmore, NSW 2360, Australia

845-572-3455 • info@plough.com • www.plough.com